635
GAR

Gardening complete.

$30.00

DATE			

GARDENING COMPLETE

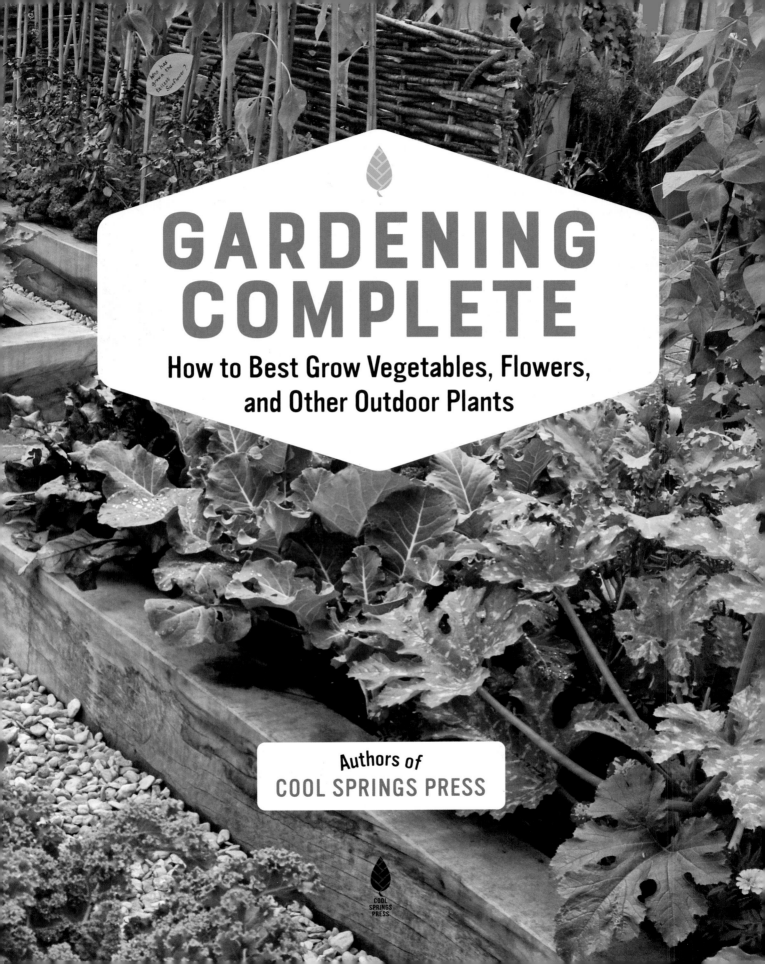

GARDENING COMPLETE

How to Best Grow Vegetables, Flowers, and Other Outdoor Plants

Authors of
COOL SPRINGS PRESS

Inspiring | Educating | Creating | Entertaining

Brimming with creative inspiration, how-to projects, and useful information to enrich your everyday life, Quarto Knows is a favorite destination for those pursuing their interests and passions. Visit our site and dig deeper with our books into your area of interest: Quarto Creates, Quarto Cooks, Quarto Homes, Quarto Lives, Quarto Drives, Quarto Explores, Quarto Gifts, or Quarto Kids.

10 9 8 7 6 5 4 3 2 1

ISBN: 978-0-7603-5765-1

Library of Congress Cataloging-in-Publication Data

Names: Cool Springs Press, issuing body.
Title: Gardening complete : how to best grow vegetables, flowers, and other outdoor plants.
Other titles: How to best grow vegetables, flowers, and other outdoor plants
Description: Minneapolis, MN : Cool Springs Press, 2018.
Identifiers: LCCN 2017035091 | ISBN 9780760357651 (pb)
Subjects: LCSH: Gardening.
Classification: LCC SB450.97 .G373 2018 | DDC 635--dc23
LC record available at https://lccn.loc.gov/2017035091

Acquiring Editor: Bryan Trandem
Content Editor: Kathy Childers
Project Manager: Alyssa Bluhm
Art Director: Cindy Samargia Laun
Cover Design: Amy Sly
Page Design and Layout: Ashley Prine, Tandem Books

Printed in China

CONTENTS

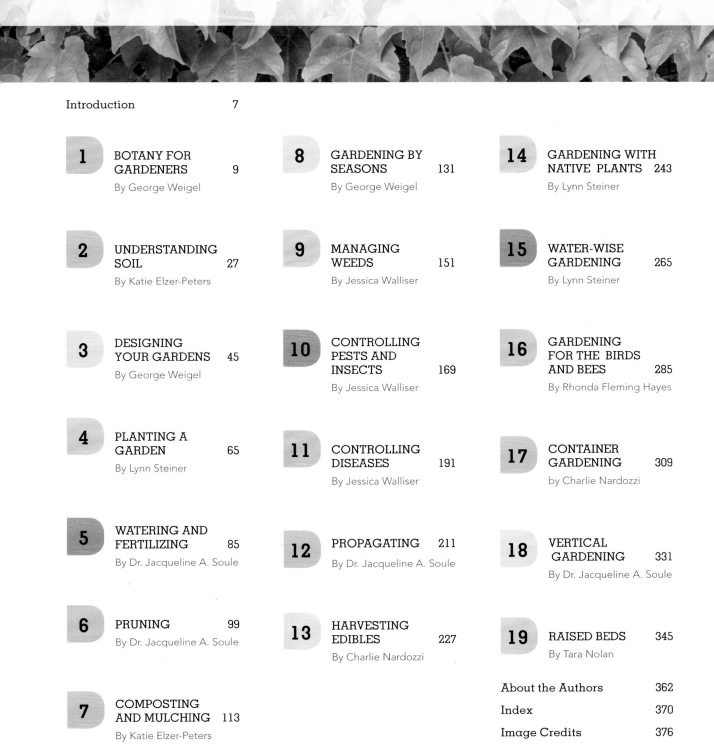

INTRODUCTION

THIS IS THE MOST UP-TO-DATE AND COMPLETE guide to basic gardening for homeowners available today. In these pages, eight of North America's top gardening experts—and Cool Springs Press authors—present 19 subjects of critical interest to anyone interested in learning or broadening their gardening skills. Whether your main interest is in designing landscapes and gardens, ornamental gardening to make your yard more attractive, or gardening to provide nutritious edibles for the family table, this book will become your definitive source of information. It is intended for serious beginning to intermediate gardeners, but even veteran gardeners will be intrigued by what these experts have to say about core gardening skills and common horticultural subjects.

Above all, this is a practical book that will both tell you and show you how to accomplish the routine activities of gardening, from planning and planting your garden, to routine care for the garden during the growing season, to dealing with pests and diseases, to harvesting fruits and vegetables. While many gardening books focus on regional plant species or devote large sections to some form of plant catalog, this book is different. *Gardening Complete* serves not only as a self-contained manual for gardening skills and information in all regions, but also as a sampler that may help you determine where to focus your gardening hobby in the future or even help you identify authors you'd like to explore further. Each of the eight authors has an impressively broad background in publishing and lecturing on gardening, and you may discover a new favorite writer in these pages. We haven't just allowed these authorities to express their individual views—we've encouraged them to do so. As is true in a healthy garden, we've aimed at diversity for this book.

This book is not an organic gardening book per se, but if you have any previous familiarity with Cool Springs Press or any of these authors, you will know that we tend to take a low-impact approach to gardening. Thus, our authors generally offer advice that is gentle to the soil, to the environment, and to beneficial insects and animals. That is not to say our authors will agree on every subject. In these pages, you may find that there is some disagreement among authors on subjects such as fertilizing or pest control. Gardeners in general are an opinionated group, and garden writers are even more so. One gardener's preferred method may not be another gardener's, and that's fine—we'd all be well advised to remember that there are always multiple ways to succeed in any endeavor.

And succeed you will if you follow the advice on the following pages. These authors have extensive experience lecturing, answering questions on radio and television call-in shows, teaching classes, and writing. They are among the most passionate gardeners you will ever meet and they have helped thousands of home gardeners just like you.

Welcome to *Gardening Complete*.

CHAPTER 1
BOTANY FOR GARDENERS

By George Weigel

BOTANY IS THE BRANCH OF BIOLOGY THAT FOCUSES on plant life. It's a hands-on science that can be very helpful to a gardener because understanding how plants work can drastically cut a yard's plant death toll.

One of the first bits of this science that gardeners encounter is how plants are named. Names matter a lot in the plant world. They're the tools that help gardeners sort out minute botanical variations and guide us to the all-important goal of getting the right plant in the right place—the not-so-secret "secret" to successful gardening.

A gardener who ignores plant names (a rose is a rose is a rose . . .) is much more likely to end up with bland tomatoes and dead shrubs than gardeners who research exactly what to plant where.

Granted, plant names can make eyes glaze over in a hurry—especially when botanists, horticulturists, and other plant geeks throw around those hard-to-pronounce Latin botanical names. But plant experts don't spout Latin just to show off (usually). They're using it because it's a standard system that ensures everyone is talking about the exact same plant everywhere on the planet.

Without it, you might *think* you're buying a native perennial flower called bluebells (*Mertensia virginica*) when you're actually getting a strappy-leafed spring bulb called bluebells (*Hyacinthoides hispanica*). Or when you're talking about your

OPPOSITE: The "bugs" you see in your garden may include the essential pollinators, such as this bee.

stunning hollyhocks (*Alcea rosea*), a farm-country gardener might say, "Sounds to me like you're talking about the outhouse plant" (also *Alcea rosea*).

WHY LATIN?

When primitive gardeners first started trying to figure out the plant world, plants were crudely named—typically by what they looked like. Early scientists began recording these plant names by 200 BC.

That worked fine until people fanned out, cultivated plants for more and more uses, and moved them to other regions. Then it became necessary to standardize names so people in one area knew what people in another were talking about.

Nailing down exact names also became more important as people began using plants medicinally. It's very helpful to know, for example, that the frilly leafed plant you're about to eat is Queen Anne's lace (*Daucus carota*) and not poison hemlock (*Conium maculatum*).

A momentous advancement came in 1753 when Swedish naturalist Carolus Linnaeus published a two-volume, 1,200-page book called *Species Plantarum*. The book laid out a system that grouped plants into a sort of family tree, primarily by their similarity to one another in flower, fruit, and leaf.

The top of Linnaeus's tree identified "kingdoms" to sort out plants from animals, fungi, and bacteria. Then the system went down a line of division, class, family, genus, and species to further group plants by increasingly intricate characteristics. A classification of "order" also is in the system, but it's more significant in animals than plants.

Linnaeus used Latin names (and some Greek ones) for his naming system because that was the international language of choice in the 18th-century scientific community. (See "Botanical Order" for more information.)

More than one plant is nicknamed bluebells, but this one is a US-native, spring-wildflower version known botanically as *Mertensia virginica*.

This is a cultivar—a variation developed from a native species. On the plant tag, it would be identified as *Salvia farinacea* 'Evolution'.

BOTANICAL ORDER

Kingdom. According to Linnaeus, Earth has five kingdoms. Plantae, or the plant kingdom, is one of them.

Divisions. These separate plants into broad groups with marked differences, such as mosses, ferns, conifers, cycads, and flowering plants.

Moss is an example of a plant division.

Classes. This level breaks down the divisions by basic botanical differences, such as number of stamens in a flower (the male fertilizing organ) and how many leaves sprout from a plant's seed.

Basic differences in plant parts, such as this hibiscus stamen or the single leaf blade of a grass, create different classes.

Families. This level starts to group plants by specific traits. For example, the daisy family (*Asteraceae*) groups plants with similar star-shaped flower clusters. The rose family (*Rosaceae*) groups plants with similar fruiting habits and showy flowers. The mint family (*Lamiaceae*) groups plants by their angled or square-shaped stems.

Rosaceae (roses) is an example of a plant family.

Genus. Each family can be broken down by even more specific traits. Genus names are often descriptive of the plants in the group, are named after the area where the plants were found, or are named after the person who discovered them.

Hydrangea is an example of a plant genus.

Species. If a plant is botanically similar in most key ways to another plant but is different enough in one or more smaller ways, it can be designated as a different species under the same genus.

A genus can have many different species, such as smooth hydrangea (*Hydrangea arborescens*), panicle hydrangea (*Hydrangea paniculata*), and oakleaf hydrangea (*Hydrangea quercifolia*).

Glauca means blue and *pendula* means weeping in this *Cedrus atlantica glauca pendula* (weeping blue atlas cedar).

THE *REAL* FUN BEGINS . . .

For gardeners, the naming system really starts to matter at the level of genus and species. These are the two-part, so-called botanical names you'll see on most plant tags. These names are generally italicized with the first part, the genus, capitalized and the second part, the species, lower case. For example, *Salvia nemorosa* is the botanical name for a blue-blooming, spiky flower.

Some plant families have just one genus while others have scores. Likewise, some genera (the plural of genus) have just one species while others have hundreds. The *Begonia* genus, for example, is one of the bigger ones with more than 1,400 individual species.

The majority of genus names are descriptive of the plants in Latin and Greek. The *Hemerocallis* genus name for daylily, for example, has its root in the Greek words

meaning "beautiful for a day." The popular *Rhododendron* genus means "rose tree" in Latin and Greek. And the sunflower genus *Helianthus* comes from Greek words meaning—you guessed it—"sun" and "flower."

Other genus names are linked to people (*Magnolia* from the 17th-century French botanist Pierre Magnol and *Euphorbia* from the 1st-century Greek physician Euphorbus), and a few relate to mythology (*Andromeda*, *Nerine*, and *Hebe*).

The species part is even more descriptive, using Latin or Greek terms for a plant's origin, growth habit, or leaf color or shape. Thus, you might guess that a plant with *chinensis* in its name is native to China, or that a plant with *pendula* in the name has a weeping or pendulous habit.

(See "What Some of Those Latin and Greek Names Mean" for more information about botanical names.)

What Some of Those Latin and Greek Names Mean

alatus = having wings

alba or **albus** = white

americana = of the Americas

angustifolius = narrow leaves

argentatus or **argentea** = silver

aureus = golden

autumnalis = relating to autumn

biflorus and **bifolius** = twin flowered and twin leafed

canadensis = of Canada

cardinalis = cardinal red

chinensis = of China

columnaris = column shaped

compactus = dense or compact

contortus or **contorta** = twisted

dentatus or **dentatum** = toothed

elegans = elegant

elongatus = elongated or stretched

esculentus or **esculenta** = edible

flexuosus or **flexuosa** = zigzaggy

floribunda = free flowering

foetidus = foul smelling

fragrans = fragrant

glaucus or **glauca** = having a grayish or blue-gray coating

globosus = rounded

gracilis = slender or graceful

grandis = showy or large

hispanicus or **hispanica** = of Spain

horizontalis = horizontal or flat

humilis = very dwarf

hybridus = of mixed parentage

integrifolius or **integrifolia** = having entire or uncut foliage

italicus or **italicum** = of Italy

lanceolatus or **lanceolatum** = lance or spear shaped

luteus or **lutea** = yellow

maximus or **maxima** = largest

mollis = soft or velvety

mucosus or **mucosum** = slimy

nanus or **nana** = dwarf or small

niger or **nigra** = black

nipponicus or **nipponicum** = of Japan

nutans = nodding

obtusus or **obtusa** = blunt

occidentalis = western

officinalis = medicinal

orientalis = Oriental or eastern

palmatus or **palmatum** = shaped like a hand (palm)

palustris = of boggy areas

pendulus or **pendula** = drooping or weeping

pinnatus or **pinnata** = feathery

plicata or **plicatum** = folded, pleated

pratensis = of the fields

procumbens = flat, prostate

pubescens = fuzzy

pungens = sharp, pointy

racemosus or **racemose** = having flowers in raceme (clustered) form

repens or **reptans** = creeping

reticulatus or **reticulata** = having netted markings

rosaceus, rosacea, rosea, or **rosaceum** = like a rose

ruber or **rubrum** = red

rugosus or **rugosa** = wrinkled

rupestris or **rupestre** = of rocks, rock preferring

sanguineus or **sanguinea** = blood red

scandens = climbing

sempervirens = evergreen

serratus or **serrata** = saw toothed

sessilis = without a stalk

setaceus or **setaceum** = bristly

spinosus or **spinosum** = spiny

striatus or **striata** = striped

strictus or **stricta** = erect, upright

sylvaticus or **sylvatica** = of the forest

tomentosa or **tomentosum** = fuzzy, wooly, furry

tuberosus or **tuberosa** = tubular, tuberous

variegatus or **variegata** = variegated

villosus or **villosa** = hairy

virgata or **virgatum** = multibranched

viridis = green

viscosum or **viscosus** = sticky, gummy

vulgaris or **vulgarum** = common

Also, whenever you see a species end in the letters ii, it's been named after a person, such as davidii (Father Armand David), hicksii (Henry Hicks), or thunbergii (Carl Peter Thunberg). Only one i is added if the person's name ends in er, such as bakeri or loebneri.

THE NAMING NITTY-GRITTY

The finest naming distinction of all happens with particular varieties or "cultivars" (short for "cultivated variety"). These are variations on a particular species—ones with traits that aren't so different to land a plant in a different species but different enough to warrant an additional nametag.

Varieties and cultivars usually appear within single quotes after the two-part genus/species name, such as *Nandina domestica* 'Moon Bay', *Cryptomeria japonica* 'Black Dragon', and *Salvia nemorosa* 'Caradonna'.

In recent decades, breeders and plant companies have begun patenting and trademarking their new introductions—giving them yet *another* name designed for clever marketing or to prevent competitors from selling the plants under the protected name. One of America's all-time best-selling landscape plants—the Knock Out shrub rose—is one example. Amateur Wisconsin rose breeder William Radler discovered this low-care rose from a single seedling in his hybridizing hobby. The actual variety name is 'Radrazz', but it was patented and introduced in 2000 as Knock Out so that only the producer, Star Roses and Plants, can sell it under that name. Similarly, the Red Beauty holly—a compact type with big berries on the branch tips—and the Rozanne hardy geranium—one of the longest bloomers of any perennial flower—are examples of top-selling patented plants with obscure variety names ('Rutzan' and 'Gerwat').

Sometimes it's hard to tell *any* difference from one variety to another. But other times, the differences are so striking in garden performance and appearance that you'll think you're looking at two entirely different species.

Trial gardens, such as this one at Penn State University's research farm, are good places to see differences in plant performance.

Monkey grass could be two completely different plants, *Liriope* (top) or *Ophiopogon* (bottom).

That's why it's worth your while to maneuver the wild world of plant name games. If you're not convinced, pay a visit to a plant trial garden. These are plots in which different versions of a genus or species are planted side by side so that evaluators can compare them. Many are open to the public at universities, public gardens, and sites run by plant societies or other plant organizations.

You'll invariably notice that in a long block of different petunias, for example, some varieties are blooming their heads off, most are good, and a few are wilted, wimpy, bug ridden, or dead. What this usually tells you is that because the conditions for all are the same, the difference is most likely in the genetics of each plant.

Doing enough homework to sort out such differences will help you be the gardener who buys the gorgeous petunia and not the wilted, wimpy one.

THE PROBLEM WITH PLANT NICKNAMES

Because "official" plant names are complex and confusing, wouldn't it be a whole lot easier to stick with more memorable names such as the "outhouse plant" instead of *Alcea rosea* or the "eyeball plant" instead of *Spilanthes oleracea*?

It would be if everyone were on the same page. The problem is that different people give different nicknames or common names to the same plant, especially from one region to the next. Before you know it, confusion reigns.

Southerners, for example, often call a particular grassy groundcover "monkey grass." One immediate problem is that they could be referring to one of several species of *Liriope* (some of which can be overly aggressive) or a species of *Ophiopogon* (a slightly shorter and more shade-preferring plant that's also commonly called "mondo grass"). In the North, *Liriope* is usually called "lilyturf" or "creeping lilyturf," even though it's neither a lily nor a turfgrass. Northerners will have no idea what you're talking about if you mention monkey grass. To make it even more confusing, some people know *Liriope* as "spider grass."

While you might see common names in articles, on garden-center signs, and on plant tags, you'll also often see them followed up with the Latin name as an accuracy backup. So, whether you're shopping for shrubs in Warsaw, Indiana, or Warsaw, Poland, the plants will be called by the same botanical name.

PLANTS AND THEIR ROLES

Go to a garden center and you'll see thousands of different plants organized by type. Usually, they're grouped not by botanical families but by what role they play in the garden and how long you can expect them to live in your climate.

You'll typically see flowers divided into an "annual" section and a "perennial" section; woody-stemmed plants such as trees, shrubs, conifers, and roses will be in a "nursery" section; a "greenhouse" or "houseplants" section will have plants that can't take a freeze; and sometimes there will be a "water garden" section with aquatic plants and water-garden supplies. Plants grown from bulbs are usually sold in bags in a "garden shop" along with sprays, fertilizers, tools, and such.

This organization helps you sort out what's what, and is a good start to help you get the right *kind* of plant in a spot that makes sense. Here's what you ought to know about each category.

Annuals and Perennials

The designations "annual" and "perennial" aren't botanical definitions. They're labels given to plants to describe whether they're going to make it through more than one season in a particular climate.

An annual is a flower that's expected to survive just one season. A perennial is a flower that's expected to live for at least three years (assuming deer and rabbits don't eat it first).

Whether a plant is an annual or a perennial varies from region to region, based mainly on how cold it gets in winter. In a frosty northern state, for example, a trailing bloomer called lantana does fine in summer but dies once freezing nights show up in the fall. However, in a warmer southern state, that same flower can live for years.

So, is lantana an annual or a perennial? Yes. It performs like and is sold as an annual in colder regions, but is considered a perennial in warmer regions. Sometimes plants such as these are called "tender perennials" because they merely act like annuals in cold climates.

Some perennial plants, such as heuchera, keep their leaves all winter in much of the United States.

Purple coneflower is a perennial plant that returns from the same roots year after year.

A zinnia is an example of a true annual, a plant that completes its entire life cycle in one growing season.

Many northern annuals are actually tender perennials in their native regions. Begonias, petunias, coleus, geraniums, snapdragons, euphorbias, callas, rosemary, dusty miller, violas, and salvias are among plants grown as annuals in the north but capable of living for years in frost-free areas. In the edible garden, tomatoes and peppers are technically tender perennials, not annuals.

On the other hand, some annuals really are "true" annuals. These are plants that go through their entire life cycle—seed to plant to flower to new seed to dead—in a single year, no matter where they're growing. Examples are marigolds, larkspur, nasturtium, cosmos, strawflowers, and zinnias.

Another category of plants—usually lumped in with the annuals in a garden center or sold as seeds—are "biennials." These are plants that take two years to complete their life cycle. They produce roots and foliage the first year and graduate into flowering and seed production the second year. Then the parent dies, leaving behind the current year's leafy offspring to flower and seed the following year to keep the cycle going.

Examples of biennials are sweet Williams, foxgloves, money plants, and hollyhocks in the flower garden and beets, cabbage, carrots, and celery in the edible garden.

Plants sold as perennials are ones that live from the same roots for three or more years—even if the plant drops its leaves and goes dormant over the winter. Most perennials *do* die back to the ground and/or lose their leaves in winter in cold climates, but some are "evergreen perennials." Examples of those are hellebores, yuccas, candytuft, lavender, some coral bells and foamy bells, and the groundcovers periwinkle (*Vinca minor*), English ivy, and pachysandra.

Examples of perennials that usually lose their leaves but survive winters in most of the United States include purple coneflowers, coreopsis, black-eyed Susans, sedum, daylilies, catmint, asters, astilbes, phlox, and goldenrod.

LEFT AND RIGHT: This *Chionanthus virginicus* could be called a fringe tree or a fringe bush, depending on how you prune it or how big you let it grow.

Trees and Shrubs

Trees and shrubs are the two main types of woody plants used in landscapes, but where does one end and the other begin? Or in other words, what's the difference between a tree and a shrub?

There's no botanical distinction between the two, and in fact, the same plant can be called a tree *or* a shrub depending on how big it is and how you've pruned it. The native American fringe tree (*Chionanthus virginicus*) and the native serviceberry (*Amelanchier arborea*) are examples of plants that naturally produce multiple trunks that grow to a big shrub-like height of 15 to 18 feet. But both also can

be pruned to a straight, single trunk, giving them a small treelike appearance.

The generally accepted definition of a tree is a plant that has a single woody stem (a trunk) that's at least 2 to 3 inches in diameter at a height of 4½ feet, plus a crown or canopy of foliage above. The plant height has to be at least 13 feet—or at least 20 feet, by some definitions.

Shrubs are generally defined as plants with multiple woody stems and heights under 13 feet (or under 20 feet, by some definitions).

Trees and shrubs are either deciduous or evergreen. Deciduous woody plants are those that drop their leaves

Maples are examples of deciduous trees that lose their leaves in winter.

Douglas fir is a needled evergreen—it has needled leaves that stay on the tree in winter.

over winter, usually after turning brilliant shades of red, gold, yellow, or orange in the fall. Examples are maples, crabapples, hornbeams, redbuds, dogwoods, flowering cherries, and most oaks.

Evergreen woody plants are those that hold their foliage all year. These can be broadleaf types, such as boxwoods, hollies, laurels, nandinas, and rhododendrons, or they can be needled types, such as spruces, pines, firs, cedars, junipers, yews, and false cypresses.

Even evergreens don't hold their leaves and needles forever, though. These plants shed their older inner foliage gradually as new growth takes place at the branch ends. Some species shed foliage that's only a year or two old, while other species hold their foliage for five years before dropping it.

Most needled evergreens are classified botanically as conifers, meaning they reproduce by seed-bearing cones as opposed to flowers. Conifers can range from super-dwarf, 2-foot balls that grow just an inch or two per year to California's centuries-old giant sequoias that can tower 250 feet tall and grow trunks 30 feet across.

However, not all needled conifers are evergreen. Some needled trees actually turn color in fall and drop all their needles every winter, *a la* maples and dogwoods. They then grow a new set of needles the following spring.

The chenille plant can grow as an outdoor shrub in tropical climates, but in colder climates, it's sold as a houseplant.

Four that you might run across in American landscapes are larches (*Larix*), bald cypresses (*Taxodium*), golden larches (*Pseudolarix*), and dawn redwoods (*Metasequoia*), stately, reddish-barked giants that were thought to be extinct before a small grove of them was discovered in China in 1944.

You'll also usually find roses sold alongside shrubs in the nursery section of most garden centers. These number in the thousands of varieties and come in types ranging from 2-foot-tall miniatures to durable, multiflowered shrub types to the sleek hybrid-tea, grandiflora, and floribunda types that collectors enter in flower shows.

One other type of plant you'll often find sold in the nursery section is the woody vine; these are plants with long arms that climb up walls and structures with their hold-fast rootlets (climbing hydrangeas, Japanese hydrangea vines, Boston ivy) or that climb and ramble by twining branches around a trellis or arbor (honeysuckle, clematis, Carolina jasmine). A few woody vines, such as climbing roses, need some training and tying to get them to stay upright on a trellis or arbor.

Houseplants

Plants commonly called houseplants are usually found in the protected greenhouse section of a typical garden center. No plant is actually native to a house, however. Houseplants are species that grow outside in tropical and subtropical climates but are versatile enough (at least temporarily) to grow inside in other climates. Many of them start to suffer when nighttime lows dip into the low 40s, and almost all will die if left outside on a freezing night.

The choices range from seasonal favorites, such as tender florist mums and poinsettias, to bloomers, such as the peace lily and orchids, to plants with colorful or interesting foliage, such as golden philodendrons, variegated Chinese evergreens, and glossy, succulent ZZ plants.

Just because tender species will die on a typical Nebraska winter night doesn't mean they're stuck growing indoors year-round outside of the tropics. Almost all will do fine when moved outside for a summer vacation. The heat and humidity then feels like home. Just get them back inside before it gets too chilly—ideally after a stiff hose-down or insecticide spray to head off bugs hitching a ride inside.

Bulbs

Some plants are easy to start simply by burying dormant bulbs in soil and waiting for the magic to happen. These include spring-blooming bulbs, such as daffodils, tulips, and hyacinths, and summer-blooming bulbs, such as gladioli, dahlias, and caladiums.

Most spring-blooming bulbs are planted in fall. That's when they put down roots and then slowly develop underground before emerging in spring to leaf out and flower. They need varying amounts of winter chill time, which is why most spring bulbs are difficult to grow in warm Southern states.

In the right setting and in well-drained soil, most spring bulbs are winter hardy and return to bloom year after year—often colonizing in the process. Examples are daffodils, Siberian squills, glory-of-the-snow, crocuses, and snowdrops. A few peter out in time and are best replanted every few years, such as hyacinths and many types of tulips.

Summer-blooming bulbs are planted after danger of frost in spring to emerge and then flower later that season.

Some, such as Asiatic and Oriental lilies, become perennials and can be left in the ground once planted, while dahlias, callas, gladioli, and cannas are among the species that have to be lifted out and stored dormant inside over winter in cold climates.

Technically, not everything that people refer to as a bulb is really a bulb botanically.

True bulbs are ball-like structures that usually narrow at the top. Leaves and flower stems emerge from there, and the roots emerge from the flat bottom (called the "basal plate"). If you cut open a bulb, you'll find a baby plant inside, ready to grow. Examples of true bulbs include tulips, hyacinths, and onions.

Corms also have a basal plate but the body has distinct rings and one or more growing points at the top. Examples include crocus, freesia, and gladioli.

Tubers don't have a basal plate, but they do have growing points called "eyes" all around their fleshy exteriors. The best-known tuber is the potato, but caladiums, cyclamens, anemones, and tuberous begonias are also tubers, not bulbs.

Dahlias are summer-blooming bulbs.

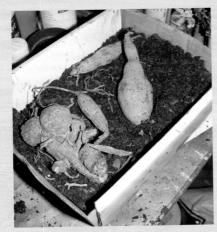

TOP LEFT: Potatoes are our best known tuber.

MIDDLE LEFT: The dahlia is an example of a tuberous root.

BOTTOM LEFT: Cannas are rhizomes.

ABOVE RIGHT: Gladiolus is a corm.

BELOW RIGHT: This tulip and its baby "bulblet" is an example of a true bulb.

Tuberous roots look similar to tubers but are actually enlarged roots that store food and cluster together while sending up shoots that flower. Examples include sweet potatoes, dahlias, and daylilies.

Rhizomes grow underground and send up flowering shoots, but botanically, these are stems that grow sideways along the soil surface or just below. Examples include irises, lily-of-the-valley, and cannas.

Water-Garden Plants

Most plants will drown in water or suffocate even when soil is too wet for too long. However, some plants are adapted to growing on the bottom of shallow ponds or even floating on water's surface with their roots dangling below.

These so-called "aquatic plants" make ideal choices for home water gardens. As with most plants, some of them can survive frozen winters in a dormant state (hardy water lilies, cattails, Louisiana irises), while others are tropical natives that need indoor water storage in cold climates (tropical water lilies, water lettuce, dwarf papyrus).

In water gardens, the non-floaters are generally grown in pots set on the pond bottom or on shelves along the pond edges.

If you don't have a pond or don't want to dig a large hole to build a water garden, you can grow aquatic plants in water-filled containers set on a deck or patio. Many small varieties do well in containers.

COLD AND THE HARDINESS ZONES

Lots of factors can kill a plant, but at the top of the heap is cold temperatures. Many plants croak when a single sub-32°F night comes along to freeze the foliage, leaving behind a pile of wilted brown mush in the morning.

Other plants can take a freeze but run into increasing risk the lower temperatures go and the longer they stay there.

To help gardeners figure out which plants are likely to survive a typical winter in their region, the US Department of Agriculture came up with a Plant Hardiness Zone Map. Updated in 2012, this map divides the United States and its territories into 13 zones based on each area's average lowest winter temperature.

Each zone covers a 10°F range, from the super-cold Zone 1 that can go down to −50 to −60°F in winter to a tropical Zone 13 that bottoms out at 60 to 70°F in an average winter.

The zones resulted from readings taken at 8,000 monitoring stations over a 30-year period, from 1976 to 2005.

Growers have assigned cold-hardiness ratings to most plants based on their ability to tolerate the average lows in a zone. You'll find those ranges listed on plant tags.

On a tag for the popular perennial 'May Night' salvia, for example, you'll find this listing: "USDA Hardiness Zones 4–9." That means 'May Night' can be expected to survive in zones ranging from Zone 4 (average winter lows of −20 to −30°F) through Zone 9 (average winter lows of 20 to 30°F).

Garden centers and mail-order retailers also use the hardiness zones as a guide to determine where they should

Waterlilies make some of the most colorful aquatic plants.

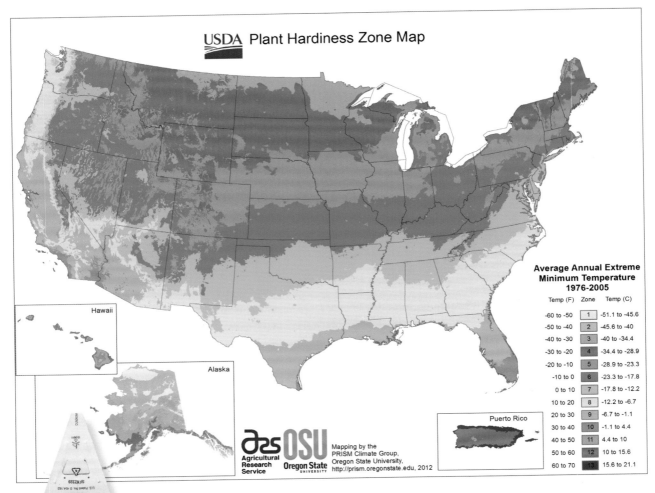

USDA Plant Hardiness Zone Map

Average Annual Extreme Minimum Temperature 1976-2005

Temp (F)	Zone	Temp (C)
-60 to -50	1	-51.1 to -45.6
-50 to -40	2	-45.6 to -40
-40 to -30	3	-40 to -34.4
-30 to -20	4	-34.4 to -28.9
-20 to -10	5	-28.9 to -23.3
-10 to 0	6	-23.3 to -17.8
0 to 10	7	-17.8 to -12.2
10 to 20	8	-12.2 to -6.7
20 to 30	9	-6.7 to -1.1
30 to 40	10	-1.1 to 4.4
40 to 50	11	4.4 to 10
50 to 60	12	10 to 15.6
60 to 70	13	15.6 to 21.1

Hawaii

Alaska

Puerto Rico

Mapping by the PRISM Climate Group, Oregon State University, http://prism.oregonstate.edu, 2012

ABOVE: The 2012 update of the USDA Plant Hardiness Zone Map divides the country into 13 growing zones.

LEFT: The plant tag of this foxglove (*Digitalis*) shows it is winter hardy to Zone 4.

FOXGLOVE
'Excelsior'
Digitalis
PERENNIAL

LIGHT	BLOOM DATE	SOIL MOISTURE
Partial sun	Summer	Moist

HEIGHT	SPACING	ZONE
36-60"	18-24"	4-8

Outstanding Features: Spikes of tubular flowers in an unusual color range, June-July.
Uses: Use for beds, borders or cutting.
Care: Prefers a moist location in part sun.

Hand water until established.

Swift Greenhouses Inc.
Home of Thrivers
Gilman, IA
50106

sell each plant. A Maine garden center in Zone 4, for example, isn't likely to sell crape myrtles rated only to Zone 6, while a mail-order grower might sell lantanas as perennials in the South but as annuals in the North.

To use the zone map as a guide, you'll need to know what zone you're in. The online version of the map is interactive, and allows users to find their zone by typing in their ZIP code. That tool and the map itself are posted on the USDA website at planthardiness.ars.usda.gov.

Keep in mind that the Plant Hardiness Zone Map shows *average* lows. Many winters never reach those lows, meaning it's possible to grow plants for years that are rated for warmer zones. However, it's also possible for a rogue winter to go *below* the average, killing plants that normally survive.

That's why the Plant Hardiness Zone Map is a good guide to survival but not the gospel word. Experienced gardeners know that every year has its share of weather curveballs and they know that each yard has microclimates—a hot spot by the west-facing brick wall, for example, or a wind-protected, afternoon-shaded spot along the east side of a fence.

Knowing your microclimates can help push the envelope with borderline-hardy plants and jack up plant-survival successes by getting the best-adapted plants in each spot. Still, if you guess wrong and see a plant struggling, there's always the shovel.

HEAT ZONES

While plant death from cold is usually sudden and obvious, plants can suffer and die from the opposite extreme—too much heat.

Heat injury is a more insidious, less understood plant menace. As temperatures rise, heat can cause flower buds to wither. It can shut down chlorophyll production, robbing leaves of their healthy green color. It can cause pollen to become nonviable, preventing popular plants such as tomatoes from setting new fruit until the weather cools. It can cause subtle chemical changes in plant leaves, rendering them more vulnerable to bug attack. And it can raise soil temperatures to the point where root activity slows and plant growth is stunted.

The late Washington plant pathologist Dr. Marc Cathey outlined those potential problems in his 1998 book *Heat-Zone Gardening*, which applied the concept of the cold hardiness zone map to the opposite end of the temperature spectrum.

Cathey, a former president of the American Horticultural Society, said that plant trouble typically starts when temperatures hit 86°F. His book divided the country into 12 heat zones, based on the average number of days each zone goes to 86°F or higher each year.

The idea, now championed by the AHS, hasn't caught on as widely as the USDA Plant Hardiness Zone Map, but many growers and websites have begun posting heat-zone ratings on plants along with cold-hardiness ratings. It's especially useful in hotter climates where heat injury is a bigger threat than damage from cold.

Find more information about heat zones and a copy of the AHS Heat Zone Map online at www.ahsgardening.org/gardening-resources/gardening-maps/heat-zone-map.

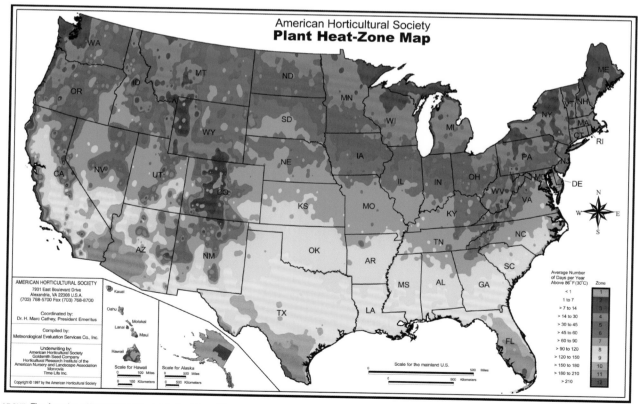

ABOVE: The American Horticultural Society's Heat Zone Map shows how hot different parts of the United States get in summer and for how long.

TOP RIGHT: Excess heat, especially paired with dry soil, can cause plant leaves to turn brown.

CHAPTER 2
UNDERSTANDING SOIL

By Katie Elzer-Peters

ALL SUCCESSFUL GARDENING STARTS WITH GREAT soil. You might be thinking, "That's an awfully bold statement there." It is, but it's true. If plants are underperforming, getting stressed, or coming under attack by insects, there's a good chance that you can reverse the unwanted trend by improving the soil.

Soil is the literal foundation for all plant life. It physically holds plants in place. But that's only the beginning. The importance of good soil runs much deeper. There's a lot going on underground. Here's how what's happening in the soil affects plant health.

Serves as a Home for Earthworms, Bacteria, Fungi, and Insects

If you looked at a bit of soil under a microscope, you'd see millions of little bacteria, fungi, protozoa, and other microscopic organisms wriggling around. If you dig around in the soil, eventually you'll run into earthworms, grubs, and other insects. The activities of this fauna support the flora growing in the soil by breaking down organic material into smaller parts (nutrients) that can be taken up and used by plants. These creatures create tunnels for air and water movement, and help keep the soil from becoming compacted. The soil provides a home for

OPPOSITE: The soil is home to more than just plant roots. Good soil includes bacteria, fungi, insects, earthworms, and other organisms.

the larvae stage of many beneficial pollinating insects as well. Understanding that the soil is full of life, and the functions that life performs, is key to ensuring its overall health and thus the overall health of the plants living in it.

Holds on to Nutrients for Plant Uptake

Soil provides plants with most of the nutrients that are the building blocks of growth. As organic materials decompose—leaves, insect bodies, twigs, and so forth—they break down into elements such as nitrogen, phosphorus, potassium, magnesium, calcium, sulfur, and more. The aforementioned soil biology plays a role in the decomposition that renders these elements available to plants. The soil particles then hold onto nutrients so that plants can take them up through their roots. (Soil also holds on to any nutrients added via fertilizer.) The physical and chemical properties of soil influence how many nutrients the soil can hold and how accessible those nutrients are to plants.

Stores Water for Plant Uptake

When you water plants, you direct the stream of water at the soil, not at the plant leaves, because plants largely take up water through their roots, not through their leaves. Water is held in the spaces between soil particles through surface tension. The smaller the spaces between soil particles, the more tightly the water is held. Pores in sandy soil are larger than pores in heavy clay soil, which is why clay soil tends to stay saturated longer than sandy soil. However,

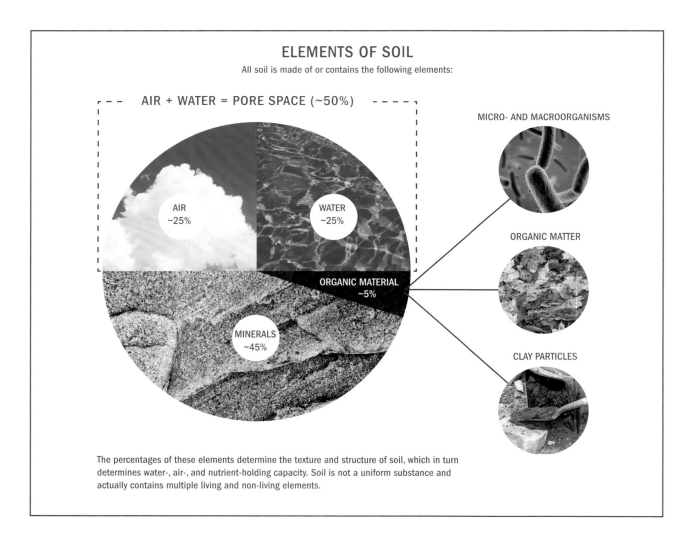

ELEMENTS OF SOIL

All soil is made of or contains the following elements:

AIR + WATER = PORE SPACE (~50%)

AIR ~25%

WATER ~25%

ORGANIC MATERIAL ~5%

MINERALS ~45%

MICRO- AND MACROORGANISMS

ORGANIC MATTER

CLAY PARTICLES

The percentages of these elements determine the texture and structure of soil, which in turn determines water-, air-, and nutrient-holding capacity. Soil is not a uniform substance and actually contains multiple living and non-living elements.

it is easier for plants to take up water from soil with large pores because the water isn't as tightly held by the particles. Achieving a good soil structure for optimum water holding (and letting go) is every gardener's goal.

Provides Oxygen at the Root Zone

Plants use carbon dioxide for photosynthesis—the process of making sugars—but they use oxygen for respiration—the process of using sugars for energy. Plants take up oxygen through their roots. When soils are oversaturated with water and there's no room for oxygen at the root zone, plants begin to rot. Oxygen availability in the soil also affects the decomposition activities of soil organisms. Lack of oxygen creates anaerobic conditions that are detrimental to certain organisms and beneficial for other harmful organisms that can cause root rot and slow down the process of nutrient cycling (and thus nutrient availability for plants).

From the descriptions of soil function, you've likely gathered that each attribute, aspect, or activity that happens in the soil is connected to another. The soil is an ecosystem and anything added or taken away affects its health, and then, in turn, the health of the plants growing in it.

Because of this interconnectivity, there is no chemical way to make up for poor soil. You can't just dump fertilizer on the soil and expect the plants to respond well long term. There's so much more to soil than the "big three" nutrients contained in most chemical fertilizers.

Let's dive a little deeper into the components of soil and how those affect soil function.

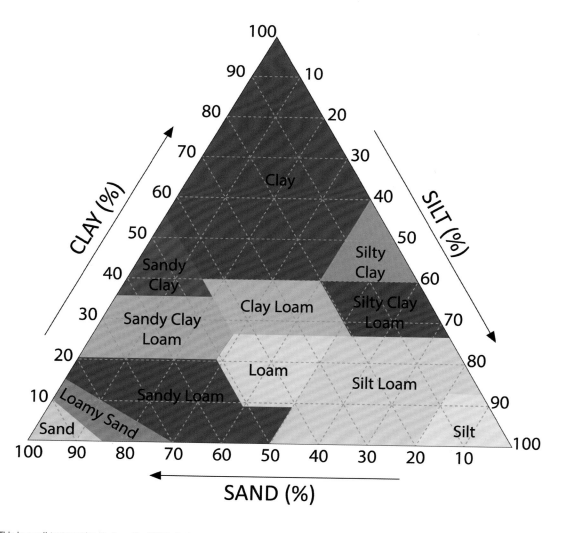

This is a soil texture triangle from the USDA. It shows the percentages of clay, sand, and silt in various types of soil.

SAND

SILT

CLAY

This photo will help you visualize the sizes of soil particles in relation to one another. You can see sand particles with the naked eye, but you'd need a microscope to see individual silt or clay particles.

SOIL PROPERTIES

All soil is influenced by the environment surrounding it. Soils underneath pine forests will naturally have a more acidic pH from the decomposition of pine needles falling on the soil. Soils in arid locations with little rain sometimes have accumulated salt buildup because those salts are not continuously washed out.

The bedrock underneath soil contributes to the soil's mineral content and qualities. You can change elements of the soil to enhance its suitability for plants, but pressure from the surrounding environment will be constant, ensuring a need for constant vigilance on the part of the gardener.

Structure

The difference between soil *texture* and *structure* is confusing because the terms are related but not the same thing. Texture refers to the percentages of different mineral particles in the soil. Structure refers to the way those particles and other elements of the soil clump together. Sandy soil doesn't have much structure—the particles don't stick together—while soils heavy in clay tend to have a blocky structure. Loamy soils are often crumbly, with just enough structure to hold plants and resist some compaction, but not so much that the soil is difficult to work.

Walking or driving on soil can disrupt its structure, as will digging and tilling. To preserve good soil structure, avoid overworking it.

Texture

Soil texture refers to the size of the soil mineral particles and the percentage of each size within a soil.

There are three sizes of mineral particles:
- Sand: the largest
- Silt: the middle size
- Clay: the smallest

Soils can be classified as one of 12 different textures, depending on the percentages of sand, silt, and clay in the soil. These textures are illustrated in the Soil Texture Triangle from the USDA (page 29). Loamy soils are the gardener's gold standard, as they have the best water-, nutrient-, and air-retention capacity, the ideal percentage of organic matter, and good structure to boot.

Soil texture can give you an indication of your soil's
- water-holding capacity,
- susceptibility to compaction,
- nutrient-holding capacity,
- workability (soil tilth),
- likelihood of erosion, and
- drainage characteristics.

There are two ways to gauge the texture of your soil at home: the jar test and the ribbon test.

Sandy Soils
- Fast draining
- Not prone to compaction
- Do not hold on to nutrients
- Little structure

Clay Soils
- Slow to drain—soils can become waterlogged
- Prone to compaction—avoid walking on, working, or driving on when wet
- Hold tightly to nutrients and water
- Usually blocky or plate-like structure

Loamy Soils
- Perfect drainage—not too fast, not to slow
- Less prone to compaction than clay soils, but more than sandy soils
- Hold on to nutrients, but also makes them accessible to plants
- Good, crumbly structure

How to Do a Ribbon Test

Take a soil sample in the same way you would for a jar test (see the next page), then moisten the soil so that it is about as moist as a wrung-out sponge. Grab a ball of soil the size of a golf ball and squeeze it between your thumb and forefinger (like you're holding a stack of money and counting it). Now, use this soil to perform a ribbon test by trying to form the soil into a narrow ribbon with your hands.

- If you can generate a "ribbon" of soil that holds together for less than 1 inch, the soil is either sandy (if it feels coarse) or silty (if it won't stay together but isn't gritty).

- Ribbons of 1 to 2 inches indicate medium texture. If it feels coarse, it's higher in sand; if it isn't coarse, it's higher in silt.

- Ribbons of more than 2 inches indicate a fine-textured (high in clay) soil.

How to Do a Jar Test

1. Gather your soil sample. You'll want to dig 3 to 4 holes throughout the yard, about 8 inches deep, and take about a cup full of soil from the bottom of each hole. Mix it up in a bucket and fill a glass jar halfway with soil.

2. Mark the level of dry soil in the jar. Add water so the jar is two-thirds full (including the water and soil). Shake the jar to mix the soil and water.

3. Allow the soil to settle for 30 seconds, then draw a line on the jar where the top of the soil hits. After 3 minutes, mark the soil line again. (It should be lower.)

4. Examine the layers. The bottom layer will be sand, the middle layer will be silt, and the upper layer will be clay. Calculate the percentage of each in relation to the original soil line and then compare those percentages to the soil texture triangle on page 29.

Soil pH

The pH number of soil is an indication of its acidity or alkalinity. The pH scale runs between 1 and 14, with most plants growing happily in a soil with a pH of 5.8 to 6.5, slightly acidic. (A 7 is neutral on the scale.) Ericaceous plants such as blueberries, hollies, rhododendrons, and azaleas grow best in a more acidic pH of 5.0 to 5.5.

If you get a soil test, it will have the soil pH in the results, along with any suggested corrective measures to adjust the pH.

If you're seeing problems with plants, always check the soil pH before fertilizing and spraying. The pH affects nutrient availability to plants, with some nutrients being more available at certain pH levels than others. Extremely high or low pH levels can also result in nutrient toxicity (too much of certain nutrients available to plants).

It is also useful to check the pH of the water that you use on your plants. If the soil pH is fine but the water pH is off, that can cause problems as well.

In addition to professional soil tests, you can also get pH testing kits from the garden center or home improvement store. (The pH of your water can affect the outcome of these tests.)

To raise the pH of the soil, you'll add lime. To lower, it you will add a form of sulfur. Add amendments to adjust pH at least one month before planting so they have time to take effect and don't burn plant roots. Below is a handy reference for adjusting pH.

Nutrient Content of Soil

Soil test reports will give you information about the nutrients contained in the soil. Remember, though, that the soil pH affects whether those nutrients are available to plants. If your plants look like they have nutrient deficiencies, make sure to take a look at soil pH before you feed them. If the pH is off, it doesn't matter how much you feed the plants; they won't be able to take up the nutrients.

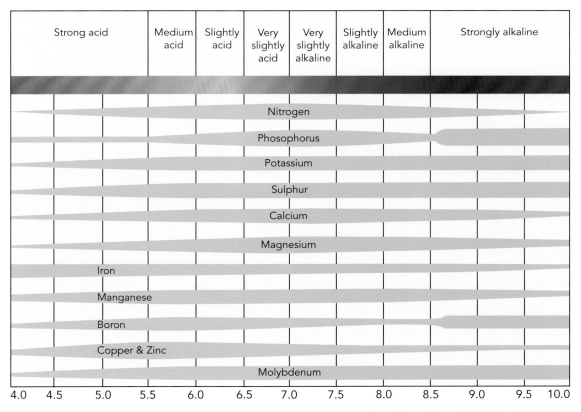

The soil pH affects whether or not plants can take up nutrients from the soil. You'll notice that the best nutrient availability is at the slightly acidic pH levels and not on one extreme or another.

Soil contains macronutrients (nitrogen, phosphorus, potassium) and micronutrients (iron, sulfur, magnesium, copper, and more). As discussed, the soil texture, organic matter content, and pH determine how much and how available the nutrients are in the soil. More is not better when it comes to nutrients, as they can reach toxic levels. Testing the soil will give you a baseline for further fertilizer inputs and any changes you need to make in order for nutrients to be more available to plants. (Learn more about fertilizing in Chapter 5.)

BUILDING BETTER SOIL

Now that you understand the components of soil, the properties of soil, and how they work together to promote healthy plant growth, you can learn about how to build better soil.

There are two parts to building better soils: practices or techniques that encourage or maintain soil health and soil inputs (such as compost or fertilizer, for example) that contribute to good soil.

CALCULATIONS FOR YEARLY SOIL ADJUSTMENTS

If your soil pH is . . .	And your soil texture is . . .		
	Sand	Loam	Clay
	. . . You need about this many pounds of LIME per 100 square feet of garden*		
4.5	12½	25	35
5.0	10½	21	29
5.5	4	8½	11½
6.5	1½	3	4½
If your soil pH is . . .	And your soil texture is . . .		
	Sand	Loam	Clay
	. . . You need about this many pounds of SULFUR per 100 square feet of garden*		
7.0	½	1	1½
7.5	1	2	2½
8.0	1½	3½	4½
8.5	3	5	6

Adapted from *Fertilizing Garden Soils* (Cornell Cooperative Extension, Chemung County)

*These requirements are based on the top 6" of garden soils. For perennials, divide this number by 3 to get the amount needed for the top 2" of soil.

Getting a Soil Test

One way to know exactly what you're working with is to take a soil sample and send it for testing through your local extension service. You can pick up soil test forms (and sometimes boxes) at the office, or print a form and instructions online.

The soil test reports differ from state to state, but they will include most, if not all of the following information:

- Nutrient content (and deficiencies) of macro- and micronutrients, with recommendations for fertilizing
- Soil texture
- Cation Exchange Capacity (CEC), an indication of how the soil holds onto nutrients
- pH (alkalinity or acidity), which impacts nutrient availability to plants
- Organic matter percentage

This type of soil test will give you a lot of information at once, and will help you make decisions for managing your soil.

This is an example of a professional soil test report.

Practices to Build Better Soil

These are the hands-on techniques that result in better soil.

Testing the Soil

A lot of this chapter has focused on soil testing. "Oh! I'll get a soil test," you say. Good! Because before you do anything other than add a light coating of compost to the garden, you need to get a soil test. Otherwise, you'll be driving blind the wrong way down a one-way street. Okay, maybe the situation isn't that dire, but you won't necessarily be doing what you need to do for better soil and might be making the situation worse in your yard or garden, or downstream. (Nutrients not needed or held in the soil get washed into waterways, causing algal blooms downstream.)

Avoid Using Chemical Fertilizers and Weed Killers

The beginning of this chapter described, in depth, the biology of soil. The soil is an entire ecosystem of living organisms. Chemical inputs wreak havoc on the insects, bacteria, fungi, and earthworms living in the soil. In addition, they don't feed the organisms living in the soil, so at the very most, they're like feeding plants a candy bar or giving a dental patient a shot of Novocain. They might produce a temporarily positive effect but those positive effects are not long lasting, while the long-term disruption of soil biology can be devastating. Organic fertilizers, including bone meal, blood meal, leaf litter, and more, however, are made from elements that feed the microorganisms, insects, and earthworms in the soil. (Learn about fertilizing in Chapter 5 and mulching and composting in Chapter 7.)

There are many organic fertilizer choices. All will contribute positively to the health of the soil and the organisms living in it. But get a soil test first.

There are some plant problems that require intervention, but it's always a good idea to start with the least impactful solution and work your way up (more about that in Chapters 9, 10, and 11). In the case of soilborne diseases and pathogens, there are cultural ways to get around the issues so that you can avoid drenching the soil with fungicides. Rotate plant families between locations in the garden from year to year. (Don't grow broccoli in the same spot four years in a row. Ditto with tomatoes.) Plant varieties resistant to diseases. Hand-pull weeds whenever possible and practice good garden care to help your plants outcompete the weeds.

Using Low-Till Gardening Methods

Tilling the entire vegetable garden before planting is so 1950s. That's because we've discovered that excessive tilling causes valuable topsoil to wash away during rains or crust over because the structure is ruined. We know how important earthworms are and we're not keen on chopping every single worm in the garden in half. Constant tilling destroys soil structure, eliminating pores for oxygen and water to stay in the soil. If you have a new garden bed or an excessive weed problem, tilling might be the only way to get the garden back in shape. (I have experienced this.) However, once you've tilled, keep that garden weeded and dig holes only to plant (or test the soil.) It really is that simple. Yank up last season's plants, shake the soil off the roots, and then plant. No tilling necessary.

Staying off Wet Soil

This practice could be expanded to "stay off all soil as much as possible period, the end." Walking around on wet soil unless it's almost complete sand is guaranteed to compact the soil. Compaction eliminates those all-important pore spaces for air and water, and leads to poor plant health.

Staying off any and all garden soil (other than the lawn) is a good idea too. It's why if you build raised beds, you're encouraged to make them no more than 4 feet wide, because 2 feet is the comfortable reach for most people without needing to step in the beds. Build pathways with stepping stones or designate pathways through large gardens to encourage your visitors and yourself to stay out of the root zones. It will make a difference over time.

Plant directly into the soil without tilling in order to avoid disturbing the soil, which can lead to erosion.

Inputs that Build the Soil

What you add to the garden helps either build or destroy the soil, so choose your inputs carefully. These beneficial gardening inputs will improve soil health over time. (Nothing natural is fast. It can take time to notice the effects. Have patience.)

Mulch

There are so many benefits to using mulch in the garden, especially organic mulch materials (shredded bark, composted leaves, grass clippings) rather than inorganic much (rubber pieces, plastic, or rocks). (Read more about mulch in Chapter 7.) Briefly, organic mulch (mulch made from natural materials) helps suppress weeds, breaks down and adds nutrients to the soil, conserves soil moisture, prevents erosion, keeps soil from crusting over, and modulates soil temperature. All those "capabilities" build soil over time.

Cover Crops

Cover crops are kind of like living mulch. Sow cover crops in landscape beds, vegetable gardens, and cutting gardens during a fallow period in that garden. Normally cover crops are pressed into service during the winter. A good rule of thumb is to sow seed one month before the first killing frost. Legumes make the best cover crops because they fix nitrogen while they grow, giving the soil an extra boost.

While the crops are still green, you'll cut them down and mix them into the soil as a "green manure."

In addition to adding nutrients to the soil, planting cover crops helps:

- reduce erosion (plant roots hold onto the soil that would otherwise be bare and susceptible to erosion during a rain),
- keep the soil surface from crusting over (which also can contribute to erosion problems),
- improve soil structure, and
- suppress weeds.

There are many common cover crops from which to choose:

- Annual rye
- Arugula
- Barley
- Buckwheat (a good source of phosphorus)
- Fava beans
- Forage radish
- Hairy vetch
- Oats
- Peas
- Red clover
- Spring or fall mustard
- Winter rye
- Wheat

LEFT: Cover crops can also be referred to as "green manure," as you'll till them into the soil while they're still growing.

RIGHT: Fava beans can be used as a cover crop.

Try to kill and incorporate cover crops into the soil before they go to seed, or you can end up with a major weed problem. You can mow down crops and till them under, till, or allow crops to be killed by freezing temperatures. Grain crops should always be mown down and tilled under before flowering.

Most of these cover crops listed above are attractive. You don't have to contain them to vegetable gardens. If you have empty space in a landscape bed, plant a row of peas or some clumps of wheat for winter interest and for the benefits they will add to the soil.

Soil Amendments

Soil amendments are, basically, anything you add to the soil to change it—improving the fertility or structure, changing the pH, and so forth. Lime, sulfur, coffee grounds, wood ash, compost, and fertilizer are all amendments. Before adding anything to the soil, get a soil test. Churning lime into a soil with an already high pH will do more harm than good.

Opinions differ on soil amendments, including what and how much you should add, and when. Soils will always move back toward their natural state. They have certain characteristics because of the vegetation growing on them and the bedrock under them. You can't change your soil full scale and expect it to stay that way. My advice is to go easy when it comes to amendments. Add a bit of lime if the pH is too low for tomatoes or spread a bit of soil acidifier around blueberries. Add some compost if the soil is full of

Worm compost is a rich source of nutrients.

2

Gardening Myths Busted: Don't Add Sand to Clay Soils

What do you get when you mix clay and sand? Concrete! (Okay, maybe not actual concrete, but that will be the consistency of the soil if you mix sand into a soil to "improve drainage.") Compost is what heavy clay soil needs to improve it. Leave the sand for the playground.

clay or entirely made of sand, and then, of course, use fertilizer for edibles. Aside from fruits and vegetables, which are high-maintenance (they're bred to do a job: produce food), select plants that will grow well in your native soil rather than plants that require constant inputs.

The benefits of compost are covered in depth in Chapter 7. There are several types:

- Composted manures
- Rotted leaves
- General yard/kitchen scrap compost
- Worm castings

Compost can be incorporated into landscape beds and vegetable gardens via mulching or tilling. Compost is the single best input you can add to the soil. All compost is chock full of beneficial nutrients, "food" for soil microorganisms, insects, earthworms, and water- and nutrient-holding organic matter. Too much organic matter in a soil can lead to waterlogged conditions, so if your soil is already high in organic matter (which you will know from getting a soil test), go easy on the compost.

Organic Fertilizers

Synthetic fertilizers are limited in scope and benefit. They're like a gulp of soda for plants—quick energy but nothing else. These fertilizers don't contain anything useful for soil microorganisms and they don't help build the soil long term. Synthetic fertilizers can also be easily washed out of the soil and into waterways, causing problems downstream. For building soil, organic fertilizers, such as blood meal, bone meal, kelp, fish emulsion, soybean meal, and others, will give you a much deeper and longer-lasting impact. Read more about fertilizers in Chapter 5.

Site-Specific Practices for Maintaining Good Soil

Here's how to put soil building practices and inputs together in specific areas of the garden.

Landscape Beds

A lot of gardeners and homeowners completely ignore landscape beds. These foundation plantings or island beds tend to have little diversity and interest. They don't have to be that way! You can have multiseason color and interest by picking out a diverse plant palette and supporting it with good soil. Here are some tips for better looking landscape beds, from the ground up.

- **Plant nitrogen-fixing plants.** There are many ornamentals in the legume family. (Pro Tip: peanuts make a great edible and ornamental landscape bed edging, and they fix nitrogen.) Wisteria, sweet peas, scarlet runner beans, lupines, and indigo plants are all nitrogen fixing.
- **Install pathways to reduce compaction.** The more you walk around in landscape beds, the worse off your plants will be. If you have to walk through foundation plantings to reach the house, lay down stepping stones and use them.
- **Mulch yearly with organic mulch (shredded hardwood/compost/shredded leaves).** This will provide a continual source of new organic matter to be broken down by microorganisms, earthworms, and insects. It will also naturally suppress weeds, conserve soil moisture, and prevent erosion.
- **Avoid working soil when it is wet.** It's so exciting to get out into the garden when the weather warms up, but in most places in spring, the ground is still thawing out and drying. Wait to plant until the soil isn't squishy.
- **Plant groundcovers.** These act as living mulch and provide all the same benefits as mulch, only you don't have to reapply every year!

Healthy plants start with healthy soil.

Vegetable Garden

If you want big vegetable garden harvests, spend time and money on building great soil. This is the one place where I throw out my rule about soil amendments and inputs. With each successive season, you're asking a lot of your vegetable garden soil. Remember that the vitamins, minerals, and nutrients you get from eating homegrown vegetables and fruits come straight from the soil (or, at least, their building blocks do). You absolutely have to replenish what the plants take out while growing. For the healthiest vegetables, make sure to support the soil with these techniques and inputs:

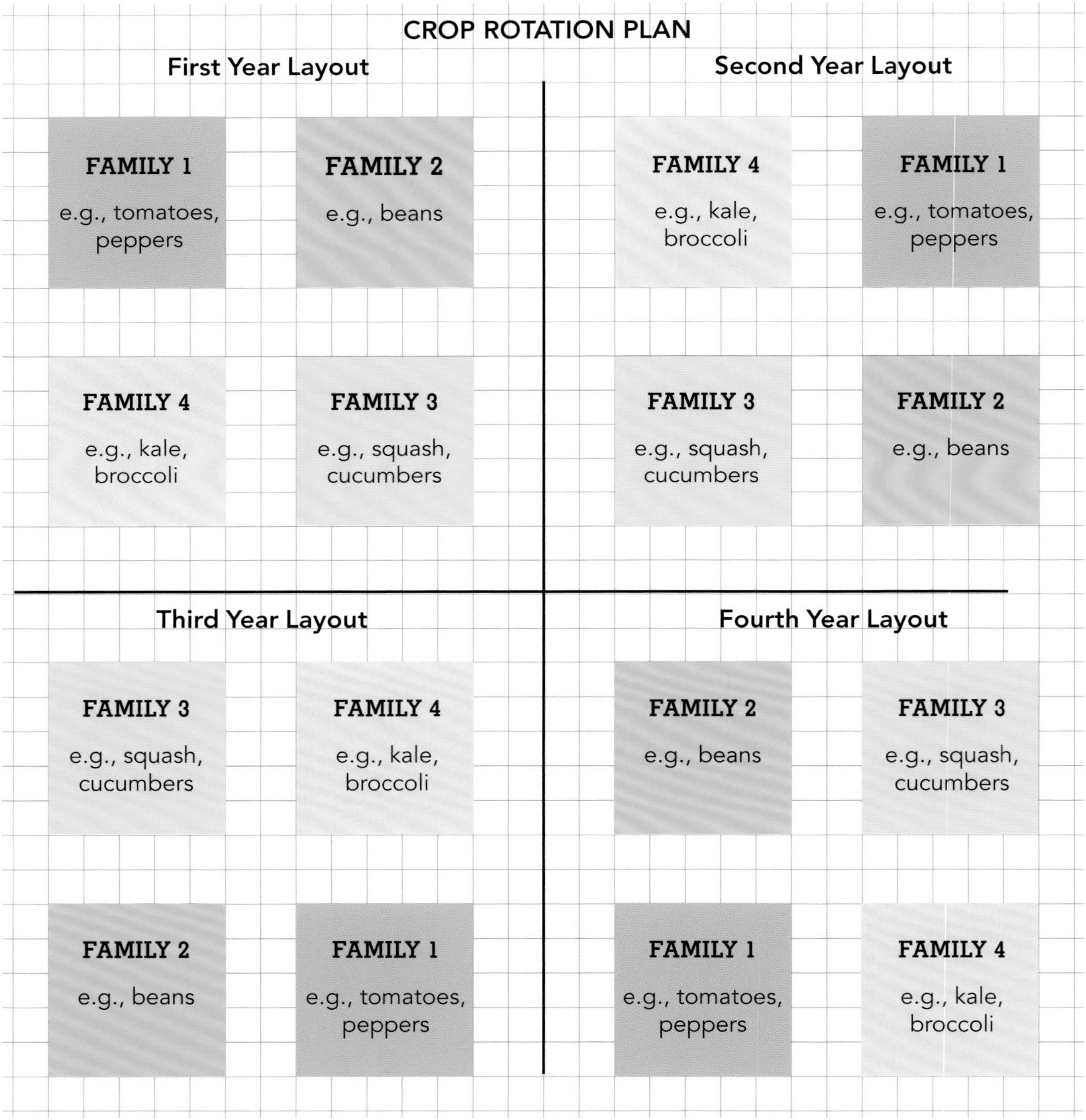

CROP ROTATION PLAN

First Year Layout

FAMILY 1	FAMILY 2
e.g., tomatoes, peppers	e.g., beans

FAMILY 4	FAMILY 3
e.g., kale, broccoli	e.g., squash, cucumbers

Second Year Layout

FAMILY 4	FAMILY 1
e.g., kale, broccoli	e.g., tomatoes, peppers

FAMILY 3	FAMILY 2
e.g., squash, cucumbers	e.g., beans

Third Year Layout

FAMILY 3	FAMILY 4
e.g., squash, cucumbers	e.g., kale, broccoli

FAMILY 2	FAMILY 1
e.g., beans	e.g., tomatoes, peppers

Fourth Year Layout

FAMILY 2	FAMILY 3
e.g., beans	e.g., squash, cucumbers

FAMILY 1	FAMILY 4
e.g., tomatoes, peppers	e.g., kale, broccoli

Rotating crops between vegetable garden plots allows the gardener to replenish depleted nutrients, and helps keep soil-borne diseases from becoming a problem.

- **Test the soil.** If you test the soil nowhere else in the garden, test the vegetable garden soil. Edibles can be so picky about their growing conditions, and most problems can be prevented or corrected by adjusting the soil.
- **Plant cover crops in rotating fallow areas.** If at all possible, plan a vegetable garden large enough that you can leave one-quarter to one-sixth of it fallow for a season and grow cover crops to improve soil structure, add organic matter to the soil, and replenish elements that have been used up.
- **Mulch the vegetable garden.** Not only will mulch break down and add nutrients to the soil, but it will also make caring for the vegetables so much easier. You won't have to water twice per day during the summer if you mulch. Less frequent watering means nutrients will stay put instead of washing out.
- **Use organic fertilizers.** They'll provide longer-lasting benefits.
- **Rotate crop families.** Soil-borne diseases cause headaches for gardeners. One way to manage those is to rotate vegetable crops. If you have four vegetable garden sections, plant one section with a cover crop, one with plants from the nightshade family (tomatoes, peppers, potatoes, eggplants), one with brassicas (broccoli, cabbage, kale), and one with other plant families (squash, beets, swiss chard, lettuce). Rotate each season. Another crop-rotation technique is to switch up the type of edible in each plot from season to season. For instance, plant a plot with a cover crop one season, a leafy green the next season, a fruiting crop (tomatoes, zucchini, eggplant) the next, and finally a root crop (carrots, turnips, parsnips). The logic behind this is that different types of crops use different nutrients from the soil. You can rotate using a bit of both techniques to avoid sucking the soil dry.

TROUBLESHOOTING SOIL PROBLEMS

Healthy soil is so important to plant health that when plant health takes a dive, the soil is the first place you should look to problem solve. "But wait, I have an insect problem," you might say. My advice would be to look at your plants. Do they seem stressed, have yellow leaves, or spindly growth? That's why (oftentimes) insects are attracted to plants, and better soil will result in healthier plant growth. Here are some common problems with plants and their root causes (pun intended) in the soil.

Poor Drainage

Topography has a lot to do with drainage. Low-lying areas of the yard are rarely going to be fast draining unless you're sitting on a heap of sand. If the soil is, overall, poorly draining, it probably has a high clay content. Work compost into the soil to improve the drainage. If this problem persists in vegetable gardens, consider growing in raised beds, where it's easier to control the soil makeup.

Compacted Soil

If you can't dig the soil to plant plants, it's probably compacted. Compost is, again, the fix for compacted soil. Work compost into the top few inches of the soil.

Weeds

Within landscape beds, rather than spraying full scale with a weed killer, hoe the weeds, hand pull, and plant groundcovers to outcompete the weeds.

Moss

Moss is a problem in highly compacted, highly acidic, nutrient-depleted soils. My personal opinion about moss is to let it be. Half of my backyard is moss. Hey—it's green and it's not taking over my vegetable gardens, so who cares. You can try to add compost to improve fertility or add lime to raise the pH, but why bother?

With gardening, it's easy to overcomplicate the issue. It's just soil, right? Well, if you have limited time and money to spend on improving your garden and landscape, every dollar and every minute allocated to building the soil will pay huge dividends over time. You'll need to intervene less if your plants have a well-drained, nutrient-rich place to call home.

CHAPTER 3

DESIGNING YOUR GARDENS

By George Weigel

DESIGNING GARDENS IS TRICKIER THAN DESIGNING the inside of a house for three reasons: For one thing, you can't just put any plant wherever you imagine it might look good and expect it to thrive. For another, plants grow, creep, die, and constantly change, so what you start with isn't what you'll end up with. Finally, while you don't have to worry about deer and groundhogs when designing other things, such as your home, you do have to worry about them eating your garden.

Fortunately, you have lots of resources for designing a garden. There are guidelines . . . plus lessons learned from the trials and errors of those who have gone before you.

And when it comes down to it, Rule No. 1 of garden design trumps all else: this is your yard, you paid for it, so it's only fair that you get to pick what you like. Design is subjective anyway. Tastes vary. One person's meadow is another person's weed patch.

Rule No. 2 is the old architecture adage: form follows function. That basically means that you should first think about what goals you have and what problems need to be solved and *then* worry about making it pretty.

OPPOSITE: This garden demonstrates great color selection and the merits of a layout featuring curved lines.

The bottom line regarding design: if you're happy with—and can sanely care for—the landscape you've created, it's right. Besides, shovels and shears can fix most mistakes.

WHERE TO START?

Assuming your goal is a doable, personally satisfying yard rather than making the cover of *Landscape Wizard* magazine, two considerations drive the process. One is what you'd *like* to do with your space. The second is what your particular conditions are going to *let* you do. Both are key to your garden plan's success.

For example, you might like the idea of a peaceful shade garden with a hammock, but if your yard resembles the Mohave Desert, the hostas and astilbes of your dreams will fry by August. Or maybe you fancy the look of palms and the fragrance of gardenias, but if you live in central Minnesota, they'll freeze-dry in winter.

Before digging your first hole or buying your first plant, think about your goals, wishes, likes, and dislikes, and especially how much maintenance you can or will devote to the yard.

A good first question to ask yourself is "How much do I like to garden?" Those who enjoy being outside with dirty hands tend to naturally gravitate toward weeding, trimming, primping, and so on and don't view any of that as work. On the other hand, those who would rather golf or read (not to mention those with bad backs and aging knees) might be better off putting low maintenance at the top of the wish list.

Knowing what you want sometimes isn't as easy as it seems. Many people can't identify up front exactly what they like, but almost everyone knows what they like once they see it. That's why it's helpful in the planning stage to browse through books, magazines, and images of landscapes to get ideas and trigger thoughts on taste. Also helpful is taking walks through local public gardens and neighborhoods to see what others have done that you like (or don't).

Think about how you'd like to use different parts of your yard before getting started on a design. A well-designed garden is a treat for the eyes, but also aims at being functional and easy to care for.

Some people prefer more formal looks with clipped hedges, straight lines, or even statuary.

Some people like an informal look with lots of plants and curved bed lines.

Planning Questions

Use these questions to help you zero in on what you might put on your garden wish list.

How do you use or want to use your yard? Do you need open space for the kids to play? Do you entertain much? Do you want a peaceful, shady retreat? How about a shed, a vegetable garden, or a pool? Do you want places to sit?

How much maintenance are you willing and able to do? If you don't like yard work and/or can't do heavy maintenance, be sure to factor that in. Even the best-designed gardens quickly fall apart without adequate maintenance. It's best to embrace your capabilities up front and match your bed sizes and plant selection to them.

Do you have a favorite style or look? Some people like formal, symmetrical gardens that are neatly trimmed. Others prefer a looser look with curved beds and naturalistic plantings or a riot of color.

Do you have any color preferences? Some people lean toward bright or warm colors, such as red, orange, gold, bright yellow, and deep purple. Others prefer cool colors, such as pink, blue, white, and lavender.

Are you looking for privacy? Are there views you'd like to block out? Need some privacy screening around a deck? Answering this will help determine where features such as fencing, walls, or tall, dense evergreens might go.

What views or focal points do you want to keep? If your backyard overlooks a lake or gives a great view of the sunset, the last thing you want is a tree or a line of evergreens that blocks the view from a favorite window or patio.

What features of the current landscape do you like or not like? In other words, what changes are in order? More color? Fill in bare spots? Tackle overgrown areas? Get weeds under control? Get rid of outdated or boring plants? Edit out bug-infested plants and pruning nightmares? Improve the view from inside?

Any specific features you'd like to add? Maybe a pollinator garden to attract bees, butterflies, and birds? A compost bin? A rain garden of damp-soil plants to solve a soggy area? A vegetable garden for fresh, organic produce? More diversity so the yard looks good in all four seasons? A few statues or non-plant focal points? A perennial-flower border? Landscape lighting?

Do you have any favorite or not-so-favorite plants or plant features? Do you want some peonies like grandma used to grow? More native plants? A rose bed? Fragrant plants around the patio? Dwarf conifers? A weeping specimen or two? Nothing that's invasive or disease prone? Nothing with thorns?

What's your budget? Don't overlook this, especially if you plan to hire out the work. Cost sometimes has a way of crimping style.

CONSIDER THE SITE

Assess your yard to determine what it might let you do. Keep in mind that it's much easier and less expensive to choose plantings that match the site you have than to alter the site to match the plants you'd like.

Most yards have a variety of conditions and microclimates, which are specific areas of the yard with somewhat different climate conditions. Perhaps the east foundation of your house gets morning sun but afternoon shade, while the foundation on the west side gets blasted by the day's hottest rays. Or maybe you have a particularly hot, dry spot along an asphalt driveway but a cool, wet area at the base of a slope. Even small differences can make a big difference in plant performance.

The better you know the intricacies of your yard, the better you'll be able to decide what kinds of gardens and plants should go where.

BELOW: Perennial-flower borders make a colorful feature along walks or property lines.

OPPOSITE: It is much easier to match a suitable use to the site, such as the water feature on an existing slope, than it is to change the site to match use.

This is especially important if you've just moved into an existing home. Resist the urge to do an immediate and total redo. You might realize too late that the ugly tree you just cut down shaded the patio in the evening or that the overgrown hollies were intentionally left untrimmed to hide the neighbor's outhouse collection.

Instead, spend a growing season observing. Pay attention to where the sun comes up and goes down. Look to see where water pools after a rain or where snow blows and piles up in winter.

You can always mulch bare areas or plant a few annual flowers until you figure out a longer-term game plan. Better to be patient and increase your odds of guessing right the first time than to "git 'er done" ASAP and end up replacing a lot of dead plants later.

Site Questions

Answer these questions to help you zero in on what might work where on your site.

How's the light? Most plants are sensitive to sunlight amount and intensity. Sun-preferring plants might not bloom in too much shade, while shade-preferers might wilt and die in full sun. Observe where it's sunny all day and how the light tracks during the day. Afternoon sun, for example, is more intense than morning sun. Note where it's shady, and keep in mind that the shade under big trees is often *dry* shade due to the roots taking moisture, so it calls for a specially adapted set of plants.

How's the drainage? This is a life-or-death matter for plants. A sunny, flat, open area usually means dry spells, while low-lying areas, depressions, and swales can mean periods of wet or soggy soil. Drought and root rot are both leading causes of plant death.

What's the condition of the soil? This includes soil quality as well as nutrition content. Sandy soil tends to drain quickly and become depleted of nutrients. Clay soil may be in better shape nutritionally but is often compacted and poorly drained. Some soils are acidic, and some are alkaline. Test and assess the soil so you'll know where you stand and what amendments might be needed before planting. (Read more about this in Chapter 2.)

How about wind? Do gusts come from a certain direction? Knowing this not only helps you avoid planting wind-sensitive plants such as Japanese maples and variegated English hollies in windy spots, but you can also identify where to plant dense evergreens to keep cold winter winds from blasting the house.

Any slopes? Slopes can create a variety of challenges. A steep slope might be too hard to mow, making it a candidate for low-care, groundcover-type plantings. Because frost rolls down a hill, the base of a slope is often a frost pocket that can kill borderline-hardy plants. South- and west-facing slopes are particularly hot because of the increased sunlight angle; they call for different plants than north- and east-facing ones.

Any animal issues? Deer can decimate a landscape overnight, so it's helpful to know if any are lurking in the area. If so, you can take preventative action by installing fencing, using repellents, or planting species they like the least. You should also assess the presence of rabbits, groundhogs, voles, chipmunks, squirrels, prairie dogs, armadillos, and raccoons.

A steep slope is an awkward place to plant lawn grass. Masses of spreading perennials would be of great use here.

What's overhead and underneath? This isn't just for aesthetics. It's a safety issue. Note where overhead lines are so you don't plant trees that will grow up into them. Have utility companies mark where buried lines are so you don't hit them while digging.

What's the character of the house and neighborhood? This might help drive the style and plantings, although it's not essential that you limit yourself only to what's the norm (remember Rule No. 1—if you like it, it's right). On the other hand, naturalistic plantings of native perennials generally are more at home in the country than around a Colonial-style house, while formal gardens with clipped boxwoods might look out of place in a neighborhood of wooded cottages.

Conditions help dictate what will work best on a site. Because most vegetables prefer full sun, for example, a sunny part of the yard would make the most sense.

"Bubbling" out a Plan

Before heading for the shovel, consider putting at least a broad plan on paper. This can be something as basic as a bubble diagram, which is a rough sketch of the whole property, that starts to translate your ideas into reality.

Draw your yard's boundaries, and then plot any existing permanent features along with their approximate size and location. This should include the house, any outbuildings, driveways, sidewalks, patios, swimming pools, and even large trees. If you have a property plot plan, use a piece of tracing paper over it to make a copy.

Then go to your wish list and begin to assign items from the list where they make the most sense. Draw blocks or bubbles to represent each use and the approximate size you're thinking of devoting to each.

At this point, don't get too specific. Think main uses and where to put them, not exact plants.

For example, you might label the front yard "public area," where you plan to do something neat and more formal where passersby frequently walk. You might include a hedge planting down the side yard where you've decided privacy is needed. You may decide that a small water feature with a flower garden would work best wrapped around the back patio. And the sunny back left corner might be the ideal spot for that fruit and vegetable garden.

This is where your wish list and the yard's what-you-can-do list come together . . . or collide.

Your first inclination for that water feature, for example, might be around the patio. But as you think through things, you might realize that the patio area is the only flat area for the kids' play set, while the slope in the back could give you a cascading waterfall that dumps into a small pond at its base.

Or you might like the eastern side yard for a vegetable and herb garden, while the sun might dictate that the brighter west side is a better spot.

Now's the time to play around with ideas. You may not be able to fit everything in, or you may need to reduce the wish-list size of that putting green to make room for that new shed. But it's much easier to erase and move pencil-drawn bubbles now than to move an actual shed later.

Dividing the outdoor space by use like this is the same technique used to play with ideas for an interior space. The living room gets assigned inside the front door, the kitchen goes along the back, the bedrooms go upstairs, and so on. If it makes sense inside, why not outside?

Outdoor Rooms

There is a garden design principle often used called building outdoor rooms. It's not the only way to plan a landscape, but it usually leads to a result that's more distinctive than the boring norm, which is to plant shrubs around the house with a tree or two in the front yard.

Just as indoor space is divided into rooms by walls, ceilings, and doorways, outdoor space can be delineated similarly.

Outdoor walls can include features such as trimmed evergreen hedges, more natural-looking mixed hedges, border gardens, fences, stone walls, and vine-covered trellises. The choice is yours, depending on how much privacy you want and how open you want each room to be.

A knee-high stone wall or border garden, for example, can give the effect of a room to an area without making it too confined or segregated.

LEFT: A bubble diagram breaks the yard into sections by use, similar to how the inside of a house is divided into rooms.

BELOW: This garden functions as an outdoor sitting room.

A vine-covered pergola serves as an outdoor ceiling (and dog-shading structure) in this garden.

Think of your outside "doors" as the way you enter and exit each outdoor area. These could be something door-like, such as a gate or an arbor, or something subtler, such as a pair of flanking tall grasses or a pair of flower pots sitting on opposing block columns.

Outdoor "ceilings" are for areas where you want overhead enclosure. These also can vary from natural coverings, such as the canopy of a shade tree or a vine-covered pergola, to more structured choices, such as an awning or sky-lighted roof.

You may not want ceilings at all in some spots, such as over the lawn where the kids play soccer or the vegetable garden.

Finally, the outdoor "floors" can range from natural materials, such as grass and mulched paths, to more structured choices, such as wood decking, paver-block patios, or brick paths.

Look to the house for cues on where to plot the boundaries of your outdoor rooms. Obvious reference points would be house corners, locations of doors and windows, and where you already have courtyards or rooms jutting out. Lining up your outdoor rooms with these is a subtle but effective way to "marry" the landscaping to the house architecture.

Get Specific

Once you've decided on the big picture, it's a matter of tackling each bubble. It's best to carry out your plan in stages, starting with your highest priority areas first. For one thing, it's easier on the back and the budget when you break one huge job into smaller bits done gradually, even if it takes several years. For another, it's more forgiving when it comes to watering in case of the Murphy's Law event where you plant the entire landscape on what turns out to be the first week of the century's worst drought.

But just as important, having a plan helps ensure you'll end up with a unified whole, even if you've done the areas bit by bit over several years.

If you're good at envisioning things on paper, get some graph paper and draw each garden in advance—in pencil. Use the scale of the graph paper: one box on the paper equals 1 foot on the ground.

You'll want to mark more specific items in your yard and plan at this stage, such as the location of hose outlets, window heights, dryer vents, downspouts, utility meters, and any other existing features that can affect plant placement. Don't trust existing plot plans for these. It's best to get your own real-life, as-is measurements.

Pencil in dots and circles to represent plants, and have fun erasing and moving until it all works out.

If you're not into using graph paper, you can do the same thing with an array of fairly inexpensive landscaping computer software that lets you transfer measurements into the program and drag scalable images of plants into various spots. Some software can even give 3D views of the future garden, although there's a learning curve involved in getting it all done properly.

If you're better working at full scale rather than using paper *or* computers, mark off your beds with rope or spray paint. Then use sticks, branches, or bamboo stakes to represent tentative placement of plants.

Work from Big to Little

A good place to start a design is to plot where you walk—or intend to walk—through an area. Whether it's a brick walk or turfgrass, pathways address an important functional need and give a logical flow to the yard as they guide from one outdoor area to the next.

Paths can be straight or curved depending on your preference and ideally they're sized at no less than 4 feet wide.

Paths also help dictate where garden beds might go, i.e., anywhere the paths are *not*. You could build an island bed along one side of a curving path, you could build beds that flank both sides of a path, or you could build a bed at the end of a path.

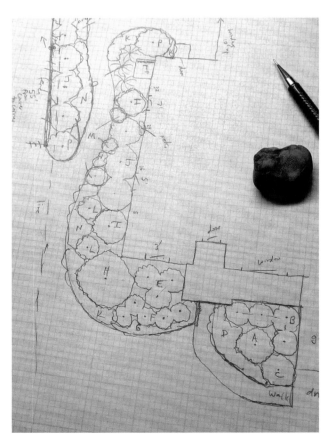

A pencil sketch on graph paper is a good way to plan plant placements before heading off to the garden center.

Plotting paths first helps determine bed shapes, sizes, and locations.

Underestimating plant sizes is the leading design blunder.

When drawing beds, think about how they'll fit into the overall landscape and how they'll look with one another. Size is an important consideration too. Go too small in a big yard, and your 4-foot circular bed will look like a drop in a big, green ocean of a lawn. Also, don't overdo it with curves. A few gentle swoops look more natural than a series of tight waves that will be a pain to mow around. A subtle technique that adds to the flow of a yard is mirroring or matching the curves in opposing beds so that it looks as if they fit together like puzzle pieces.

Once the paths, bed sizes, and bed shapes are drawn, place the biggest and/or most permanent elements. These include hardscaping elements, such as arbors, pergolas, and retaining walls, as well as anchor plants, such as trees, weeping-evergreen specimens, and tall shrubs that flank pathways.

Refer to your wish list again. This is where you can solve needs you've identified and carry out your goals by specific placements. If you're designing around the patio, for example, one of the first elements might be to erect a vine-covered trellis to put screening between you and the neighbor's patio. Or you might be able to keep the setting sun out of your face

in the evening by strategically placing a single shade tree. Or the situation might call for a trio of dense evergreens along the property line to block wind gusts coming from an adjacent open field.

Remember, form follows function: solve issues first, then make it pretty.

Keep Plant Size in Mind

Want to guess the leading design blunder? It's placing plants too close to one another as well as to walls and other structures.

What counts is how big a plant is *going* to get and how fast it's going to get there. Make your planting plan according to the mature sizes listed on plant tags, not by how plants look when you purchase them.

When planting next to a wall or structure, divide the mature width in half (because a plant will grow out on both sides from the center). Plant no closer than that distance. For example, a holly that will get 8 feet around should be planted a minimum of 4 feet away from a wall.

To determine how close to space plants, leave enough room so that they can grow to their mature width without interfering with another plant. For example, plant hydrangeas that grow to a mature size of 4 feet in diameter at least 4 feet apart.

If two plants of differing sizes are being planted next to one another, add the two mature widths together and divide the total in half to determine minimum spacing. A 6-foot-wide viburnum and a 4-foot-wide hydrangea should be planted no closer than 5 feet apart (6 plus 4 equals 10, 10 divided by 2 equals 5).

Planning for height is easier. If your window sill is 3 feet off the ground and you don't want to obstruct the view, look for plants that top out at 3 feet tall—unless you don't mind regular trimming.

In borders and foundation plantings that you view from only one angle, arrange your plants so that the tallest ones are in the back, layering down to the shortest ones in front.

In an island bed that allows you to see plants from all angles, place the taller plants toward the middle and the shorter ones around the perimeter.

Be especially careful when planting along property lines. Plants growing over neighbors' properties can be the source of neighborly spats. And don't create a hazard by obstructing driveways with big plants.

Remember that plants really never stop growing until they're dead. Like people, they usually just slow down with age.

This garden sticks mainly with chartreuse as the dominant color, making it largely monochromatic.

This purple-leaf smoke bush adds color to the garden even when it's not in bloom.

The burgundy stems of these sedum are a perfect color echo for the burgundy-leafed coleus underneath.

PLAN FOR COLOR

Color is one way to group plants. You have lots of freedom with this because coordinating color in garden design is like beauty: it's in the eye of the beholder. Some beholders see clashes with even slight variations in hues, while others are okay with any color pairing—especially when it comes to flowers.

It's hard to go wrong if you stick with a monochromatic (one-color) garden, such as a white garden with all-white flowers or a yellow garden with nothing but yellow bloomers.

A step more adventuresome is pairing two or more colors from the same color family.

Warm colors are brighter, more saturated, and more attention-grabbing—red, gold, bright yellow, orange, and hybrid colors that have warm-color parents, such as salmon, apricot, and chartreuse.

That means you'll usually be fine pairing a red flower with a gold one and/or an orange one.

Cool colors—especially pastels—are soft and relaxing: pink, blue, lavender, and soft rose. These are calming colors, like what you'll find in doctor's offices. You can successfully pair a pink flower next to a blue one.

Green, white, silver, and black are neutral colors that work with most any other flower.

When choosing colors, don't limit yourself to flowers. You'll find lots of plants with colorful leaves as well as interesting bark and fruit color. An additional benefit of using plants that don't flower: leaf color lasts much longer than many flowers.

For plantings used as a backdrop by a house or other structure, try to coordinate those plant colors with the structure's colors. For example, if your house has a blue door or blue shutters, look for a few plants that bloom blue or that have bluish foliage. Or if your house is red brick, consider a warm-colored plant scheme with red, gold, yellow, orange, and burgundy.

To help with matching, use paint chips. Pick chips that match the house trim, then take those to the garden center to hold up alongside prospective plants.

Another color trick is looking for color "echoes." This is when a color in one plant matches the color in another, such as the burgundy leaf of a coleus that's the spitting image of the burgundy throat of a particular daylily.

If you don't have a good eye for color matches, get a color wheel. These are inexpensive and sold at art-supply stores. They show which colors pair nicely together.

The wheel also shows which colors are opposites of one another, such as blue and yellow or purple and orange.

When pairing plants, try to vary textures, such as contrasting a rounded dark-leaf heuchera (rear) with a planting of fine-leafed 'Angelina' creeping sedum.

These columnar yews are an example of one type of plant form.

When done in moderation, exact opposites pair together as nicely as different colors of the same family.

MIX FORMS AND TEXTURES

A second way to mix and match plants is with their form and texture.

Form is the shape of the plant, including narrow uprights (columnar), broader pyramids, vase-shaped plants that flare out at the top, weepers with arms that hang down, ball-shaped plants, plants with branches that seem to spray up and out, and ground-hugging creepers.

Texture is the tactile quality of plants. It could be how they feel when touched or how you perceive they might feel according to their appearance, such as plants with rounded leaves, plants with lacy or frilly leaves, or plants with spiky or strappy foliage.

Gardens generally look best when plant forms and textures are varied and contrasted. Plant all rounded plants or all spiky ones, and the feel is monotonous—too much of the same thing over and over again.

Instead, if you're planting rounded-leaf coral bells, consider pairing it with fine-leafed creeping sedum instead of another rounded-leaf plant.

Or, if you're planting a bed of ball-shaped boxwoods, pair them with a bladed plant, such as liriope or Japanese forest grass, or a spiky upright, such as salvias or irises.

WHAT PLANTS WHERE?

Unless you're thoroughly familiar with plants, plan to do some homework to pick the best plants for each site. Plant selection makes a huge difference, so it pays to invest time zeroing in on superior varieties.

Lots of resources can help with this, but the best ones are those closest to you. That's because plants perform markedly different from region to region. What's a great choice in dry Arizona may rot out in a Carolina bog.

Start by paying attention to plants that are doing well in local public gardens and neighborhoods. Pick the brains of local Master Gardeners, garden-center staff, and local veteran gardeners. Lean toward the plant suggestions and plant lists from regional sources, such as local extension services, regional gardening magazines and websites, and local plant societies, garden clubs, garden writers, and bloggers. Consult your region's Cool Springs Press garden guide, which is a series of books written by local experts focusing on the best landscape plants for each state or region.

Get to know the traits of the plants that are best for your region, such as sizes, bloom colors and times, light needs, and site preferences. The goal is to arm yourself with a workable list of plants that are likely to do well in your climate, soil, and setting. Refer to that list as you draw a plan and choose specific plants for specific spots.

Don't worry if you guess wrong on the first attempted planting. If you see a plant struggling, try to figure out why. Often, moving a plant to a sunnier or shadier or wetter or drier part of the yard can turn a struggler into a thriver. Even if a plant dies, examine why it died and chalk it up to experience.

This Black Lace elderberry has a fine, lacy texture to its leaves.

ABOVE: This "pot couple" gives a personal and fun finishing touch to this garden.

OPPOSITE: Flowers can add a pop of color to make edible gardens more attractive.

FINISHING TOUCHES

Finally, think about accessorizing the landscape by adding focal points and other non-plant items. They add a nice finishing touch to a garden and put your personality into the mix. Examples include statues, fountains, ornate pots, sundials, birdbaths, benches, or even antiques and found objects from a garage sale.

Here are some ideas for where to add them:
- At the end of a path or where a path veers off, to draw your eye down the path
- Lined up with windows, where they tie into a house feature but also can be seen from the inside
- Where two different plant masses meet
- As the centerpiece of a flower garden
- Under a low-hanging tree, especially where a branch seems to point at your object

EDIBLE LANDSCAPING

Just because you can eat a plant doesn't mean it's ugly and has to be relegated to a hidden back corner. Many edibles are as good-looking as ornamental plants and are fair game anywhere in the yard.

One option is to make primarily edible gardens more attractive by mixing flowers in with them. Marigolds, celosia, and dwarf zinnias, for example, add pops of color to green-leafed beds of cabbage, lettuce, and carrots.

Edible gardens also can be designed in more ornamental ways. For example, lay out the raised beds in patterns; use attractive wooden gates and picket fences instead of chicken wire; add hardscape features, such as wooden obelisks for vine supports and a bench or two; and tuck in a few focal points, such as a sundial, a birdbath, or a small statue.

When planting, use the same principles as in the ornamental garden to mix and match edibles. Rather than line

up vegetable crops in rows or blocks by themselves, look at the plant colors, textures, and forms and interplant them in mixed arrangements. A cluster of spiky onions, for instance, might look good in front of taller pepper plants and flanked by trios of rounded red lettuce. Or look to the purple leaf color in purple sage as a good partner for the lavender blooms of eggplant or the purplish stems and leaf veins of 'Redbor' or 'Red Russian' kale.

A second strategy is to mix edibles in with the existing landscape. Because most edibles are annuals, they can be tucked seasonally into openings among shrubs and between flower clusters. You won't even need a separate vegetable garden with this approach.

Again, look to neighboring plants for cues on what edibles might look best where. If you have a cluster of spiky ornamental grass with an opening next to it, how about a rounded cabbage with purple leaves? Or flank a yellow rose with a pair of hot peppers that will produce small red fruits. Substitute edibles altogether where their traits make sense, such as using blueberries as a colorful border hedge or a band of chives, thyme, or oregano along a path.

A third option is mixing edibles with flowers in containers. Rather than filling a big pot or window box with annual flowers, look to the herb and vegetable section of the garden center to design a mixed "veggimental" pot.

When you're using edibles in the landscape, have a plan for when you harvest: when the red lettuce or purple cabbage is ready to eat, have another crop or flower ready to go in the harvested space.

Edibles Worthy of Ornamental Treatment

Here's a list of some of the most attractive edible plants.

Plants with colorful foliage or stems: golden oregano, kale, lemon thyme, lettuce, malabar spinach, mesclun, mustard, okra, orach, pineapple sage, purple basil, purple kohlrabi, radicchio, red cabbage, sage, silver thyme, Swiss chard

Plants with colorful fruits or flowers: beans, blueberries, cauliflower (especially purple or orange), chamomile, chives, cucumbers, currants, dill, eggplant, gourds, grapes, hardy kiwi, lavender, melons, nasturtiums, okra, pansies, peas, peppers, squash, strawberries, tomatoes

Plants with interesting texture or form: asparagus, bok choy, brussels sprouts, cardoon, carrots, celery, chives, corn, dill, fennel, globe artichokes, kale, kohlrabi, leeks/onions, okra, parsley, rhubarb, rosemary, tarragon

OPPOSITE: Most edibles do well in containers, where plants such as these peppers and cabbages pair well with mums and a boxwood.

CHAPTER 4
PLANTING A GARDEN

By Lynn Steiner

PUTTING PLANTS IN A FRESHLY PREPARED GARDEN bed is truly one of the most fun aspects of gardening. Planting reflects the optimism and anticipation that all gardeners feel. Your garden may not look like much on planting day, but you can imagine what will transpire as the weeks and years go on. The rewards may come as quickly as a few weeks when you harvest some radishes to many years down the road when you enjoy the shade of a mature tree. Whether you are putting a few seeds in the ground or filling a large garden bed with container-grown plants, you'll want to give your new plants the best start possible by using proper planting techniques.

"The right plant in the right place" is a common garden mantra, and for good reason. Let's take that one step further and say "the right plant *properly planted* in the right place." Just as important as choosing the best plants is planting them correctly. In this chapter, you will learn about the different ways to purchase plants as well as how to start plants from seed. There is detailed information about the proper planting techniques for annuals, perennials, bulbs, vegetables, shrubs, and trees—everything you need to make sure your garden is off to a strong start!

OPPOSITE: Planting is the foundation of a good garden and good planting is a matter of proper technique using the most basic of tools.

BUYING PLANTS

Start by choosing high-quality plants. You can get plants from a variety of sources. Most will probably come from traditional garden centers and nurseries, but some will also come as gifts from friends' and families' gardens, local plant sales, the local grocery store, and even from a previous residence. While it is fun to get plants from a variety of sources, the best way to get good plants is to shop at a reputable nursery or garden center. When you visit, observe the growing conditions and talk with the staff to see how knowledgeable they are. In most cases, you get what you pay for. High-quality plants may cost a bit more, but they usually get established more quickly and are better plants in the long run.

Plants are available in several different vessels. Most annuals and vegetables are sold in cell packs, while perennials are usually sold in individual pots. Woody plants are sold as bare root, container grown, or balled and burlapped. Container-grown plants with a well-established root system are usually the best way to go with perennials and woody plants. They become established quickly and give you a better-looking garden sooner. If cost is a concern or if you are planting a lot of one species, such as a hedge or a groundcover, consider using seeds, bare-root plants (without soil), or plugs, if you can find them. Plugs are small, cone-shaped pots, usually about 2 inches in diameter and about 5 inches long. They are often sold in six- or nine-packs like annuals. Plugs usually establish themselves rather quickly and do just as well as container plants in the long run.

TIMING

In most areas of the country, the best time to put most plants in the ground is spring. This gives them ample time to become established before they have to endure their first winter in the ground. Rainfall is also usually more abundant in spring.

But container-grown summer- and fall-blooming flowers and most woody plants can be planted in spring or fall—actually, all season long if you are diligent about watering when needed. You may also need to provide shelter from the sun for a few weeks. Fall planting should be finished at least six weeks before hard-freezing weather occurs.

In cold climates, it is a good idea to put down a winter mulch of weed-free straw or leaves after the ground has frozen. This helps ensure that the new plants will remain firmly planted in the soil through winter freeze-thaw cycles.

It is best to plant or transplant early-blooming species right after they flower, usually in late spring. Bare-root plants shipped by mail-order nurseries should only be planted in spring.

Ordering Plants by Mail

Mail-order shopping is convenient and provides you with a larger selection of plants. Here are some tips for success:

- Order from a reputable nursery that has a refund or replacement process.
- With perennial plants, order from a nursery with the same climate as you have.
- Order early for a better selection.
- Specify a shipping date so plants don't arrive before you are ready to plant them.
- Unpack plants as soon as they arrive and examine them carefully for any problems.
- Plant as soon as possible after receiving plants.

If you plant in the heat of summer, you may need to provide some type of shading until the plants become established to prevent excessive water loss.

When purchasing annuals, look for healthy seedlings that haven't outgrown their container. Don't buy them too early. These young plants require daily watering and regular fertilizing and the garden center or nursery is often better able to give this regular care than you are at home.

Make sure the plants are well watered in their containers right up until the time they go into the ground. Bare-root plants should be soaked in water for a day or two before planting. Planting can be a traumatic experience for even the toughest of plants. Try to plant on an overcast day; misty rain is perfect. If cloudy weather isn't in the forecast, transplant later in the day. This will help reduce water loss from the new transplants.

NEW PLANT CARE

When planting a large garden, try to avoid stepping on the soil as much as possible. Covering the prepared soil with mulch before planting will help protect the soil and it is usually easier to lay down mulch before the easily damaged young plants are in place. Start in the middle and work your way out. Pull away the mulch and prepare a planting hole deep enough so that the plant will go into the ground at the same level as it was growing in the nursery container. Then gently replace the mulch back up around the plant, keeping it a few inches away from the stem itself.

New plants must have adequate water. Give your newly planted garden a good soaking right after installation regardless of the soil moisture level, and plan to water as needed to keep the soil evenly moist until plants are well established. New plants growing in sandy soil may require watering every couple of days for the first few weeks if there is not adequate rainfall.

If you've prepared your soil properly and amended it as needed, newly planted gardens don't need fertilizer. You run the risk of burning the roots and you will also encourage weeds. And there is a very good chance that a granular fertilizer will wash away before the plant roots have a chance to take it up.

Plants from Seeds

There are many reasons gardeners choose to grow plants from seeds. It offers you a much wider range of varieties than you would find at local nurseries. It can also save you money: Instead of buying three small pots of your favorite annual, you can buy a pack of seeds for about a third of the price and get more plants than you can find room for. And if properly stored in cool, dry conditions (the refrigerator works fine), many seeds will last two years or even more, stretching your investment even further. Seeds are also more flexible in terms of shipping and planting, providing you with a longer planting window than container-grown plants. Finally, watching a plant grow from a seed you planted yourself is a very rewarding experience—a true sense of accomplishment for any gardener.

The easiest way to start plants from seeds is to do like we did as children: plant seeds in the spot we want them to grow. This works well for cold-tolerant and fast-growing vegetables (such as lettuce and radishes) and annuals or perennials that do not tolerate root disturbance when transplanting (such as morning glories and lupines). Here are some general rules of thumb:

- Bury seeds only about as deep as their diameter.
- Sprinkle soil on top of the seeds, pressing gently to ensure they have contact with the soil. A few seeds need light to sprout, so cover them sparingly.
- Sprinkle water on the seedbed whenever the surface is dry until all the seeds have sprouted.

It is best not to direct seed warm-season annuals and vegetables, most perennials, and woody species. Warm-season annuals and vegetables require 6 to 12 weeks to reach flowering or fruiting size, so direct seeding wouldn't give you a usable plant until mid- to late summer. Most perennials take at least two growing seasons to become established from seed; woody plants take even longer. In the meantime, weeds can move in and make it difficult to differentiate between good seedlings and bad plants.

For plants that require a longer period of time to reach flowering or fruiting, indoor seed starting is a rewarding endeavor. You can go the cut-down milk carton route like you did as a child, but you will have better luck if you start with some specific equipment and the right space.

Growing plants from seeds is a simple, easy, and inexpensive way to acquire garden plants.

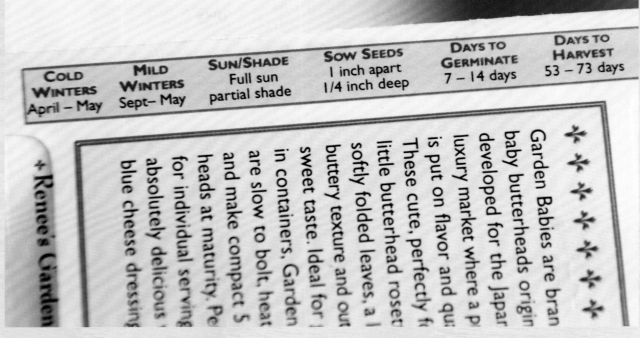

COLD WINTERS April – May	MILD WINTERS Sept– May	SUN/SHADE Full sun partial shade	SOW SEEDS 1 inch apart 1/4 inch deep	DAYS TO GERMINATE 7 – 14 days	DAYS TO HARVEST 53 – 73 days

Garden Babies are bran... baby butterheads origin... developed for the Japan... luxury market where a p... is put on flavor and qu... These cute, perfectly fi... little butterhead roset... softly folded leaves, a l... buttery texture and out... sweet taste. Ideal for j... in containers. Garden ... are slow to bolt, heat ... and make compact 5 ... heads at maturity. Pe... for individual serving ... absolutely delicious ... blue cheese dressing...

+ Renee's Garden

To make sure your plants are garden ready at transplanting time, read each seed packet carefully and make a list of start dates. Your goal is to have strong, stocky vegetable plants and annual flowers with buds just ready to open when you put them in the ground.

Sow the seeds at the appropriate time. Most warm-season annuals should be seeded indoors 6 to 8 weeks before the last spring frost, but some require 10 to 12 weeks or more, which means they need to be sown by mid-January to have garden-sized blooming plants by mid-May. On the other hand, seeds sown too early result in leggy (tall and weak-stemmed) plants that don't transplant well. A popular way to get seeds is from mail-order catalogs, so make sure you order yours in plenty of time.

Use a proper container. You can use almost any container that will hold soil and has drainage holes to get rid of excess water. Just make sure it is clean and sterilized. You can reuse the cell packs that purchased plants come in for starting seeds or potting up seedlings. Just make sure you clean them first; most will survive a run in the top rack of the dishwasher.

Use the right planting medium. Even the best garden soil is not a good choice for starting seeds indoors. It is too heavy and it is often contaminated with weed seeds or disease organisms, which can prove fatal to seedlings. A better bet is to purchase a commercial soilless seed-starting mix. These mixes are well drained, have good aeration, are sterile, and often provide small amounts of nutrients.

Provide adequate light. Lighting is crucial when starting seeds indoors. Winter sun alone is usually not strong enough to produce healthy seedlings. You need to provide artificial light in the form of an inexpensive shop light fixture holding two 40-watt fluorescent tubes. Suspend the fixture over a bench or table, making sure you can raise and lower the lights as needed as the plants grow.

Harden off before transplanting. Hardening off is the process of acclimating your tender, indoor-grown seedlings or store-bought transplants to the harsher conditions and brighter light awaiting them in the garden. A week or so before planting outdoors, start exposing your plants to outside conditions. Set them outside in a shady, sheltered spot for a couple of hours. Gradually increase the time they spend outdoors and the amount of sunlight they receive over the course of the week. Keep a careful eye on the young plants. It doesn't take much for them to wilt or even die if they get too much wind or sunlight too quickly.

Starting Seeds Indoors

1. Fill containers to within about a ½ inch of the top with a sterile soilless mix and place in a tray of water to saturate the soil.

2. Carefully sow the seeds on the moistened surface and cover with the appropriate amount of medium. Some seeds need light to germinate and should only receive a light dusting of the medium.

3. Put the container in a plastic bag or cover it with plastic and seal it to maintain humidity. Place in a warm spot out of direct sunlight; the top of a refrigerator or freezer works well. Check daily for germination. You may need to open the bag for a little while to prevent excessive moisture buildup, which can lead to damping-off disease.

4. Remove the plastic bag when the seedlings first appear and place the container under fluorescent lights, leaving about 1 inch between the tops of the plants and the light. Adjust the light as needed to keep it 1 to 3 inches above the seedlings as they grow. Maintain evenly moist soil by misting or bottom watering, which won't disturb the tiny plants.

5. When seedlings have one or two sets of leaves, use a small, pointed scissors to thin out excess seedlings. Avoid pulling the unwanted seedlings because it can uproot nearby seedlings.

6. Transplant seedlings into individual pots when they have two sets of leaves, gently prying seedlings out of the soil and separating the roots. Place the pots back under lights.

If the roots of annual plants have grown together, or if the plants are not growing in individual cells, carefully cut the soil into sections using a sharp knife or scissors. With individual plants in peat pots, you can peel away the top of the pot, then plant the pot itself in the soil.

PLANTING ANNUALS

Annuals are used in many ways in the landscape. They are often planted in groups or drifts in flower gardens, spacing plants 6 to 8 inches apart. They are staples in container gardening. Some larger annuals can be planted as single specimens in the mixed border, but usually it is best to plant a minimum of three plants for the best show.

You can start annuals by seed (see "Plants from Seeds" on page 68), or you can purchase them. Most annuals are sold in cell packs of six to nine plants, but they are also available in individual pots and in flats (large trays that hold a number of plants). Look beyond the flowers when buying annuals. You want plants that are stocky and have healthy green leaves. They won't necessarily have to be the largest plants or have the most flowers. Smaller plants with unopened flower buds will usually suffer less transplant shock and do better in the long run.

Knowing your average last frost date is crucial with annuals because most shouldn't be transplanted into the garden in spring until all danger of frost has passed. Even if they are not injured by low temperatures, tender annuals will not grow well until the soil warms. Cool-season annuals (such as cabbage and broccoli) will tolerate lower temperatures, but even they don't like a hard frost. They usually can be planted outdoors about a week or two before the last expected frost date. (Find out your average last frost date on your state's university extension service website.)

To plant annuals from a cell pack or flat, gently squeeze out the individual plants from the container. Do not grab plants by their tender stems or leaves. The less the roots are disturbed, the faster the plant will become established. Put the individual plants in the soil at the same level they grew in the pack, or maybe just a little deeper. Never bury any leaves. If plants are leggy (tall and spindly), you may want to pinch off the tops to encourage a bushier form as they grow.

Planting under Large Trees

Be careful when planting under a large tree. Many trees are very sensitive to surface root disturbance. If you will be planting right under a tree's canopy, it is best to dig individual planting holes and add organic matter to holes as needed rather than till or dig up the entire area. Do not change the grade by adding soil on top of tree roots.

PLANTING PERENNIALS

The backbone of flower gardens and mixed borders, perennials usually are best planted in drifts of five to seven plants. They also can be used in container gardens and then planted in the garden. Some perennials have a shrub-like structure, making them open to use in foundation plantings and shrub borders.

Perennials typically are sold in individual pots, which can range in size from 4 inches up to 2 gallons or more. Obviously, the larger the container, the larger the root system and the quicker you will get to your desired effect. Often a perennial in a larger container can be divided into several smaller plants, providing you with more plants for your dollar. Look for plants that are compact, healthy, and actively growing. Most likely they won't be in flower, which is just fine. Plant spacing depends on each individual species and how long you want to wait for your garden to fill in, but about 12 inches is generally good for most herbaceous perennial plants.

Before putting perennials in the ground, place the containers in your prepared garden to see the big picture. You may find that you didn't quite buy enough plants to cover an area, in which case you may want to space them farther apart, or you may find that you have too many of some plants and need to use them in other areas of your garden. Because some plants have extensive root systems and don't like to be moved once they are established, you need to give careful thought to placing them.

PLANTING SPRING BULBS

Nothing cheers a gardener more than the sight of showy spring bulbs after a long winter. But it takes a bit of planning to enjoy these spring beauties because they must be planted in fall. Purchase bulbs while supplies are good during September or October. They can also be ordered by mail at any time for fall planting. Always go for the largest bulbs you can afford to get larger and more flowers. The bulb should be firm and free of blemishes; avoid any that are shriveled, bruised, soft, or moldy. It is best to plant bulbs as soon as you get them. If you have to store them for a few days, put them in a cool area below 60°F until you're ready to plant.

Most bulbs are long-lived perennials, so it is important to prepare the bed well before planting. Bulbs will rot if they stand in water, so make sure there is good soil drainage. In heavy soil, incorporate 2 to 3 inches of organic matter to a depth of 10 to 12 inches. Remove all weeds and debris before planting. The soil pH for most bulbs should be between 6 and 7 (read more about soil pH in Chapter 2). Permanent bulb plantings should be fertilized by mixing a slow-release complete fertilizer or bone meal mixed with an application of quick-release fertilizer at the rate of 1 to 2 pounds per 100 square feet in the rooting area at planting time.

In general, plant the bulb at a depth that is three to four times the width of the bulb. Set the bulbs in place with their pointed ends up and gently press them into the soil. Large bulbs should be spaced 3 to 6 inches apart, small bulbs 1 to 2 inches. Cover the bed with 2 to 3 inches of organic mulch after planting.

PLANTING VEGETABLES

Nothing says success to a gardener better than harvesting fresh vegetables. Like annuals, many vegetables are sold in cell packs of six to nine plants. Some are sold as individual plants and some are grown from bulbs, such as onions and garlic, or rootstocks, such as asparagus. Some are best started from seeds sown directly into the soil, such as radishes, carrots, lettuce, beans, and peas, because they don't transplant well.

Frost Dates

It's crucial to know the first and last frost dates of your region when planting vegetables. These dates will help you determine when to sow seeds and plant tender plants outside in spring as well as how late in the season you can plant for a fall crop. Seed packets list the typical number of growing days required for a variety, either from seeding or from the transplanting date. Visit the website of your state university extension service to get more accurate information for your specific area. They usually have frost dates listed with information on vegetable gardening.

OPPOSITE: Spring bulbs should be planted in groups of at least 12, and more if you can afford it. The smaller the bulb, the more you should plant. Do not plant bulbs in a straight line or a single circle around a tree or shrub. Large drifts of one or two colors look better than a hodgepodge mix of many different colors.

Planting a Perennial Garden

1. Before removing plants from their containers, place them in the prepared garden to see how they will look together and to make sure you have enough plants to fill the space.

2. Dig a hole about twice as wide as the container and deep enough so the plant is just a little higher than it was in the container to allow for soil settling.

3. Potted plants need to be carefully removed from their containers. Place your hand over the top of the container, placing the stem between your fingers. Turn the container upside down and tap or press on the pot as needed until it slides off the rootball. If you must tug it out, pull it by its leaves rather than the stem (if a leaf comes off, no harm done; damage the stem, and the plant will not survive).

4. Gently loosen some of the side and bottom roots to encourage them to grow into new soil. Place the plant in the soil and fill in with soil, and firm around the plant. If the plant was grown in a loose soil-less mix, shake off the excess and plant it like bare-root plants.

5. Water the entire garden thoroughly to settle the soil around the roots. Check back after the soil has settled to see if you need to add more soil so the plant will be at the correct level.

A well-planted vegetable garden can provide a bounty of vegetables from spring well into fall.

Onions are often planted from sets, which are actually small dormant bulbs. They are somewhat cold-tolerant and should be planted about 4 weeks before the frost-free date. Gently push the sets into the softened ground, pointed end up, so that you can just see the top of the set.

Direct Seeding

Many vegetables and herbs do best when direct-seeded into the garden. Prepare your seed bed or rows by loosening the soil to a depth of 6 to 12 inches, depending on your crop. For tiny seeds, moisten but don't soak the soil before planting; watering after planting can wash the seeds away. Do your best to evenly space the seeds in the row or bed. The seed packet will tell you how far apart to plant them. Don't sweat it if you plant them too closely, however. You will just need to do some thinning after they come up.

Cool-Season Vegetables

Cabbage, broccoli, lettuce, and other cool-season vegetables require cool temperatures to do well and many actually have better quality when grown in cool weather; it's said that the frost "sweetens" them. They will languish in the heat of summer. They should be planted in early to mid-spring and again in mid- to late summer for a fall or winter crop. Warm-season vegetables, such as tomatoes, squash, and peppers, should not be planted outside until all danger of frost has passed and the soil has warmed up to at least 50°F.

Second Plantings

After harvesting early-maturing vegetables such as salad greens, radishes, peas, and spinach, you can plant other crops in the same space for fall harvest. Unfortunately, nurseries don't usually carry vegetables after spring, so you will have to direct seed or start your own transplants. This is when it's really important to know the average first frost date in your area in order to calculate when to plant these late vegetables so they'll mature before being killed by cold weather.

Before sowing these second crops, turn over the soil and mix in some balanced fertilizer to replace what earlier plants have used up. Leftover debris such as stems or roots from the first planting can cause problems in seed germination if they aren't removed or allowed to break down, so wait a week or two before seeding the second crop or be sure to remove this material as completely as possible.

Succession Planting

Leafy vegetables, such as Swiss chard, kale, and beet greens can be planted in succession every few weeks over the course of the spring and summer to provide a steady supply of young leaves. Lettuce tends to bolt and taste bitter when grown in the heat of summer, so just enjoy it in spring or wait until temperatures cool to plant a late crop.

Shade from taller plants may help improve the quality of summer-grown lettuce, as will selecting varieties suited for warm weather.

Spacing

Vegetable gardens are typically planted in rows, but this isn't always the best way to maximize space. While it's important that plants have adequate spacing between them, this doesn't always have to come in the form of rows. Many heat-loving plants such as cucumbers and melons are often sown three to five seeds in hills, which promotes warming of the soil and improves soil drainage.

Intercropping

Intercropping—growing two or more crops together that mature at different times—increases yields and can also help reduce pest problems if the crops are from different families. To be successful, you must pick vegetables and herbs that mature at different rates, some quick, some slower. They should also have similar needs for watering, feeding, and pest control, and you must be able to harvest the early crop without damaging the later crop. Some root crops can be quite disruptive when they are being pulled out of the soil. Here are some combinations to try: leaf

---

Vegetable Planting Preferences

Many vegetables can be direct seeded but others should be put in the garden as transplants. Follow these guidelines.

Direct Seed (these do not transplant well)
- Beans
- Corn
- Okra
- Peas

Transplant Carefully (minimal root disturbance)
- Beets
- Carrots
- Cucumbers
- Pumpkins
- Spinach
- Summer squash
- Swiss chard
- Turnips
- Winter squash

Easily Transplanted
- Asparagus (when dormant)
- Broccoli
- Brussels sprouts
- Cabbage
- Cauliflower
- Celery
- Collards
- Eggplant
- Kale
- Kohlrabi
- Lettuce
- Onions
- Peppers
- Tomatoes

lettuce with tomatoes, peppers, bulbing onions, pole beans, or late-season cabbage; green onions with tomatoes, peppers, or basil; spinach with brussels sprouts or garlic; and radishes with peppers or tomatoes.

PLANTING SHRUBS

Shrubs, vines, and small trees are typically sold in containers, balled and burlapped, or bare root (without soil). Bare-root plants are the most wallet friendly, but you must plant them before they start growing in spring. Container-grown plants are the most popular and most flexible with regard to planting times. They can be planted anytime during the growing season but the cooler, wetter weather in spring and fall usually gives the best results. The fewer or smaller the leaves are, the faster a shrub will recover from transplanting. Balled-and-burlapped specimens are large and fill out a garden quicker but they are also the most expensive and can be challenging to plant. They should be planted in spring or fall as soon as possible after purchase.

Hole Diameter

Ideally, the diameter of the planting hole for woody plants will be at least twice the size of the root ball. By loosening and improving the soil in a larger circle, you will provide a nice, friable soil that is conducive to outward root growth. If your soil is very sandy or very heavy, amend it with a good amount of organic matter, such as compost or well-rotted manure. Mix this organic matter thoroughly with the planting-hole soil.

Hole Depth

Planting depth is an important step in success. Planting too deep or too shallow can lead to problems. For container-grown or balled-and-burlapped plants, the hole should be no deeper than the depth of the root ball so the plant will be at the same level as it was growing in its container. An exception is if you are planting in heavy, poorly drained soil. Then it is a good idea to plant so the top of the root ball is an inch or two above the soil line. This helps prevent the roots from becoming waterlogged in wet soil.

Make maximum use of your space by seeding a crop of quick-growing lettuce in between rows of later-maturing crops, such as peppers.

For bare-root plants, dig the hole wider and deeper than the largest roots. Make a cone of soil in the bottom of the hole and spread the roots out over the cone. Gently add soil as needed to keep the plant's crown at the right level, making sure to fill in the hole completely with soil to avoid air pockets where the roots may dry out.

Spacing

Space shrubs and small trees according to their mature size, which will be listed on the plant tag. Unless you are planting a hedge, give new plants plenty of room to expand to their full width without crowding.

Watering

Newly planted shrubs should receive an inch of water each week for their entire first growing season. Plan to water if rainfall isn't adequate. If autumn is dry, continue watering until the first hard frost. Once fully established—after 3 to 4

years—most woody plants should only require supplemental watering during dry spells.

Staking and Fertilizing

Staking is generally not needed for newly planted small trees. They actually grow stronger and are less likely to break if they are grown without support. Wait a year to fertilize any newly planted shrubs, and do so only if a soil test indicates a need or the plant shows signs of a deficiency.

PLANTING LARGE TREES

Like shrubs, large trees may be sold in containers, balled and burlapped, or even bare root. A fourth way to purchase a tree is to have it dug up and planted with a tree spade. This gives you a larger tree faster, but it's usually much more expensive. Because most trees are not easily moved once established, make sure the tree you select is a good match for your site.

With container-grown shrubs, look for specimens with healthy branches and good leaf development.

With trees, examine your specimens for symmetrical branch arrangement and overall shape before buying.

Planting a Container Shrub

1. Dig a planting hole twice as wide as the rootball but no deeper. The plant should sit at the same place it was growing in the container or perhaps an inch or so above the surrounding soil to allow for settling.

2. Place the container on its side and roll it on the ground while tapping it to loosen the roots. Upend the container and gently pull it off the plant roots.

3. Use your fingers to loosen any roots that may be matted, gently untangling them. Roots that are tightly coiled should be cut apart and loosened.

4. Set the shrub in the hole. Gently spread the roots wide so they are pointing outward as much as possible. Backfill the hole with the original soil.

5. Mound the soil to create a ridge around the plant to hold water. Water well and cover the soil with organic mulch, keeping it a few inches from the shrub.

Planting a tree is a long-term investment, so it is important to start with a healthy, nicely shaped seedling with a gentle taper to the trunk, well-spaced branches on all sides, and a single dominant branch, which will be the "leader." A single-leadered tree not only looks better but it also will be stronger. Most trees that have a double leader will eventually split because of the weak *V*-shaped crotch. If you do end up with a double-leadered tree, prune out the weaker leader. It may look funny at first, but the other leader will soon straighten and become the single dominant leader.

Hole Diameter

As with shrubs, the planting hole should be two to three times wider than the tree's root mass but no deeper than the plant is growing in the container. You want the trunk flare to be near the soil level. Do not place the tree so deep that any part of the flare is covered with soil. If anything, err on the side of planting a little shallow, because there is usually some settling of the roots and you will probably be adding a generous layer of mulch.

Root Care

Planting time is your one chance to make sure the roots are growing outward and not in a circling pattern, which can cause problems down the road. Break the roots apart or even cut some away, if necessary, to get a nice outward growth. Unless your soil is unusually bad, it is best not to amend the soil. Roots growing in cushy, amended soil are hesitant to venture out into the poorer native soil. You want your tree to have roots extending out in all directions, both for the health of the plant and to provide stability.

Staking

In most cases, newly planted trees should not be staked. While staking encourages a straighter trunk, it can result in a weaker tree. It is better to allow trees a little movement to encourage stronger trunks and healthy root systems. Trees planted on a very windy, exposed site, however, may benefit from staking for their first season or two, especially if they are top heavy. Any stakes should be removed as soon as the tree has rooted well, usually after the first year.

To properly stake a tree, string wire through a section of garden hose to protect the bark from injury. The wire should hold the tree firmly without putting undue pressure on the trunk. The staked tree should still be able to sway somewhat in the wind.

Planting a Balled-and-Burlapped Tree

1. Dig a hole no deeper than the depth of the rootball but at least twice as wide, preferably three or four times wider. Loosen the soil, breaking up clumps and removing any rocks.

2. If the wrapping is real burlap, simply cut and remove the fabric on top of the ball and peel the burlap down the sides so it stays below the soil line. It will eventually decompose. Synthetic burlap must be removed completely. If there is a wire basket surrounding the rootball, remove it.

3. Place the tree in the hole and adjust the hole depth so that the plant is about 1 inch higher than it was planted in the nursery to allow for settling of soil. Use a shovel handle laid across the hole to help determine the proper depth.

4. Shovel in soil around the rootball, stopping to tamp down the soil when the hole is half full.

5. Fill the rest of the hole with loose soil and tamp down again to ensure good contact between the soil and the roots.

6. Soak the planting area with water. Once the soil has settled, build up a 2- to 3-inch basin around the plant to catch rainfall and irrigation water. Do not build a basin if your soil is very heavy and doesn't drain well.

7. Apply 2 to 3 inches of an organic mulch, such as shredded bark or wood chips, keeping the mulch a few inches away from the trunk.

CHAPTER 5
WATERING AND FERTILIZING

By Dr. Jacqueline A. Soule

IT IS BEST TO CONSIDER HOW YOU WILL WATER your plants long before you plant them. Watering the garden is not as simple as turning on the tap. Even xeriscape yards still need water. (Read more about xeriscape in Chapter 15.)

Plants need water so that they can photosynthesize and make the food they need for life and the defensive compounds to fight off disease and insects. This comes before they make pretty flowers or tasty fruit for us to enjoy. Plants that become overly stressed by lack of water—even if the soil only dries for a day or two—are more likely to suffer from disease and pest infestations or become weakened and die.

Luckily, even with water restrictions, you can have a lovely garden if you practice some simple water-conscious care. Then, when your plants do need water, you will be able to provide water in the right place, to the right depth, for the right amount of time, and at the right time of day.

OPPOSITE: A classic galvanized watering can isn't fancy, but can serve basic watering needs just fine.

HOW TO WATER

In many areas of North America, up to three-quarters of household water use is for the landscape. Watering your yard efficiently is one of the best and easiest ways to save water. Proper watering will also keep your garden and all your plants healthy and beautiful throughout the year.

Because drought is a reality for many of us, it pays to learn correct watering techniques. You will also need to know how good your soil is at holding water, which is generally related to the amount of organic matter in the soil. There is also the factor of how easy it is for the plants to remove the water from the soil. Plants are genetically set to fall into three loose categories: hydric, mesic, and xeric. Hydric plants live in marshes and wet areas, mesic plants live in areas with ample soil moisture, and xeric plants live in areas that tend to have dry soils. Xeric plants are highly efficient at getting water out of dry soils, while mesic plants have a harder time absorbing scarce water.

This difference between xeric and mesic plants makes it hard for the beginning gardener to know how much water plants will need. Furthermore, the two terms are relative—not absolute. In Idaho, yarrow is sold as a xeriscape plant, yet in Arizona it's considered a mesic plant! To top off this issue, how much water you need to apply depends on your soil, the weather conditions, time of year, size of the plants, and stage of life for the plant (is it flowering or going dormant for the season?). Location matters too—think about what "full sun" means in Maine compared to Florida.

Avid gardeners constantly putter in the garden, responding to plants' needs, but if you have a busy life, you may not have an hour or two every day to fuss with garden things. I will warn you that you do need to spend *some* time, at least at first, learning what it takes to care for your plants. Know this—every gardener has killed plants. Don't get discouraged! Do try again. (It took me six tries until I added enough sand to my soil for thyme plants to thrive.) Good resources include local extension services and the Cool Springs Press regional garden guides.

A watering wand gently applies water without washing away plants. Plus, it's fun to use.

Annuals, such as pansies, wildflowers, and small vegetables such as radishes, have shallow roots and need water only to 1 foot deep. Perennials, such as daylily or ornamental grasses, larger vegetables such as tomatoes, and shrubs such as roses and raspberries, should be watered to 2 feet deep.

"Tweeners" are those large shrubs, such as lilacs or vitex, climbing roses, and vines such as wisteria. Consider them to be trees and water to a depth of 3 feet.

Trees have absorbing roots that easily reach 3 feet deep. Shallow-rooted species, such as maples and mulberries, can be encouraged to send their roots deeper by infrequent but deep watering in times of drought.

Water to the Right Depth

As plant roots grow, they age and grow bark. Only the most distant reaching root tips are capable of absorbing water. This means that the older the plant, the deeper the roots—within limits. For the home gardener, you only have to consider three depths, depending on the type of plant.

Water in the Right Place

Established plants have their water-absorbing roots at the drip line of the plant, which is beneath the outer edge of the plant's canopy, not close to the trunk or stem. The anchoring roots are next to the stem or trunk and they aren't capable of absorbing water.

DEEP WATERING PLANTS

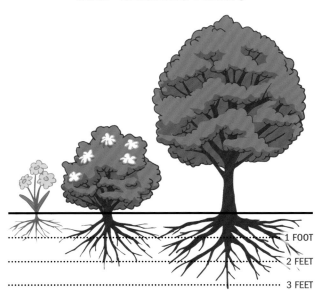

1 FOOT
2 FEET
3 FEET

Water to the correct depth for the type of plant.

PLANT DRIP LINES

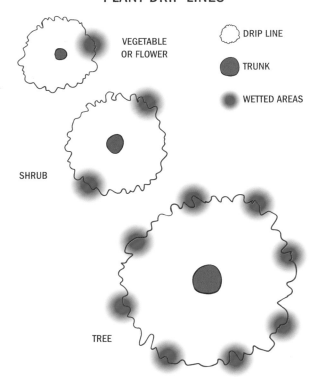

VEGETABLE OR FLOWER

SHRUB

TREE

DRIP LINE

TRUNK

WETTED AREAS

Watering in the right place means applying irrigation water under the edge of the plant's dripline. With vegetables and flowers, this can be a single watering spot under the outer edge of the dripline. With shrubs and trees, it's best to water in several spots around the perimeter of the dripline. For a shrub, two or three spots will suffice, but a tree is best watered at many spots spaced a few feet apart.

When you water a plant, either by irrigation or garden hose, it is best to apply the water out at this drip line, right where the plant has the type of roots that can use it. The water will spread through the soil. Gravity pulls the water down to the water-absorbing roots and the texture of the soil will help the water spread horizontally as it soaks into the soil. How many places around the drip line you need to place irrigation emitters or wet with a hose depends on your soil.

Water for the Right Amount of Time

All soils absorb and hold water like a sponge. The water then typically moves both horizontally and downward through the soil, though it can vary with different soil textures.

Sandy soil absorbs water quickly but will also dry quickly as the water is pulled down by gravity. Water has little horizontal spread in sandy soil, so you will have to water in more locations around the drip line of the plant to ensure a thorough watering.

Clay soil holds water longer than sandy soil, but it is slow to move downward and horizontally. It stays wet longer than a sandy soil. It is best to apply water slowly to allow it to percolate downward. You will also need to water less frequently.

Loam soil is what gardeners aspire to. Loam soils offer a good balance of both downward and horizontal water spread.

Water at the Right Time

It's better to water all plants deeply and only as frequently as they need it. Instead of watering a tiny bit every day, water less often and as deeply as the roots grow—but only after the soil down there dries out. This may be as seldom as once a week or even once a month—yes, even in the desert!

The best time of day to water is first thing in the morning, when plants wake up for the day. This is especially true for many plants in areas of ample sunlight and in the dead of summer. Many plants perform all the photosynthesis they need for the day by 10:00 a.m. and spend the rest of the day just hanging out. Water applied at the end of the day (after you get home from work) has all night to evaporate before the plants wake up the next morning and need it.

COMPARATIVE WETTING PATTERNS

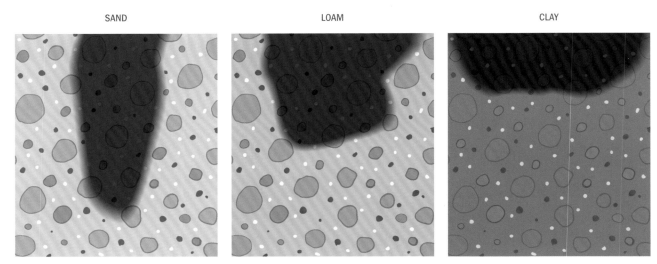

SAND   LOAM   CLAY

Different types of soil transfer water in different patterns. One inch of water will soak into about 12 inches in sand, 7 inches in loam, and 5 inches in clay.

How to Gauge How Deep the Water Goes

A direction to "water until the water reaches 3 feet deep" may sound impossible at first, but you can quickly learn what the soil in your yard is like.

I use sturdy foot-long knitting needles, but a long, narrow screwdriver will work. There is a tool called a soil probe, but unless you move often or test soil for a living, save your money.

Before watering, use the knitting needle or long screwdriver to see how far it will go into soil. Next, water for 20 minutes and then see how deep the probe will go easily into the soil. If it goes in 4 inches, you can calculate how long you need to water for the proper depth: to water to 1 foot deep, multiply 20 minutes (the time it took to reach 4 inches) by 3 (4 inches x 3 = 1 foot). The result: it will take 60 minutes for the water to go 1 foot deep. In such soil, trees will need 3 hours of watering for moisture to reach 3 feet deep.

Here's How to Recognize Plant Water Stress

Ironically, some signs of overwatering are the same as signs of underwatering. Over time you will learn to recognize these signs of water stress.

Signs of Underwatering
- Soil is dry and hard to dig.
- Older leaves turn yellow or brown and drop off.
- Leaves are wilted or drooping and do not recover after sundown.
- Leaves curl around the mid-vein, especially seen in grasses.
- Stems or branches die back.

Signs of Overwatering
- Soil is constantly damp.
- Young shoots are wilted.
- Leaves turn lighter green or yellow throughout.
- Leaves remain green yet are brittle and may crumble.
- Algae or mushrooms appear on or around plants.

Watering Must-Haves

There are three things worth installing for any garden watering system to preserve your watering equipment and ensure your water supply in the house is safe:

Pressure regulators help regulate municipal water to a pressure level that helps preserve the life of hoses, sprinklers, and irrigation emitters.

An outdoor water or debris filter catches all the little gritty debris that is common in virtually any municipal water supply. This helps extend the life of watering devices, including sprinklers, spray nozzles, and irrigation emitters.

A back-flow preventer prevents the hose or irrigation system water from being sucked back into your home or the municipal water supply. (I unknowingly emptied a fish pond into the dishwasher once.) It is required by law in many municipalities.

A pressure regulator and debris filter can greatly extend the life of your hoses, sprinklers, and irrigation systems.

Harvest Water

Even in areas of high rainfall, there is often a dry season or recent shifting weather patterns to consider. There are a number of passive and active systems for harvesting rainwater (local laws permitting). These topics are covered more completely in Chapter 15.

Squash often wilt in the afternoon to conserve water. If you water in the afternoon, much of the water is not used by the plant because it shuts down at night.

COMMON WATERING TOOLS

Having a few simple tools on hand will make watering your plants an easy task instead of a tedious chore. Following is a list of the basics. If you live in an area of low or unpredictable rainfall, irrigation systems are an excellent way to ensure plants get the water they need.

Garden Hose

In some areas, a garden hose is the main tool for watering plants. It's worth the money to buy a top-quality 25- to 50-foot, heavy-duty, no-kink hose. Longer hoses should be avoided unless you really need one. They tend to get in the way.

Hose Manifold

A hose manifold allows you to connect two (or more) hoses to a single spigot.

Soaker Hose

Soaker hoses are porous hoses made of fabric or plastic that lay in the garden and can connect to the faucet via an irrigation line or garden hose. The sewn fabric ones have a longer life in sunlight and can more easily be taken up and stored in areas that freeze. Soakers can also be buried under soil or mulch so that the water is delivered where the plants need it—at the roots.

Watering Wand

For gardeners both young or old, a watering wand makes watering easier and adds some fun. The long, rigid handle lets you reach overhead to hanging pots, the tops of vertical gardens, and over rows, or down near the base of a plant without bending over.

Rain Head

Also called a water breaker, this is used on the end of a hose or watering wand to disperse the flow of water so that it is gentler and less likely to disrupt soil, seeds, and delicate seedlings. These are helpful for vertical garden systems.

Hose End Shut Off

This small device is handy if you are hand watering and notice a plant to deadhead or a weed to pull. You temporarily shut off the water right where you are then easily resume.

Water Sprinkler

There are many types of sprinklers, including those that rotate in some manner and those that are static. Avoid spraying water up into the air if the relative humidity is less than 50 percent. You will lose as much as half the water to evaporation.

Tip for Success with Water Devices

Two things to keep on hand are Teflon pipe tape and spare hose washers. If you use Teflon tape on all your hose threads, your watering devices (wands, sprinklers) won't stick together. Summer heat causes hose washers to deteriorate rapidly and develop leaks, leading to unwanted puddles. Keep some extras on hand and replace as needed.

Microdrip tubes have drip emitters every 6 inches, making them optimal for watering vegetable gardens and flowerbeds. Because they are smaller in diameter, they are more flexible and less obtrusive than soaker hoses.

IRRIGATION SYSTEMS

An irrigation system can save money and time compared to hand watering. It does not need to be elaborate. A simple garden hose can feed one irrigation line and be moved as needed. Quick connectors help the process.

Irrigation has come a long way in the last few years. With all the newer products available, an irrigation system is not difficult to install or maintain. They are now so lightweight and flexible that they can be easily drained and rolled up for winter storage in areas of freezing winters or drained and left in place. It is worth it to visit a store that specializes in irrigation and purchase industry standard equipment. It makes troubleshooting and repairs much easier.

Irrigation systems are generally laid underground, but with the newer UV-resistant materials, they don't need to be. For vertical gardens, an irrigation system may be suspended from support structures. For vegetable gardens, you may wish to have a removable irrigation system featuring microemitters.

INTRODUCTION TO FERTILIZER

Plants make all their own food. That is what photosynthesis is all about. To feed themselves, plants need specific chemical elements or minerals out of the soil. If your soil lacks certain chemicals or elements, you can improve it by adding fertilizer. People speak of fertilizer as "plant food," which is an oxymoron and wrong to boot. Think of fertilizer as the *vitamins* that plants need so they can make their food. (And while they are at it, plants make food for us too!)

Essential Elements

The essential elements plants need for life are oxygen (O), carbon (C), and hydrogen (H), which they get from air and water. Then there are all those other chemical elements that are essential to the plant for completing all its life stages, such as forming flowers and making fruit. Nutrients are divided into macronutrients and micronutrients, based on the *amount* needed by the plant. All are equally essential.

Almost all fertilizers contain the macronutrients that plants need for life: nitrogen (N), phosphorus (P), and potassium (K). You can purchase fertilizer in more forms than you can shake a stick at and they come with a bewildering variety of labels, but—by government mandate—the N-P-K amounts will be listed, and in that order.

Ready to Use

FERTIFEED
All Purpose Plant Food

12-4-8

FertiFeed Ready To Use All-Purpose Plant Food
Net Weight 4lb. 12oz. (2.15kg)

GUARANTEED ANALYSIS
Total Nitrogen (N)..12%
    12.0% Urea Nitrogen
Available Phosphate (P_2O_5).................................4%
Soluable Potash (K2O)..8%
Manganese (Mn)...0.05%
    0.05% Chelated Manganese (Mn)
Zinc (Zn) 0.05%
    0.05% Chelated Zinc (Zn)
Inert Ingredients...76%

Information regarding the contents and levels of metals in this product is available on the Internet at http://www.regulatory-info-sc.com.

KEEP OUT OF REACH OF CHILDREN

By government mandate, nitrogen (N), phosphorus (P), and potassium (K) are always listed in the same order.

Plants are complicated living beings and need far more than six elements for life. This is what makes hydroponics, aquaponics, and even vertical and container gardening so challenging. Often a single element lacking can mean failure of a system. This is also why people are proponents of using organic rather than synthetic fertilizers: the required traces are more generally available. Some of the following information is the product of recent scientific studies and has not made its way into textbooks yet.

Nitrogen is needed to make the amino acids used in every cell of the plant. It also is needed for chlorophyll molecules and proteins for growth and energy transport. Nitrogen stimulates vegetative growth. Deficiency symptoms include pale green or yellow-green leaves and dwarf or stunted plants. Too much nitrogen can result in no flowers.

Phosphorus is required for anything to do with DNA, RNA, and the membranes of new cells, thus maximum flower and fruit formation. It's essential at seeding time for rapid root and stem growth. Deficiency symptoms include leaves that are stunted with purple or red discoloration. In some cases, leaf petioles or stems will become stunted and discolored as well.

Potassium is needed as a catalyst for many metabolic reactions and is required for growth and development, including the thickness of plant cell walls. This helps a plant resist the stresses of heat, cold, drought, and disease. Potassium helps build stronger stems and deepen flower color. Deficiencies are indicated by weak stems and yellowing and browning of leaves at the tips. Leaves may also rumple and turn under at the edges.

Types of Fertilizer

The key thing to remember when buying fertilizer is that reading fertilizer labels is just like reading labels on a can of soup. Instead of listing the calories and carbohydrates that humans need to eat for life, fertilizer labels list the elements that plants need to make their own food.

For optimal health, pest resistance, and fruit and vegetable production, plants will need all the macronutrients and micronutrients listed on the chart on page 93. Different plant species have slightly different needs, and these needs will change at different stages of life. This is one more reason why there is such a massive array of fertilizers available.

Fertilizers can be based on either synthetic or organic components. Organic fertilizers come from formerly living

Elements Required by Plants

Do not be daunted by this list of nutrients and their chemical symbols! This chart is provided to help you troubleshoot if you have problems in the garden. For example, manganese is needed so plants can use the fertilizer you apply. Zinc is needed to formulate fruit. If you aren't getting good fruit production after adding a phosphorus-rich fertilizer, you might consider a soil test or simply add a fertilizer high in zinc, such as many of the seaweed-based fertilizers.

After water and air, these *macro*nutrients are critical to a plant's survival.

Nitrogen (N)	Needed for photosynthesis	**Manganese (Mn)**	Required for enzymes for photosynthesis, use of nitrogen
Phosphorus (P)	Needed for flower and fruit production	**Zinc (Zn)**	Essential for coenzymes in all cells
Potassium (K)	Needed to build good root systems	**Boron (B)**	Needed for transfer of sugars within the plant, critical for good roots
Calcium (Ca)	Regulates cell membranes	**Iron (Fe)**	Catalyst for making chlorophyll, part of many enzymes
Magnesium (Mg)	Center of the chlorophyll molecule, needed for many enzymes	**Copper (Cu)**	Needed for oxidative enzyme
Sulfur (S)	Necessary for amino acids and coenzymes		

Along with macronutrients, there are also *micro*nutrients. Micronutrients are *necessary* but not critical for basic survival. Many of these are used in wound healing and defensive compounds and thus are required when plants are pruned often.

Iodine (I)
Sodium (Na)
Chlorine (Cl)
Cobalt (Co)
Fluorine (F)
Vanadium (V)
Chromium (Cr)
Nickel (Ni)
Arsenic (As)
Selenium (Se)

The elements of this last group are used for things not essential to survival of the individual plant but are helpful to make all the secondary chemicals a plant needs for defense from pests and disease. Plus, they help with details such as fragrance, seed coats, and the like. Some of these can cause problems in too high of concentrations.

Aluminum (Al)
Silicon (Si)
Titanium (Ti)
Germanium (Ge)
Bromine (Br)
Cadmium (Cd)
Tin (Sn)
Tungsten (W)

Soil health is improved by the use of fertilizers from organic rather than synthetic sources. A good population of earthworms both aerates the soil and fills it with nutrient-rich castings produced by the worms.

While there are many fertilizer options, one option is to garden organically, amending soil with ample natural peat moss or compost so the micronutrients are incorporated into the soil.

beings—generally either plants or animals. Animal-based fertilizer can be byproducts from processing animals, such as blood meal, bone meal, and fish emulsion, or from animal waste such as composted steer manure, chicken manure, or bat guano. These tend to be rich in many of the micronutrients that plants need, such as boron or zinc. Confusingly, organic fertilizers many not be formulated organically for growing an organic garden. The Organic Materials Review Institute (OMRI) has clear-cut guidelines about how fertilizers must be handled to be certified for organic gardening.

Vegetable-based fertilizers include compost, granulated seaweed, and crop residues such as cottonseed meal or composted mushroom farm substrate.

Mineral fertilizers include rock phosphate, greensand, lime, sulfur, and powdered boron. Such minerals release very slowly over a period of time and benefit soil microorganisms. These are generally used in agricultural fields.

Synthetic or chemical fertilizers are acceptable if sufficient organic material has been added to the soil to hold the nutrients. Plants don't care where their nutrients come from as long as the nutrients are in a usable or available form. The drawback is that chemical fertilizers can burn plant tissue and roots if improperly applied. Synthetic fertilizers may also include harmful salts that can build up in the soil over time.

Whenever possible, use organic fertilizers. Your garden will benefit from this in the long run. Think of synthetic fertilizer as a candy bar—it provides quick nutrients to the plants, but the effects wear off quickly.

Which fertilizer you purchase is something you have to choose for yourself. Consider your tolerance for fussing with application methods, your desire to nurture your soil over time, and your wallet. Some avid gardeners may have five or twelve different kinds of fertilizer tucked away in the garden shed. You can probably stick with two, a general-purpose fertilizer and a bloom/fruiting fertilizer.

FERTILIZER APPLICATION

Fertilizer is sold to be placed into the soil or used as a foliar spray for application to the foliage or leaves of plants. The problem with foliar sprays is that plants are not designed to absorb nutrients through their leaves (unless they are carnivorous plants). Foliar sprays can burn plants, even when used as directed—especially in low-humidity climates or when days of sun are in the forecast. The bottom line is that foliar sprays can be safe when used as directed, but foliar feeding for the home gardener is not recommended.

Fertilizer is offered in three main forms—liquid, powder, or granules. Liquid fertilizer is mixed with water (in

TOP: The proper amount of fertilizer with regularly timed applications is crucial for healthy fruit production.

ABOVE: Called "side-dressing," sprinkling fertilizer on the soil alongside the plants and gently raking it in will help your vegetable garden produce bountifully.

Tip for Success: Less Is More for Fertilizers

Follow the label directions. Ideally, err on the side of caution when using fertilizers. Too much can easily kill the plant you wish to help, even if it is an organic fertilizer. It is always safe to use half as much twice as often.

a can or bucket) and watered into the soil. Powdered and granular forms are generally spread directly onto the soil. As tempting as it is to spread them and walk away, it is not the best gardening practice. Spread the fertilizer, and then water or rake it into the soil. Alternatively, dissolve the fertilizer in water first and use this dissolved fertilizer to water with. Why? Because wind may blow the fertilizer onto plant leaves, burning them, or rain can wash it into lakes and streams, encouraging algal blooms that kill fish. Birds often eat dry fertilizer, thinking it is a new form of seed, and it can kill them. In general, you paid good money for the fertilizer, so why waste your money?

NUTRIENT DEFICIENCIES

If your plant leaves are turning unusual colors for the species (purple, yellow), they might have nutrient deficiencies. Nutrient deficiencies are tough for the novice gardener to diagnose, but it's usually possible to identify a nutrient deficiency with a careful look at the plant.

The diagram on the following page shows the symptoms caused by the most common nutrient deficiencies.

SYMPTOMS OF PLANT NUTRIENT DEFICIENCIES

BORON: Discoloration of leaf buds. Breaking and dropping of buds.

SULPHUR: Leaves light green. Veins pale green, no spots.

MANGANESE: Leaves pale in color. Large and small veins dark green, tissue between veins crinkled.

ZINC: Leaves pale narrow and short. Veins dark green. Dark spots on leaves and edges.

MAGNESIUM: Paleness from leaf edges. No spots. Edges have cup-shaped folds. Leaves die and drop in extreme deficiency.

PHOSPHORUS: Plant short and dark green, in extreme deficiencies turn brown or black. Bronze color under the leaf.

CALCIUM: Plant dark green. Large and small veins dark green, tissue between veins crinkled.

IRON: Leaves pale. No spots. Major veins green.

COPPER: Pale pink between the veins. Leaves wilt and drop.

MOLYBDENUM: Leaves green/ lemon yellow/orange. Dead spots appear between veins. Leaf may become sticky underneath.

POTASSIUM: Small spots on the tips, edges of pale leaves. Spots turn rusty. Tips curl.

NITROGEN: Stunted growth. Extremely pale color. Mature leaves light green/yellowish. Appear burned in extreme deficiency.

Celebrate and Fertilize

When it comes to fertilizer, applying it just three or four times per year can keep your garden healthy and happy. How to remember when? Just think "Happy Holidays to my Garden!" and celebrate by fertilizing on these noteworthy days.

- **Zones 11, 10, and 9:** St. Patrick's Day, Memorial Day, and Labor Day (skip the Fourth of July or Canada Day—it's too hot)
- **Zones 8 and 7:** Tax Day (April 15), Memorial Day, Fourth of July or Canada Day, and Labor Day
- **Zones 6 and 5:** May Day (May 1), Memorial Day, Fourth of July or Canada Day, and National Sneak Some Zucchini onto Your Neighbor's Porch Day (August 8)
- **Zone 4 and 3:** Memorial Day, Fourth of July or Canada Day, and National Sneak Some Zucchini onto Your Neighbor's Porch Day (August 8)

Gardening with Epsom Salt

Epsom salt is the gardener's friend twice over, or maybe three times. It contains two macronutrients plants need to thrive. Plus, gardeners can use some Epsom salts in the bath to soak away aches after a long day.

Why Epsom Salt Works

Epsom salt is simply magnesium sulfate. Both magnesium and sulfate are macronutrients crucial to healthy plant life. Magnesium plays a critical role in photosynthesis because it is the center of the chlorophyll molecule. It is also needed for germination and cell-wall formation. Sulfate (a mineral form of sulfur) helps the plant make more chlorophyll molecules, and helps release other soil-bound minerals.

How to Use Epsom Salt

For the vegetable garden, scatter 1 cup of Epsom salt per 100 square feet and work or water it into the soil before seeding or planting. For flower beds and container plants, dissolve 1 tablespoon of Epsom salt per gallon of water and use this to water once a month.

Shrubs, especially evergreens such as Indian hawthorn, honeysuckle, azalea, and Texas ranger, benefit from 1 tablespoon of Epsom salt per 10 square feet of bush area once a year in spring. Sprinkle this around the drip line of the shrub and dig or water it into the soil. Treat trees the same way.

WHEN TO FERTILIZE

Fertilizer should be provided to landscape plants when they are actively growing but not too close to the time when it might freeze in your area. Fertilizer stimulates new growth, and such tender growth is more susceptible to frost damage. Fertilize no later than 1 month before the average first frost date. (Your local extension service should have the information.) The last frost date marks the time to begin fertilizing again in the spring.

Avoid excessive fertilizer on plants that are actively producing flowers, fruits, or nuts. If a nitrogen-rich fertilizer is applied, plants may drop many of the flowers or fruit they have started and switch to growing leaves. Fruiting fertilizers carry their own hidden problems, in that too much may cause the plant to drop some of its developing fruit and just concentrate on making a few really large ones. Read and follow label directions. If in doubt, use less than called for.

FERTILIZER EXCEPTIONS

Some plants are stunted by fertilizer. Members of the legume or pea family work with soil bacteria to take nitrogen out of the atmosphere. If you give them nitrogen-rich fertilizer, they may stop growing. This means that garden peas and beans are best not grown in your highly enriched garden bed! In the flower garden, sweet peas are affected by excessive fertilizer. A number of trees and shrubs are legumes, including locust, redbud, mesquite, and Mexican bird of paradise. These plants still need the P and K (and all the other parts of fertilizer), just not the N.

Cacti and other succulents have slow metabolisms. Always use fertilizer at half the recommended dose on them. Avoid acidifying their soil, as they tend to come from alkaline soils.

New evidence shows that fertilizer should not be applied to newly planted plants. Fertilize at least 2 weeks after plants are rooted in and established. Use root growth promoters if you desire, but not general fertilizer.

Always read and follow label directions for any chemical compound, including fertilizer application. Too much fertilizer can kill the plant you wanted to help. If you are in doubt, err on the side of caution. Apply half-strength fertilizer twice. Wait 2 weeks in between doses for plants to show you that you got the dose right or wrong.

CHAPTER 6
PRUNING

By Dr. Jacqueline A. Soule

THERE ARE TWO EQUALLY IMPORTANT REASONS TO prune: for the safety of people and property near the plant and for the health of the plant. Plants will grow better and produce more flowers and fruit when pruned according to the few simple guidelines that are covered in this chapter.

Pruning involves the selective removal of certain parts of a plant, such as branches, buds, flowers, excess fruit, or, occasionally, roots. It's one of those jobs where less is more.

Less pruning saves you money. Plants don't have to spend energy healing all the cuts and recovering, so they need less fertilizer and less water. And less pruning means less yard waste, which means fewer taxpayer dollars spent on landfill space. Less pruning also saves you time—less time pruning and more time enjoying your yard.

Proper pruning reduces the chance of weakened growth, including the potential loss of large tree limbs that might damage your home or car as they fall.

So how can you learn how to prune in a way that saves you money and time and produces healthier plants? You really only need three things: an understanding of plants, the right tools, and the knowledge to use those tools properly in the right place at the right time.

OPPOSITE: Regular, routine pruning keeps you connected to your garden plants and keeps them looking their best.

UNDERSTANDING PLANTS

The key to pruning lies in understanding that plants have genes that tell them how to live and grow. The genes determine if a plant will be tall or small, have many branches or few, and have big leaves or small. When you prune, the plant can only recover in certain genetically determined ways.

Appearance

All plants have a particular appearance specific to their species. Shrubs and trees have shapes, forms, and sizes that are genetically predetermined. Shapes are varied; for example, trees can be round like the white oak or pyramidal like the pin oak. They can also be columnar like the Lombardy poplar, oval like the sugar maple, or V-shaped like the American elm.

Then there is the overall form, such as angular, weeping, or spreading.

As for size, every species has a mature height and width that is optimal for that species, and plants will always try to reach their optimum.

All these size and color factors must be considered when selecting a plant and planting it in the landscape, but also when pruning it. If you do not like the form, shape, color, or habit of a plant, do both of you a favor and remove it from your life now and install a plant you will be happy with. In the long run, it will cost you a great deal less time, money, and aggravation.

All plants have a natural shape, form, and size to which they will grow.

Buds contain meristem cells that can grow into whatever the plant requires.

Cut just above a bud or node to encourage the plant to rebloom.

Biology

Plants are uniquely different from animals in many ways, especially due to their meristem cells. These cells are found virtually everywhere in plants and can grow into anything the plant needs—branch, bark, or blossom. It's as if humans could grow new arms or legs as needed. While meristems cells are found throughout the plant, they are especially found in buds. This fact is key when it comes to pruning.

Meristem cells reward proper pruning by growing into new flower buds on roses or new bark over a wound. Meristem cells respond to poor pruning by forming troublesome water sprouts or unsightly witches' brooms.

Growth

Plants grow taller and wider by growing all around their edges, which, thanks to their meristem cells, they can do. They control all this growth through a suite of plant hormones.

When it comes time to prune, remember the need for leaders in the plant's life. Find a bud that is pointing outward or in the direction that you want new growth to follow, and then cut just above it. You have just removed the old leader and the bud meristem will become the new leader. ("The king is dead, long live the new king!") If you desire no growth at all in a particular direction, then just be sure to cut flush with the main stem, not in the middle of a branch.

As long as you understand that leaders are very important to plants, your plants will respond well to your pruning care and grow robust and lovely.

When You Cut, Cut Flush

It doesn't matter if you are pruning living wood, cutting off a dead limb, or simply taking off spent flower stalks. You need to consider the tissue you are leaving behind. Remember that plants have meristem cells everywhere! When cutting side branches off a tree or shrub, this means you need to cut flush with the trunk and not leave a large stub that is hard for plants to heal over. When cutting a rose for a vase, cut just above a node or bud—which is in the joint of a leaf and the stem. This allows the meristem cells inside the bud to grow into a new flower.

Cut flush with a branch to prevent side shoots from trying to become leaders.

THE RIGHT TIME TO PRUNE

6

Timing is critical for pruning. Rather that hacking away because it is spring cleaning time and you want everything to look tidy, it is best to think ahead and plan your work based on what is best for the plant. There are several things to consider.

Age of the Plant

I was taught by an old Vermonter that when pruning, you should "catch 'em young and bring 'em up right." The smaller the branch that is cut (i.e., the younger the branch), the easier it is for the plant to seal off the wound and heal over the area. Sealing and healing limits the possibility of fungi, bacteria, or insects attacking the plant. Also, if you shape plants when young, you won't have unsightly scars from removing larger branches later.

Note that you do need to be gentle with young plants. Avoid removing more than 20 percent of their mass at once. Once they are older, you can remove more at one time up to 30 percent.

Prune at the right time of year to avoid creating wounds that fail to heal and weep resin or sap for years.

Right Season

The proper time of year to prune varies widely, or wildly, or even both! There are around a half million species of plants. Many of these plants must be pruned when dormant, some will survive if pruned when dormant, and a large number should *never* be pruned when dormant. Which is which? The topic is still being researched, discovered, and discussed. But there are some guidelines.

Plants from the temperate regions can be pruned when dormant. If a plant has tropical genes, do not prune it when dormant. The easy way to know if your plant is tropical is to look at its frost tolerance. If the plant isn't hardy below 26°F, it's got tropical genes. If it is not hardy in USDA Zone 7 or colder, it has tropical genes.

Depending on the species, many temperate plants can be pruned either during dormancy in winter or, for species where winter frost can harm a recently pruned plant, after flowering is completed. In Zones 6 and cooler, autumn pruning should be avoided, as the spores of disease and decay fungi are abundant at that time of year. Also, pruning stimulates new growth that can be damaged by cold.

Some woody plants, such as maples and mesquites, tend to bleed profusely from cuts. Some, such as magnolias and bottle trees, callous over slowly. These species are best pruned during active growth seasons when they can more readily heal. For more help with this topic, the non-profit group Plant Amnesty (www.plantamnesty.org) offers a number of regional guides online. In general, whether a plant is temperate or tropical, you can prune out dead wood any time of year.

Timing for Flowers

You should avoid pruning right before a plant is about to flower. The rule of thumb is to prune two seasons before bloom. But I just told you to avoid pruning in autumn, so now what? Early spring bloomers, such as redbuds, dogwoods, sennas, and forsythias, are pruned after bloom is done. Roses bloom later in the spring and are pruned in fall or winter when they are dormant. Prune fall-blooming plants in spring.

WHAT TO PRUNE

Remember that pruning is for the health of the plant or for human safety. The following types of pruning will help.

Dead Wood

Deadwooding refers to removing dead branches. It helps both the appearance and health of a plant. With dead wood removed, light can get in to all the leaves. Deadwooding is also a good way to "clear the deck for action"—pruning action, that is. Once the deck is clear, you can see what living branches may or may not need pruning. Generally, deadwooding can be done at any time of the year. Cut out dead branches by cutting the wood flush with the remaining wood or down to just above a bud.

Spent Flowers

Similar to deadwooding, deadheading refers to removing spent plant tissue—in this case, spent flowers. By removing flowers that are done blooming, the plant will not spend energy making seeds and will instead spend energy to produce more flowers. To deadhead, look for a bud and cut off the spent flower head just above it.

Removing dead or damaged branches makes it easier to see what further pruning may be required.

By removing flowers that have finished blooming ("deadheading") you encourage the plants to make more flowers instead of spending energy making seeds.

Pruning Tools

The old adage "buy cheap, buy twice" is especially true when it comes to cutting tools. Always try to purchase top-quality tools. They are easier to use and require less effort to operate, making pruning less of a chore and lessening your chances of injuring yourself. Good tools make clean cuts, which are healthier for the plant.

Scissors. Really good garden scissors are more precious than gold. Use them to prune small herbaceous plants, cut twine, open bags of fertilizer, cut flowers for the home, and so on. I hide mine from the hubby.

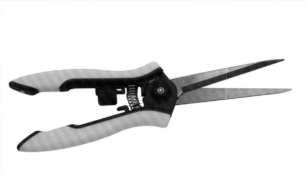

Snips. Snips are somewhere between scissors and hand pruners. Their scissorlike cutting action is offset by their spring (like hand pruners). Snips are great for thinning and deadheading small shrubs and roses.

Hand pruners. Hand pruners are for pruning small branches, harvesting vegetables, deadheading, and thinning fruit. Find the one just right for your hand.

Pruning saw. These are used for cutting larger branches and come in several styles. If you are training your plants correctly when young, you should not need one.

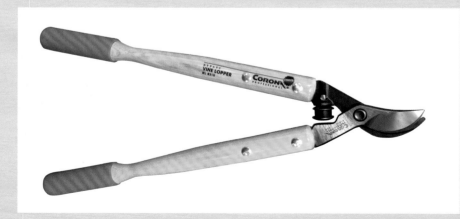

Loppers. Loppers are basically long-handled hand pruners. Use them to prune larger branches. They also can be used to cut large branches into smaller pieces for disposal.

Crossovers

Branches may cross back through the center of a plant in a quest for light. Although not so much of a problem when plants are young, it can cause problems later on. Remove branches heading into the center of a plant when they are small. This may be all the pruning you need to do on a young plant for the entire year.

Winter is a good time to observe the structure of deciduous trees and see if there are any branches crossing back through the tree. If there are, plan to prune them out at the best pruning time for the type of tree.

Bad Angles

For long-lasting durability in most tree species, branches should grow at about a 45-degree angle. If you have to choose, keep the limb with the better angle. Some species have narrower angles, such as elms, hawthorns, and striped maples. You will have to work with the nature of the tree or shrub and remove what looks out of the norm for that plant.

Rubbing Branches

When one branch rubs on another, the plant is injuring itself. Scarring and weakening of the wood occurs. Remove one of the two branches. You also need to see if one is crossing over back through the tree and which has the better crotch angle (the angle between the trunk and the branch).

Poor crotch angles (those that are too narrow) can cause limbs to break during high wind or in an ice storm. Remove limbs before they become an issue.

Branches that rub against each other inflict wounds and allow easy entrance for disease or insects.

Step 1: The first cut is about a foot out from the trunk. Cut upwards roughly halfway through the branch. Move several inches further out and make the second cut downward. At some point, the branch will break and fall.

Step 2: Tidy the area by cutting where the branch emerges from the tree—at the branch collar. Ideally, slightly cut through the bark underneath the severed limb first to score it so that when you cut off the rest of the limb, the bark will not tear.

PRUNING TREE LIMBS

Occasionally it becomes necessary to remove large limbs. This work must be done carefully because branches can be quite heavy. The Internet abounds with (painfully funny) videos of people who neglected to consider this fact. You need to protect not just yourself and your property, but also the tree itself. If pruned improperly, you can severely damage the tree, which can lead to disease and the need to remove the entire tree.

PRUNING SHRUB ROSES

Pruning roses is about timing, amount, and place on the plant.

Timing

Prune when roses are dormant, 8 weeks before the last frost date in your area.

Amount

You'll reduce your big fat rose bush to three to six main branches, also called canes. Some varieties will have up to 10 canes. Start by removing any dead canes as well as small, twiggy growth. Remove any canes that are crossing through the middle of the bush or rubbing against other canes.

Now look at your bush and pick out the best canes that remain. Smart carpenters measure twice and cut once. So

do smart pruners. Measure with your eye from two different directions before you cut.

The main canes are going to be short—around 1 foot tall. The exact height depends on the type of rose bush. Pretend you're a hungry giraffe and chomp down at least half of the plant. Because you are a smart giraffe, you'll leave enough so the plant has enough energy to grow lots of sweet flowers to enjoy later.

The final height and number of canes depends on the rose type.

TYPE	HEIGHT AFTER PRUNING	NUMBER OF CANES
Hybrid Tea	8 to 12	3 or 4
Grandiflora	up to 18 inches	up to 6
Floribunda	6 to 12 inches	up to 10
Miniatures	reduce to one-third of original height	4 to 6 canes

Place

Look for a new bud near the base of the canes you have selected to remain. The bud is usually pinkish. Select one about a foot above the ground and on the outside of the cane. Because this bud will grow into a whole new cane, you want the right one—one that will grow outward, opening the shape of the rose bush and letting light into the central portion of the plant.

Cut at a slight diagonal about ¼ inch above the bud. Cut just enough to help shed rainwater once it's healed.

SPECIAL CASES FOR PRUNING

They say that there are exceptions to every rule, and pruning plants is no exception to that rule! The guidelines provided above are good guides, but special situations abound.

Rejuvenation Pruning

Rejuvenation pruning can help shrubs that have become leggy and full of dead patches. Different species need it on different timetables. Some species respond better to gradual rejuvenation or renewal pruning over several years, whereas other species do best with extreme rejuvenation pruning all at once.

Gradual Rejuvenation Pruning

Also called *renewal pruning*, this gradual process can restore overgrown shrubs with tangled growth and dead central branches. They will flower less and less as time goes by. These can be renewed through a gradual rejuvenation process in which one-third of a shrub's growth is removed each year over three consecutive years. Many deciduous and evergreen shrubs respond well to gradual rejuvenation pruning, including barberries, pyracanthas, forsythias, honeysuckle, hydrangeas, lilacs, and mock oranges. This type of renewal pruning can also be used on some evergreen shrubs, such as boxwoods, cherry laurels, and rhododendrons. Yews need such help once every decade or so.

Cut just above the next living bud when pruning. New growth will be jump-started at the bud point.

Renew a long-established shrub by cutting one-third of the stems to ground level.

Extreme Rejuvenation Pruning

Some plants grow best with an extreme rejuvenation pruning on an infrequent basis. In some species, it is because in nature they are subject to periodic wildfires, such as Cleveland sage or Texas ranger, or eaten to the ground every so often, such as sand cherry or perennial sage. In the garden, you need to do this once every three to five years—chop the entire plant back all at once, generally to 6 to 12 inches high. This results in new growth that is full and even throughout the entire plant. Deciduous shrubs that tolerate extreme rejuvenation pruning include redstem dogwoods, forsythias, hydrangeas, privets, honeysuckle, elderberries, spireas, lilacs, rosemary, creosote, wormwoods, damianitas, and brittlebushes.

Over time, the lower branches of many shrubs become shaded by their own top growth and lose their leaves. Rejuvenation pruning is required.

One year after the entire shrub was cut to 6 inches tall, this plant is bushy and full.

Pruning Ornamental Grasses

Most people think of woody plants needing pruning, but there are many other garden plants that require periodic cutting back. Ornamental grasses need extreme rejuvenation pruning once a year. Think of it as a military crew cut for the clump of grass.

Timing. Do this right after the last frost day in your area. If you do this too soon, plants may be frost damaged, but if you wait too long, you may kill new growth.

Amount. If the species reaches less than 1 foot tall, cut the entire plant down to 4 inches tall. Grass species that grow 1 to 2 feet should be chopped down to 6 to 8 inches. Grasses over 2 feet should be cut to 8 to 12 inches high. This may seem extreme, but the goal is to remove all older brown growth and open the central crown to sunlight. Use the pruned tops for mulch or compost them.

Just after the last frost date in your area, remove unsightly dead stems and older growth on ornamental grasses.

Cut ornamental grasses short enough to expose the central crown to sunlight.

Freeze and Frost Damage

Every so often, an unexpectedly hard freeze or an ice storm can wreak havoc in the garden. While you may want to rush around and tidy up right away, it is best to give plants a chance. Remove torn limbs but leave frosted foliage. Wait until one month after the official last frost date in your area to give damaged plants a chance to display new growth. After this date, go ahead and prune what you must. You may have to break the 30-percent rule.

Crown and Canopy Thinning

Selectively removing a number of branches in the crown of trees makes sense in two cases: in orchards where fruit production is important and on urban street trees growing with inadequate root systems.

In orchards, canopy thinning increases light that penetrates to the central fruit and enhances fruit quality. In the city, street trees with limited space to grow supporting and anchoring roots may require crown thinning to reduce the

It's best to hire certified arborists for major tree work. They have the training and tools to do the work correctly, plus insurance in case things go awry.

wind resistance of the tree. This is best left to an arborist, because lopping off the wrong sections can make the situation worse and cause the tree to overbalance and fall.

The myth that you have to "thin the crown" of every single tree is unfortunate and widespread. The story goes that you need to thin the crown of large trees so they don't blow over in the wind. It is an ideal story with which to scare homeowners—convincing them to spend money on tree care they generally don't need. Reputable licensed arborists do not condone the practice. If trees haven't developed anchoring roots, it might be a good idea, but if you give them enough space to grow and water them correctly, this isn't a problem. Don't plant too big a tree for the space. Water at the drip line (the edge of the canopy where the feeder roots grow). These feeder roots develop into anchoring roots. If you water at the trunk of a tree, you encourage feeder roots to grow in toward the tree until the anchoring roots are just a ball under the trunk and don't—can't—anchor anything.

A study of urban blow downs in Southwestern cities showed that lack of good anchoring root structure was a contributing factor in over 90 percent of the cases.

Canopy Lifting

When trees loom over a space we wish to use, it may be time to lift the lowermost tier of the canopy. Once trees are mature enough (established for three years), remove the lower branches to a given height. Don't remove more than 30 percent of the plant's mass at a time or you may kill it.

Canopy lifting is also called skirting a tree, as if we were lifting its skirts. This introduces light to the lower part of the trunk. In a number of species (especially those with tropical genes, such as citrus or olive), this alerts the meristems to grow new branches to shade the trunk. Also called water sprouts (or occasionally suckers), this growth should be caught as soon as possible and stopped.

Removing Water Sprouts

Water sprouts are upright shoots that arise from the trunk of a tree. They originate from the meristem buds hidden in the trunk. Water sprouts often develop in trees in response to sunlight damage or improper pruning. Water sprouts by their nature are not as strong as regular branches. These shoots are more subject to diseases and pests.

Your first instinct may be to cut them off, but it's better to remove the meristem tissue underlying the sprout. If the sprout is small enough this is easy. Firmly grasp the water sprout as close to the base as you can. Turn it clockwise as you pull, and it should come out with the lump of latent bud. Your tree should not resprout in the same spot. Note that this is a twist, not a backwards yank. The clockwise twist more effectively disrupts the cellular growth process.

You may have to remove water sprouts a number of times before the tree stops producing them.

Vista Pruning

This special type of pruning is done in rare cases where the home and tree are on a slope with a desired view. A window of view can be opened by removing several limbs rather than completely skirting a tree.

Pollarding

Back in the days when we wove baskets to carry things and needed pliable wood for use around farm and home, pollarding was done to stimulate thin pliable branches. Pollarding is not needed in the modern yard—it just repeatedly damages trees and leads to their early demise, generally from pests or disease.

Try to plan ahead and remove limbs before they become large. The tree will heal better and the trunk will not be marred with scar tissue as this one is.

Pull water sprouts when they are small, removing the meristem cells in the trunk that form them.

CHAPTER 7
COMPOSTING AND MULCHING

By Katie Elzer-Peters

GROWING A PRODUCTIVE AND BEAUTIFUL GARDEN comes down to the soil, as discussed in Chapter 2, and building soil involves adding organic materials to the garden. Compost and organic mulch are the two best inputs for building soil.

Compost is, essentially, a miracle material for the garden. There's almost no problem that can't be solved with compost. Soil draining too fast? Add compost to retain water. Nutrients leaching out? Add compost to keep them in. Soil too heavy and sticky with clay? Add compost. Soil largely made up of sand? Add compost. Landscape plants declining? Add compost. Vegetables growing slowly? Add compost. For healthier vegetables and a lush landscape, regularly add compost to the soil or mulch with compost.

Mulch (both organic—compost, shredded hardwood, or grass clippings—and non-organic—gravel, black plastic) offers additional benefits to compost, including moisture retention, weed suppression, and providing the "finishing touch" to the garden.

Here's how to keep your garden growing and looking its best with mulch and compost.

OPPOSITE: A homemade bin made from scrap materials creates nutritious compost when you add the proper organic materials and turn them regularly to keep air and moisture circulating.

COMPOST

Eventually, any natural material that has been left outside will decompose. But piling together yard waste, leaves, and kitchen scraps speeds up the process of decomposition and results in a (somewhat uniform) product called compost that improves garden soil when properly applied.

You can buy compost or make your own. Making your own is a way to use up yard and kitchen scraps that would otherwise be trashed.

The benefits of making and using compost in the garden are many:

- Recycle kitchen and yard scraps—cut down on municipal waste fees and keep biodegradable items out of the landfill.
- Improve soil structure and reduce compaction.
- Elevate water and oxygen-holding capacity.
- Increase nutrient availability to plants by providing the microbes, insects, and other life forms in the soil with raw materials to break down.
- Save money by making your own soil amendments.

Making Your Own Compost

Compost is made from green materials, which are high in nitrogen, and brown materials, which are low in nitrogen and higher in carbon. When you're building and adding materials to a pile, try to keep a carbon to nitrogen ratio (C:N) of 30:1, which ends up being about 2 parts brown materials to 1 part green materials. If your pile skews higher in green than brown or vice versa, it isn't the end of the world, but it might start to either emit a foul smell or be slow to break down.

Here are the various materials appropriate for composting by category.

Any covered bucket will do for a kitchen compost pail, but you can buy them with carbon filters to keep the smell down between trips to the compost pile.

Brown Materials

- Shredded newspapers
- Dried leaves
- Sawdust
- Wood chips
- Paper bags
- Paper towels
- Twigs
- Tea bags
- Straw
- Wood ashes

Green Materials

- Grass clippings
- Coffee grounds
- Weeds (only if you have a hot pile)
- Green leaves
- Kitchen scraps (vegetable peels)
- Eggshells
- Fresh rabbit, chicken, goat, horse, or cow manure

Green materials, such as lawn clippings, are high in nitrogen.

Brown materials are high in carbon.

What NOT to Compost

There are items you don't want to compost because they either won't break down or might introduce pest, weed, or disease problems into the garden if the compost pile doesn't reach a high enough temperature. Never compost human or pet waste, regardless of the type of compost operation you're running. (This does not include standard animal manures.) You can end up introducing bacterial and viral diseases into the garden that are harmful to human health. You should also avoid composting diseased or infected plants, as you can end up spreading the plant diseases to the rest of the garden. Just throw away diseased plant material.

Don't Compost These Items

- Meat or animal products (including dairy products)
- Diseased/infected plants
- Weeds (unless the pile is hot)
- Pet waste, including litter
- Pig manure
- Coal ashes (too heavy on chemicals)
- Seeds

Compost Methods

To create something so simple—decomposed plant materials—there are actually quite a number of techniques you can use. Depending on the amount of time, energy, and space you have, some methods will better suit your needs than others.

Slow, Cool Compost Piles

The other name for this method would be "make a pile and let it rot." Most home compost piles are going to be slow, cool compost piles. It can take up to a year for compost made via this method to be ready. Add material to the pile as it becomes available from the kitchen, the junk mail pile (just don't compost glossy paper), the lawn mower, and more. Try to keep in mind the 2:1 brown-to-green-materials ratio mentioned earlier.

Hot Piles

Hot piles produce usable compost faster, but they require more work and careful tending. Hot piles should reach temperatures high enough (145°F) to kill weed seeds and disease organisms from animal manures. You can build a hot pile in a three-sided bin or as an open pile. Select a level, somewhat shady spot for the pile.

It's important to take the temperature of compost to ensure the pile is heating enough to kill pathogens.

Bin Composting

If you're serious about processing a large volume of yard and kitchen scraps, you might want to invest in a triple-bin compost system. These are three conjoined bins, open on one side. Compost in each bin will be at a different stage of decomposition.

A three-bin system is set up in the following way:
- Bin 1: New materials
- Bin 2: Compost that is "cooking"
- Bin 3: Finished compost

Start by building a pile in bin 1. You can build it all at one time or as materials become available. When the pile in bin 1 is hot, turn half of it into bin 2 and let it cook. Continue to add materials to bin 1. Turn bin 2 on the hot/cool cycle that you'd use for a hot pile. When it is done, move it to bin 3 and move half of the material from bin 1 to bin 2 and repeat the process.

A single-bin compost setup that doesn't rotate should be managed like a hot or cool compost pile—whichever works for you.

Compost Quick Tip

Chop up or shred materials before adding them to a compost pile or bin so that they will break down faster. Smaller pieces mean more surface area for the microbes to devour.

How to Build a Hot Compost Pile

1. Gather materials. You will need to start with enough brown and green materials in a 2:1 ratio to build a pile that is at least 3 feet tall by 3 feet wide.
2. Chop and shred the materials.
3. Begin building the pile. Start with a layer of sticks, wood chips, or other airy, bulky brown materials. For a 3×3-foot pile, start with a 4×4-foot base.
4. Layer materials, alternating 2 parts brown with 1 part green.
5. Water each layer so that it is about as damp as a wrung-out sponge.
6. Finish with a layer of brown material and cover the pile.
7. Check the temperature every couple of weeks. It should heat up. If it has not, add more green materials and a bit of water and check again after a week or so.
8. Turn the pile after it has cooled down.
9. Check the pile for another heating and cooling cycle. Once the compost doesn't heat upon turning, it's ready for use.

ABOVE: A cool compost pile requires both green and brown material and should be occasionally turned.

BELOW: Compost bins keep the pile contained.

A compost tumbler is basically a bin that rolls or turns.

Tumbler Composting

You can buy tumblers on stands that are easy to turn, or you can make your own by drilling holes (for aeration) in a 55-gallon drum with a lid.

Fill the tumbler about two-thirds full with the same 2:1 ratio of brown materials to green materials, and water the materials so they are as damp as a wrung-out sponge. Then turn the tumbler once a day. The compost inside should heat up and cool down several times while it cooks. It will take from two to four months to finish.

The advantage to using a tumbler is that all the compost is contained. The disadvantage is that you can only really have one batch of compost cooking at a time.

Sheet Composting

Sheet composting is another type of passive composting. You create layers of green and brown materials on the surface of the soil and let them break down in place. The finished "pile" or "sheet" should be around 18 inches tall and include several 1- to 2-inch layers of green and brown materials. Add materials as you have them, but always top a layer of green materials (such as kitchen scraps) with brown materials (such as wood chips, straw, or shredded paper). You will be able to plant into the sheet compost area between six months and one year after the initial build.

Trench Composting

This type of composting is similar to sheet composting, only instead of creating layers of compost on top of the soil, you bury the layers. You can dig a hole or, if you have a lot of material, dig a trench and fill it with a 2:1 ratio of green and brown materials. It will take about a year for you to be able to plant directly into a compost trench. One way to trench compost without eating up part of your garden is to dig a trench where the garden paths are and pile the compost in the path/trench. Top with soil and some wood chips, and you won't even know the compost is there.

RIGHT: Trench composting builds compost directly into the garden bed.
BELOW: Sheet composting is like making lasagna—with yard waste!

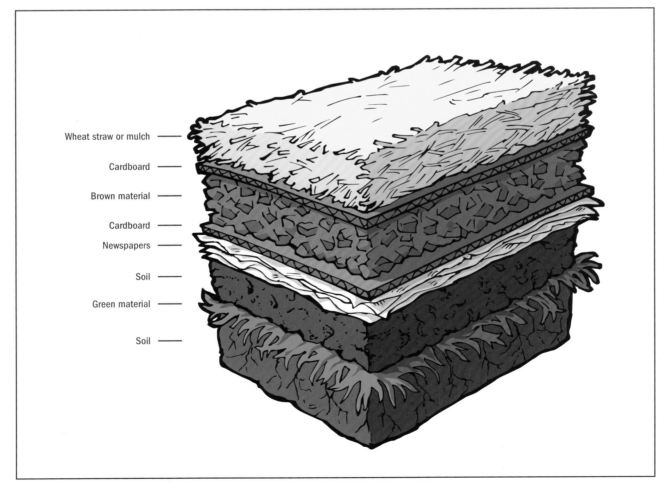

Wheat straw or mulch —
Cardboard —
Brown material —
Cardboard —
Newspapers —
Soil —
Green material —
Soil —

Worm Composting

Worm compost is a magical elixir for the garden. Worm castings (worm poop) are like liquid gold, especially for vegetable gardeners. Worms are fairly easy to tend. You want to make sure they don't get too hot, too cold, or too wet. Otherwise, as long as you feed them regularly, they'll produce plenty of valuable compost for the garden. Here's how to be a vermicomposter (worm composter):

Buy worms. The best worms for worm composting are red wigglers because their preferred environment is easy to recreate within a worm compost bin.

Make or buy a worm bin. You can buy triple-decker worm bins that encourage worms to move from the bottom layer up as they eat the available food. If you have the space, interest, and money for one of these setups, they're pretty convenient because you don't have to try to separate the worms from the finished compost. They'll just move up to the new layer where there's food.

Single worm bins are easy to make. Get a large plastic container that's around 1 foot deep by 3 feet wide by 2 feet long. Drill holes the size of a quarter around the bottom edge of the container, about 1 inch from the bottom. Cover the holes with some screen. (These are drain holes, but you need to cover them with screen so the worms do not escape.)

Fill the bin with bedding. Shredded office paper or newspaper makes excellent worm bedding. Wet it so it is about as moist as a wrung-out sponge and line the bottom of the bin to a depth of 8 inches. Add a couple of cups of garden soil for grit, and then the worms. A pound of worms can eat ½ pound of food per day.

Set the bin in its permanent location. Worms will do best in a shady location with temperatures between 55 and 75°F.

Feed the worms. To keep odors and issues to a minimum, feed worms vegetable and fruit scraps, bread, cereal, coffee grounds, and egg shells. Do not feed worms meat or dairy products, oils, peanut butter, citrus peels, onions, or pet waste. Add about ½ pound of food at a time and bury it under the bedding. Wait until the worms have mostly eaten the food before adding more food.

Worm Bin Problems and Solutions

- Bedding is too wet: add more bedding
- Worms are dying: cut back on the amount of food added, add bedding, and remove some of the worms
- Bin is dry: add water
- Bin is attracting flies: cover the food with additional bedding
- Fruit flies are multiplying: stop adding fruit peels and add bedding

Red wigglers are the ideal worm for worm composting.

Harvest and use the compost. The easiest way to do this is to move all the contents of the bin over to half of the bin and fill the second half with fresh food and bedding; the worms will scoot over. You can remove the top third of the worm bin and set it aside and then dump the contents of the bin into the garden, fill the bin with new bedding, and replace the worms that you removed. You can also dump the entire contents of the worm bin onto a clean sheet of newspaper. Form it into little piles. The worms will move to the bottom of the piles, and you can remove the tops of the piles and use them in the garden.

Composting Manure

Manure is not the same thing as compost. Manure is waste from animals, while compost is decomposed vegetable matter. You cannot apply fresh manure to the garden, as it will burn plants. (It also likely has harmful pathogens.) To render manure usable, compost it with brown materials such as sawdust or wood for several months. Turn the pile occasionally. Horse, cow, chicken, sheep, and rabbit manures are the most commonly available and recommended for home gardeners.

Composting Leaves

Composted leaves, called "leaf mold," are excellent as mulch and soil amendments. Simply shred the leaves and pile them up. Let them sit over the winter, turning occasionally. They'll be ready to use by spring!

RIGHT TOP: Fresh manure can burn plants and transmit pathogens. Always compost manure before using it in the garden.

RIGHT BOTTOM: Leaf compost is one of the best things you can add to the garden to improve the look and quality of your landscape.

Compost Troubleshooting

- **Smelly pile:** Either the pile is too wet or it's filled with more nitrogen-heavy materials than carbon materials. To fix the problem, add more dry brown materials.
- **Pile is not shrinking/cooking:** The pile might be too small.
- **Pile is damp and sweet smelling:** It needs nitrogen.

- **Pile is damp and rancid smelling:** It needs carbon.
- **The pile is dry:** It needs green materials or to be watered. The pile might need aeration, and will benefit from being turned.
- **Pile is attracting animals:** It needs to be covered and/or it may have the wrong ingredients in it.

No garden is complete without the finishing touch of mulch.

MULCH

Next to compost, there's no better addition to the garden than mulch. Landscape beds, flower garden borders, and vegetable gardens all benefit from a 2- to 3-inch layer of mulch.

It takes a little bit of money, time, and elbow grease to mulch the garden, but the benefits are huge:

- Conserves soil moisture
- Reduces erosion
- Prevents soil crusting
- Incorporates organic matter
- Suppresses weeds
- Modulates the soil temperature
- Tidies the look of the garden
- Prevents soil from splashing onto plant leaves and spreading fungal diseases

I think a garden never really looks "done" until it has been mulched, but that's me.

Choose mulch that works well with your surrounding landscape. Pine straw in the desert would look ridiculous. (It would also, most likely, not be available.) Red lava rock in New England looks out of place, where a tumbled stone would not.

Get the most from your mulch by using the right type for your garden situation. Broadly, mulch can be categorized as inorganic (not made from natural materials and/or will not break down and add nutrients to the soil) and

organic (made from natural materials that will break down and add nutrients to the soil). Technically, stone is a natural material, but it doesn't add massive amounts of nutrients to the soil other than a few minerals that might leach from the stone. For most situations, good old shredded hardwood or, when available, composted leaf mulch is best.

Stay Away from Landscape Fabric

Landscape fabric, a woven plastic fabric sometimes used to block weeds in new landscape plantings is not mulch and should not be used like mulch. While the fabric will suppress weeds for a few months, eventually it will be rendered ineffective by mulch, dried leaves, and other organic materials settling on top. Weed seeds will blow in and sprout on top of the fabric, and you'll have twice the mess. Once landscape fabric is down, you have to use a knife to cut a hole in it in order to plant anything in it. Plant roots grow into it and anchor it to the ground. It's a big mess that's better to just avoid in the first place.

Buy in Bulk

If you have more than a small landscape bed to mulch, it's most cost effective to buy mulch in bulk. Search for a local supplier and get their rates for delivery. Bulk mulch is usually sold by the cubic yard. To decide how much to order, measure the square footage of the area you are mulching (length × width = square footage).

Find a mulch calculator online and enter the square footage you want to cover and the depth you want the mulch to be. The calculator will give you an estimate in cubic yards (and sometimes cubic feet) of how much you need.

Save money—buy in bulk!

Organic Mulches

Organic mulch will, over time, break down and add nutrients and beneficial structure to the soil. Because it breaks down, it has to be reapplied. Some materials used for organic mulch, such as compost, could also be considered soil amendments, but this section discusses these elements and their functional use as mulch rather than as a strict soil amendment.

When buying bagged mulch, take care to note whether there are any weed-killing chemicals in it. Chemical use is a gardener's personal choice, but you wouldn't want to use mulch with pre-emergent-weed-killing additives anywhere you plant new plants, particularly where you've planted seeds. If you're going to use mulch with those types of additives, use it around established plants.

Compost

While you could technically mulch a garden with any type of compost, from worm compost to mushroom compost, most types of compost are most beneficial when worked into the soil. However, partially composted chopped leaves, a blend of composted manures, and coarse garden compost (that might still have some decomposing to do) make great mulch. Apply a layer 2 to 3 inches deep in the spring and the fall. Compost is a great mulch for any landscape or garden area, including vegetable gardens.

Using compost as mulch does double duty. It performs all the functions of mulch while adding nutrients to the soil.

Fresh Wood Chips

There is occasionally some hand wringing about using fresh wood chips as mulch. People get concerned that because the chips are fresh and, therefore, high in carbon, they'll tie up nitrogen from the soil as they decompose. That is true—at the immediate point where the wood chips meet the soil. Fresh wood chips will not, at the level of soil where most plants are taking up nutrients, tie up enough nitrogen to cause deficiencies in plants. This would not be my first choice of mulch for a vegetable garden, as the edibles could be more shallowly rooted than landscape plants and will have some roots in the zone where nitrogen is tied up. However, you can make up for that by adding a little extra organic fertilizer. If fresh wood chips are your only choice for vegetable garden mulch, go ahead and use them. One bonus with fresh wood chips is that they shouldn't have any weed seeds in them. If you can, try to verify that the mulch isn't made from pressure-treated wood scraps, which have chemicals that can kill plants. Fresh wood chips are usually fairly lightweight and don't compact, although they can sometimes float away during a heavy rain. Apply a 3-inch layer in spring and fall.

TOP: Wood chips are a cheap and plentiful mulch option.

BOTTOM: Shredded mulch is one of the most attractive mulch types.

Dyed Wood Mulch

Dyed mulch is not my favorite. In addition to red, you can find mulch dyed black, brown, and other colors. Usually dyed mulch is made from fresh wood chips, so it should be used in similar situations—not in the vegetable garden, for example. Who knows what chemicals are in the dye that has been used? Do you really want that on your veggies? Probably not. Reapply when the color fades.

Shredded Hardwood

This type of mulch is probably the most popular. It's made from the shredded bark of hardwood trees (not pine trees), is usually dark brown in color, and has an earthy scent. Sometimes it is partially composted. You can find varying textures—triple ground is the finest and my choice when using hardwood mulch. Use shredded hardwood in all landscape and garden situations. It will also compact and stay in place on gently sloping hills and, during a heavy rain, wash away less than fresh wood chip mulch. Typically, an application of 3 inches in the spring is enough for the year.

7

ABOVE: Take care not to add more than an inch of grass clippings at a time when using it as mulch.

RIGHT: Make sure you're buying straw, not hay, if you plan to use it as vegetable garden mulch.

Shredded Leaves

Leaves are a great natural mulch that add tons of nutrients to the soil. Worms love leaves! If you have lots of hardwood trees and want to make your own mulch, invest in a shredder. They're inexpensive. Whole leaves dry out and blow away or, depending on the weather, can become heavy mats that can harbor pest and disease problems. Shredded leaves break down quickly and will need to be applied in the spring and the fall. If you shred all the leaves in the yard and apply some in the fall as mulch, you can compost the rest until spring and reapply as leaf mold. Apply a 2- to 3-inch layer as a mulch.

Grass Clippings

These are most often used as a mulch for vegetable gardens because, while they add nitrogen to the soil, these clippings are not the most attractive type of mulch for a large landscape bed. Apply grass clippings no more than 1 inch deep in vegetable gardens. Take care to keep the clippings away from the stems of the plants. Let the clippings dry out before adding any more. Large buildups of grass clippings can create thick mats that prevent water from penetrating the soil. Extreme heat can also build up in a thick mat of clippings.

Straw

This mulch is also most often used in vegetable gardens. Some people grow entire gardens in straw bales or use straw to build potato towers. Straw is excellent for retaining soil moisture, but it is less helpful with weed control. It's hard to achieve total soil coverage with straw—it is slippery and coarse—so weed seeds still receive enough light to germinate. Straw can also come with its own weed seeds that, once established, can be hard to control. Apply straw in a 2- to 3-inch layer and reapply as it breaks down. The mulch will become slightly compacted after a rain.

Pine straw is a popular and plentiful mulching material in the southeastern United States.

Pine Straw

You'll see pine straw used as mulch in landscape beds in the southeastern United States where longleaf pines, loblolly pines, and slash pines are part of the natural landscape. Some people simply rake up "pine straw" (the dead pine needles shed by the trees) to use as mulch in their own gardens. Pine straw can also be bought in bales composed of flakes (smaller sections of straw). Pine straw is pretty fluffy when you first spread it in the landscape, but it does eventually pack down. Use it in landscape beds and around acid-loving plants such as blueberries, camellias, azaleas, hollies, and rhododendrons.

Paper

If you feel that you must use some sort of weed block "fabric" in addition to another type of mulch, paper is a better alternative than landscape fabric. You can actually buy biodegradable paper rolls of weed block. Sheets of plain (not glossy) newspaper also work well to block weeds. If you want to use large sheets, always mulch on top with another organic mulch to help prevent the paper from drying out completely, as paper is sometimes difficult to re-wet when it dries. Shredded newspaper can be an effective vegetable garden mulch if kept damp (so it doesn't blow away).

Pine Bark

This mulch comes in different sizes, from small fines to large nuggets. I prefer the look of "pine bark fines" over the large nuggets. The smaller pieces tend to stay in place better during a rainstorm as well. Apply a 2-inch layer of pine bark as a mulch in the spring.

Inorganic Mulches

Inorganic mulches provide many of the benefits of organic mulches, but they don't add any nutrients to the soil, and if they break down, it is into a waste product rather than a soil additive.

Gravel/Stone

Once you put down gravel, you are not going to want to pick it up (it's heavy), so use it to mulch permanent plantings. House foundations are good locations for gravel or stone mulch. Stone soaks up heat and can create small microclimates where it is used. That is a plus if you are growing marginally hardy plants, but it can be a minus if you're growing thirsty plants in a hot climate. Choose stone that matches the colors and natural stones where you live. Otherwise, the mulch will stick out like a sore thumb. Apply stone in a 1-inch layer and stay on top of any weeds that pop up. You can use a blower or a soft broom to remove any leaf debris that may land in the planting bed.

Pine bark is available in a variety of sizes, from small "fines" to large nuggets about the size of a deck of cards.

ABOVE LEFT: Gravel mulch creates a microclimate, elevating the temperature in the immediate area where it is used.

ABOVE RIGHT: Only use lava rock where it makes sense with the surrounding environment. In the desert, it's a good choice. In a naturally wooded area, not so much.

RIGHT: Black plastic is most beneficial when used as a weed suppressant in the vegetable garden.

Lava Rock

Red rock made from a volcanic product is more porous than stone and will break down slightly over time. It does soak up some water, so it will help with moisture retention better than stone. It is sharp, so use it where you won't have to weed or plant frequently. I would also caution you to only use any red-colored stone in an area where it will blend with the house or the natural environment. For example, red lava rock in a beach garden near pure white sand will look out of place.

Plastic Sheeting

The most common colors of plastic sheeting are black and red. The only place to use this mulch is in the vegetable garden and it must be used in conjunction with drip irrigation. Plastic mulch is excellent for weed suppression, soil moisture retention (provided that the plants are irrigated), and elevating soil temperature. In the home garden, plastic mulch would not be a first choice unless you're trying to grow tomatoes and other heat-loving crops in a cooler environment.

Rubber Mulch

Rubber mulch is common on playgrounds. Often made from recycled tires, this mulch comes dyed in every color of the rainbow. Because it doesn't break down and add nutrients to the soil but will degrade and potentially leach chemicals into the soil over time, it isn't the best choice for anything

Helpful Tools for Mulching

- Pitchfork or hay fork
- Hard rake
- Shrub rake
- Spade
- 5-gallon bucket

other than, perhaps, a pathway in a public park. I do not recommend using rubber mulch in the home landscape.

Whichever type of mulch you decide to use, remember that it should be the frame for the picture (the picture being the flowers or landscape plants) and not the main feature. If you look at a mulched garden and the first thing you notice is mulch, you might want to reconsider your choice of colors or materials.

Applying Mulch

Usually you'll mulch the garden and landscape in the spring and/or fall. Spring mulching helps tidy up the garden, suppress summer weeds, and conserve moisture. Fall mulching, especially at great depths, can help keep the soil warmer and contribute to better overwintering of plants. It also helps prevent soil erosion from winter rains and, in warm areas, keeps winter weeds to a minimum. The type of mulch influences how often it needs to be applied and to what depth, both of which are noted in the individual mulch descriptions.

Apply most mulch at a depth of 3 inches per application. The exceptions are rocks/gravel, grass clippings, pine straw, and rubber mulch. Rocks, rubber mulch, and grass clippings are deep enough at 1 inch. Pine straw is fluffy; when applied it will initially be about 6 inches deep, but it will pack down.

Follow these guidelines:

- Take care with your back. Always lift with your legs and take a break if your back is straining. If you don't want to use a pitchfork and wheelbarrow for bulk mulching, a 5-gallon bucket is a good way to transport mulch from the pile to the landscape bed.
- Dump piles in the landscape beds and use a hard rake to spread it. A smaller shrub rake comes in handy to even out mulch around plants.
- Start at the back of the landscape bed and work out so that you don't get footprints in the fluffy, newly applied mulch.

- Keep mulch away from the plant stems and tree trunks because this can cause plants to rot. Do not make mulch "volcanoes" around plants.

How to Spread Pine Straw Mulch

Pine straw mulch is common in the Southeast. There's a trick to spreading this type of mulch without making a mess.

To add the pine straw to the landscape, simply snip the twine holding a bale together, and the bale will break apart into clumps called "flakes." Sprinkle the flakes around the landscape bed or trees, being careful to keep the straw near the ground. If you fling pine straw around above your waist, you'll end up with needles hanging all over your shrubs, and that's annoying to clean up!

The newly spread straw will be fluffy and it will most likely escape the landscape beds. To tidy up the beds, you'll want to rake and tuck the straw to keep it in place. Using a hard rake, pull the straw into the edge of the landscape bed. Step on the straw on top of the rake, and then, leaving your foot where it is, pull the rake out. This bunches up the straw at the edge of the bed.

To tuck the straw, after raking, plunge a sharpened spade or shovel into the ground about 1 inch inside the landscape bed. This will trap the edge of the straw in the soil and will keep it from blowing out of the bed. You can use a chopping motion to do this.

Rake mulch evenly across the landscape bed.

Gently pull mulch away from plant stems so the stems do not rot.

Spreading pine straw mulch.

CHAPTER 8
GARDENING BY SEASONS

By George Weigel

ASK GARDENERS WHAT'S IMPORTANT TO THEM IN the landscape and "four-season interest" usually shows up near the top of the wish list. Most people like the idea of gardens that change with the seasons *and* look good in all of them. That's doable, even in climates buried under snow for much of winter or baked to a crisp during triple-digit summers.

Seasonal change is most dramatic in regions with four distinct seasons. There, yards can take on four different looks per year while showing subtle differences day by day.

In warmer regions with climates more akin to two seasons—a long, hot summer followed by four to five months of cool to moderate temperatures in winter—the changes are less abrupt and dramatic but still worth embracing.

In all climates, plants naturally change in response to temperatures rising and falling and to daylight that lengthens and shortens. Some plants are seasonal. They make a short appearance before going dormant the rest of the year (such as spring-blooming tulip and daffodil bulbs) or they enter and leave the scene each year (such as annual flowers and most edibles). Others run through a cycle each year, starting with fresh young leaves, then flowers, growth, and fruits before ending with a glorious fall leaf-color change.

OPPOSITE: Season-long color is possible in a garden planted with long-blooming species and flowers that bloom in each of the seasons.

Beautyberry is barely leafing when gardeners are shopping in spring, but it matures into this berried beauty by fall.

It all adds up to a dynamic mix that's a lot like a botanical symphony. Think of your role as the conductor. Be ready, though, for the weather to have a big say in your all-season symphony. Not only do seasonal changes vary widely from region to region, but also the timing of changes can vary by weeks from season to season, even in your own yard.

An early spring, for example, might have cherry trees blooming and daffodils popping up two or three weeks earlier than usual. A sudden cold snap in autumn could shorten the fall foliage display, while a long, gradual cooling could extend it. In other words, you can't be so exact as to count on your mophead hydrangeas to bloom on June 22 every year.

On the other hand, weather affects the entire landscape, so if one plant is early, odds are everything else will be early. Some years, weather vagaries compress bloom times, causing plants that usually bloom at different times to bloom in concert. Other years, a surprise late frost will zap buds and lead to no magnolia or hydrangea flowers and no apricots or peaches.

Because there's very little gardeners can do about erratic weather, go with the flow and enjoy each unique season! Most plants are resilient enough to survive ill weather effects and go back to their usual behavior when conditions stabilize.

DO YOUR HOMEWORK

While most gardeners want all-season interest, it's easy to end up with a yard that looks good in flashes (most often in spring), but then has long periods with little change, color, or interest. The main reason for that is most people tend to plant shop in April or May. Masses go to the garden center every year at the same time and naturally gravitate toward what looks good then . . . or is on sale. That leads to spring-loaded landscapes that look great in April or May but then fizzle the rest of the year.

One solution is to shop in different seasons. Go back to the garden center throughout the growing season, especially when your yard is looking barren. Snoop around the plant benches at different times to see what's attractive each time. That beautyberry bush that produces beautiful metallic purple BB-sized fruits in fall, for example, is a pot of bare branches in April.

Another option is to visit local public gardens. You'll no doubt find plants doing something interesting at a time when your yard is snoozing. Plants are usually labeled at public gardens, making it easy to know what to buy. Public gardens also let you see what plants look like when maturing in actual garden settings as opposed to growing in small pots. And if you stick close to home, what's doable at the local public garden is likely doable in your yard.

Take walks around nearby neighborhoods at different times of year to see what others are growing that would add interest to your down times.

IT'S NOT JUST ABOUT THE FLOWERS

While flowers are likely to grab your attention first, don't overlook the leaves. Blooms are fleeting, but colorful leaves and needles add interest much longer—sometimes all year long. Because of the lure of wire-to-wire color, foliage has become a hot item in plant breeding.

Look no further than the glut of coral bells (*Heuchera*), foamflowers (*Tiarella*), and that marriage of the two— foamy bells (*Heucherella*)—as evidence of the color that leaves can bring to a landscape. Hundreds of new varieties of these three have hit the market in the last 20 years, offering leaf colors ranging from silver to burgundy-marked gold to nearly jet black.

Breeders have been developing new colorful-leafed versions of many other old favorite perennials, such as silver-leafed versions of false forget-me-nots, gold-leafed bleeding hearts, and dark-leafed cranesbill geraniums.

Coleus is the star of color-leafed annuals, although you'll also find silver-leafed dusty miller, black-leafed ornamental hot peppers, burgundy-leafed alternanthera, and gold- and black-leafed sweet potato vines, among others.

More foliage color is showing up in the nursery as well. In addition to long-popular blue spruces and golden false cypresses, you'll find native ninebark shrubs in golden-apricot and dark-burgundy forms, Leyland cypresses with golden needles, and weigelas in your choice of green leaves, black leaves, golden leaves, or white- and rose-variegated ones.

Another element to consider is bark. When leaves are off deciduous woody plants in winter, bark can take center stage. That's when plants such as the glowing stems of red-twig and gold-twig dogwoods and the smooth coral-red trunks of coral bark maples (*Acer palmatum* 'Sango Kaku') are at their best.

Other trees offer interest in their peeling or mottled bark. Among the choices are birches, Kousa dogwoods, paperbark maples, and Persian ironwoods.

ABOVE: This 'Stoplight' foamy bells, a cross of foamflowers (*Tiarella*) and coral bells (*Heuchera*), has two-toned foliage all season.

RIGHT: The stems of red-twig dogwoods turn dark red in fall and winter.

Plants with Colorful Foliage

8

Trees

- Beeches (burgundy, purple, cream/pink variegation)
- Crabapples (burgundy)
- Crape myrtles (burgundy)
- Japanese maples (red, gold)
- Kousa dogwoods (gold variegation)
- Redbuds (burgundy, apricot/gold)
- Smoketrees (burgundy, gold)

Evergreens

- Arborvitae (gold)
- Boxwoods (gold, white and gold variegation)
- Cedars (blue, gold)
- False cypresses (blue, gold)
- Hollies (gold and white variegation)
- Junipers (blue, silver, gold)
- Leyland cypresses (gold)
- Nandinas (red, gold)
- Osmanthus (white variegation)
- Pines (gold, gold striping)
- Spruce (blue, gold)

Flowering Shrubs

- Abelias (white and gold variegation)
- Barberries (red, burgundy, gold)
- Bush honeysuckles (black, white variegation)
- Caryopteris (white variegation)
- Deutzia (lime/yellow)
- Elderberries (black, gold)
- Fothergilla (blue)
- Hydrangeas (burgundy, white variegation)
- Ninebarks (burgundy, apricot/gold, nearly black)
- Shrub dogwoods (white variegation)
- Spireas (blue, gold)
- St. John's wort (burgundy/green, blue, gold)
- Sumac (gold)
- Weigelas (white variegation, burgundy, nearly black)
- Willows (white variegation)

Perennials and Grasses

- Astilbes (burgundy)
- Asters (dark burgundy)
- Big and little bluestems (blue)
- Bugbane (dark burgundy, nearly black)
- Coral bells (you name it)
- Creeping sedum (gold, blue, white variegation)
- Euphorbia (white variegation, burgundy accents)
- False forget-me-nots (silver, silver variegation)
- Fescues (blue)
- Foamflowers (red markings)
- Foamy bells (gold, red veining, tea-colored)
- Hardy geraniums (burgundy)
- Hibiscus (burgundy, nearly black)
- Hostas (gold, lime, blue, gold/white variegation)
- Indian grass (blue)
- Irises (white variegation)
- Jacob's ladder (white variegation)
- Japanese forest grass (gold, gold/white striping)
- Lamium (white variegation)
- Lavender (silvery gray)
- Ligularia (dark burgundy)
- Liriope (gold, gold and white variegation)
- Lungwort (white variegation)
- Miscanthus (white and gold striping)
- Russian sage (silvery gray)
- Salvias (burgundy/purple)
- Sedges (gold and white variegation)
- Solomon's seal (white variegation)
- Switchgrass (blue, burgundy accents)
- Yuccas (white/gold variegation)

Colorado blue spruce is a needled evergreen with powdery blue needles.

St. John's wort is a shrub that comes in versions with gold and bluish foliage as well as this one, 'Albury Purple', which has burgundy-tinged leaves.

Japanese forest grass comes in varieties that have green, gold, and gold- or white-variegated blades.

DIFFERENT WAYS TO GET ALL-SEASON INTEREST

The most change and interest will come from a landscape filled with many different kinds of plants that do different things at different times. A side benefit of diversity is that it aids beneficial wildlife, such as pollinating bees, butterflies, birds, and the "good" bugs that eat "bad" bugs. Wildlife thrives when there's a steady supply of host plants, pollen plants, nectar plants, and fruiting plants throughout the year. They'll go elsewhere if/when your landscape takes a siesta.

Stick with One Species

A simple approach to creating interest in different seasons is to plant different varieties of just a few species. Often, different varieties bloom at slightly different times or have other features that can spread out interest.

For example, if you like irises, instead of planting 20 of the same kind, plant rock-garden types (*Iris reticulata*) for late-winter bloom, native crested irises (*Iris cristata*) for spring bloom in the shade, and several kinds of Siberian (*Iris sibirica*) and bearded iris (*Iris germanica*) for bloom later in the spring. Also consider a variegated-leaf iris for season-long foliage interest and a reblooming type for fall flowers.

Kevin Kelly's Pennsylvania front yard changes markedly throughout the season, thanks to plentiful plants of many kinds.

Spring-blooming bulbs add color to a landscape while many plants are just waking up from winter dormancy.

Fill the Voids

A more planned approach is to evaluate what each part of the yard looks like in each season, then purposely seek plants that add interest to the voids. Make notes as you see the landscape change week by week, and do your improvements at prime planting times.

If you notice, for example, that beds are slow to get started in spring, the solution might be an early-blooming witch hazel or star magnolias, a few patches of daffodils or crocuses, and a cluster of hellebores, which are the first perennials out of the gate in winter. If you're hitting a dead zone in the dog days of summer, dwarf panicle hydrangeas, coneflowers, Russian sage, and sedum might fill the blooming void. And if your yard is going out in a fizzle instead of a sizzle in fall, maybe it could use a maple tree, a few fothergilla bushes, and some patches of goldenrod, asters, and mums.

If you're starting from scratch, think what your prospective plants will do throughout the year. When do each

bloom? For how long? Are you including anything with long-lasting features, such as colorful foliage or bark, that will bridge bloom gaps? Are there any times in the plan when little will be going on?

You can always go back and make additions later if you miscalculate. But at least giving thought to seasonal change at planning time will help avoid loading up with, say, five perennial flower choices that all happen to bloom in May.

You can bridge gaps between the bloom of perennials and woody plants by planting annual flowers. Most annuals bloom nonstop from the day you plant them until frost kills them.

In warm climates, it's possible to keep gaps filled all season by using warm-season annuals from spring through fall and switching to cool-preferring pansies, dusty miller, lobelia, snapdragons, and dianthus in winter.

Don't overlook containers for filling gaps too. These can be changed seasonally for four different looks per year.

Choose Hard-Working Plants

Especially in smaller spaces, maximize all-season interest by leaning toward hard workers. These are plants that either do something interesting for a long period of time (such as those colorful leafers and barkers) or that do more than one thing in one time.

Many plants are action-packed enough that they don't need coordinated neighbors to pick up the slack. For example, oakleaf hydrangeas (*Hydrangea quercifolia*) are native shrubs that produce large, white cone-shaped flowers in late spring that turn pink in early summer. The leaves resemble large oak leaves (bigger than an outstretched hand), turning from green to deep burgundy in the fall. Then when the leaves drop in fall, oakleaf hydrangeas reveal their peeling, cinnamon-colored bark throughout winter.

Another example is viburnum. Most of these produce white or pink fragrant "snowball" flowers in spring. Then the plants develop red, gold, blue, or black berries in late summer that ripen in fall, often changing color in the process. Most viburnums also have leaves that turn rich shades of gold and burgundy in fall before dropping. A few have evergreen foliage for winter interest.

Some other good hard-workers include:

Virginia sweetspires (*Itea virginica*). A native shrub with arching, white, bottle-brush flowers in June; long-lasting glossy red fall foliage.

Ninebarks (*Physocarpus opulifolius*). A native shrub with nearly black or apricot-gold summer leaves; small, pinkish-white snowball-like flower clusters in late spring followed by reddish fruits; rusty-red or gold-red fall foliage.

Ornamental grasses. Many types develop tan to pink seed clusters in late summer as well as foliage that turns shades of gold to burgundy in fall. Foliage is generally brown over winter but can be left standing for texture, movement, and birds' nest building.

Japanese stewartias (*Stewartia pseudocamellia*). A small tree with white summer blooms, multicolored fall foliage, and flaking, mottled bark in winter.

Kousa dogwoods (*Cornus kousa*). A small tree with white or pink June flowers, deep-red fall foliage, and red, bumpy, marble-sized fall fruits.

Oakleaf hydrangea is a plant that does more than one thing in one season, offering flowers, colorful fall foliage, and peeling bark in one package.

8

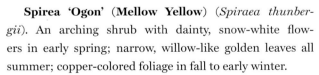
Stewartia is a tree that flowers in late spring (top), then turns multiple shades of bright leaf colors in fall (above), and even looks good in winter with its mottled, flaking bark (right).

Spirea 'Ogon' (**Mellow Yellow**) (*Spiraea thunbergii*). An arching shrub with dainty, snow-white flowers in early spring; narrow, willow-like golden leaves all summer; copper-colored foliage in fall to early winter.

Multiseason plants such as these are much easier for all-season planning than trying to knit together a nonstop array of two-week wonders. Those are plants with one-dimensional interest that might last only a week or two out of the entire year. That interest is often stunning enough that they're nonetheless in widespread use in US gardens. Among them are forsythia (mounds of golden blooms as winter ends), azaleas (beautiful flowers in assorted colors in early spring), peonies (showy, rose-like flowers in mid-spring), lilacs (fragrant pink or purple cones in late spring), and burning bush (fire-engine-red leaves in fall). The short

interest time doesn't mean that old-fashioned favorites such as these have no place in an all-season garden. But if your plan is overly reliant on them, you're more likely to run into voids.

A Bed for Each Season

Another approach to all-season interest is planting gardens dedicated to each season. Rather than sprinkle plants with multiseason interest throughout the beds, this approach concentrates same-season peakers in the same bed.

The advantage is gardens with maximum "wow," because everything is screaming with interest around the same time. The downside is that while one garden is singing, the rest are barely humming.

Spirea 'Ogon' (Mellow Yellow) blooms white in early spring (above left), then has fine-textured golden foliage all summer (above right), and finishes the year with a fall-foliage show that's coppery in color (top).

FOUR-SEASON PLANT GUIDE

8

With seasonal gardens, the idea is to load up with plants that bloom or show off in some way within the same season. Whether you're going that route or just trying to shore up existing shortfalls, here's a season-by-season rundown.

Spring Interest: Hard to Go Wrong

You'd almost have to *try* to be boring to come up with a springtime yard without color. So many plants flower from April through June that it's hard to avoid at least occasional splashes of color. Spring is also the most changeable time of year because many spring plants poke up quickly and bloom for just a few weeks to beat the arrival of summer heat. Change is noticeable more at a daily pace than a weekly one.

Six Linchpins of the Spring Landscape

1. **Spring-blooming bulbs.** Tulips, daffodils, hyacinths, and other colorful spring bulbs are lead actors in spring, but the catch is that you have to plant them the fall before. Missed your chance? You can still buy potted, blooming bulbs from the garden center in spring, but they'll be much more expensive than dormant bulbs. Warm-climate gardeners are stuck with buying potted bulbs (or with buying prechilled bulbs to plant) because spring bulbs need a cold period over winter to initiate flowering.

   To spread out bulb interest, plant different varieties that bloom at different times. Snowdrops, crocuses, winter aconite, and rock-garden irises are the earliest, followed by Siberian squill, daffodils, hyacinths, glory-of-the-snow, and species tulips, then late-spring-blooming tulips, grape hyacinths, Spanish bluebells, and, finally, alliums. For best impact, plant bulbs in clusters or wide bands as opposed to single files.

2. **Flowering trees.** A majority of trees put on their floral show in spring. These offer some of the yard's most dramatic color, although tree blooms tend to last only two or three weeks. Plant several that bloom at different times, especially redbud, dogwood, crabapple, cherry, and American fringe tree.

3. **Spring-blooming shrubs.** A string of both deciduous and broad-leaf shrubs bloom from the time winter is winding down until summer, starting with late-winter bloomers, such as witch hazel and forsythia,

Witch hazel is one of the season's first woody plants to flower.

Pansies are very cold hardy and can go in the ground well before spring's last frost.

Summer annuals such as this bed of petunias, blue salvias, and verbena usually bloom nonstop until frost kills them.

peaking with May's flurry of azaleas, rhododendrons, and fragrant viburnums, and leading into June's roses, Virginia sweetspire, and mophead hydrangeas.

4. **Spring-blooming perennials.** Almost all perennials are sending up fresh and often colorful foliage by May, but many bloom from late March into June. Among the choices are salvias, false forget-me-nots, foamflowers, irises, bleeding hearts, sweet woodruff, barrenwort, dianthus, and veronica.

5. **"Wildflowers."** Spring is peak time for the bulk of native perennials, such as columbine, Virginia bluebells, crested irises, trout lilies, and creeping phlox. Bloom times tend to be short, but plant a selection so that one hands off to the next. Be ready to fill gaps with annuals or flower pots, because some of these go dormant by June or July.

6. **Cold-tolerant annuals.** Get a jump on frost-free time by adding new annual flowers that can tolerate a freeze. These include pansies, violas, snapdragons, annual dianthus, nemesia, and dusty miller. Northerners can plant these as soon as the ground thaws in early spring, while Southerners can grow these all winter into May.

Summer Interest: A Breeze?

Summer is a season that can go either way—really, really good or really, really bad. It's when you'll have a ton of choices in flowers (especially nonstop-blooming annuals) as well as a good selection of summer-blooming shrubs.

However, if you've fallen into the spring-loaded plant trap or don't pick plants that can take your summer's heat and potential drought, summer can go downhill quickly from spring's freshness. Keep the garden watered and weeded and you have the potential for a season that's just as colorful as spring.

Seven Key Elements for Building Summer Interest

1. **Annual flowers.** These are the stars of the summer garden. Most annuals can't take a freeze, but give them warmth, fertilizer, and a steady supply of moisture, and they'll bloom their heads off for months.

   Just match your picks to the site, such as marigolds, celosia, angelonia, vinca, and zinnias for your sunniest spots and begonias, coleus, impatiens, browallia, and caladium in your shadier spots.

   In sizzling-summer climates, lean toward varieties best equipped to take the heat, including vinca,

Different perennial flowers bloom at various times in summer.

angelonia, zinnias, petunias, marigolds, wax begonias, dusty miller, geraniums, and blue salvias.

As with spring bulbs, mass them for the most impact, or spot them in mixed beds to ensure color while perennials and shrubs are handing off to one another.

2. **Pots, hanging baskets, window boxes.** Annuals are the usual stars in these too, but don't overlook perennials with colorful foliage (coral bells, false forget-me-nots, creeping sedum, hostas, etc.)

Tropicals look great in summer pots as well, so browse the houseplant section of garden centers in addition to the annuals benches.

Another strategy is to move potted houseplants you already own outside. Place them on the deck, patio, or porch for a "summer vacation." Most of these are tropical or subtropical natives that appreciate the outside heat and humidity more than staying inside

all summer. Shaded to partly shaded spots outside are best for most of these, because the leaves of indoor-adapted plants will bleach in sudden bright light.

3. **Summer-blooming perennials.** Lots more perennials kick into peak form after the spring bloomers finish. These include daylilies, black-eyed Susans, coneflowers, coreopsis, hardy (cranesbill) geraniums, yarrow, Russian sage, catmint, bee balm, and gaura.

Lean toward the longest-blooming varieties you can find (breeders have been working on extending perennials' bloom times) and plan for a succession of bloomers from late June through late September.

Also pick a few with colorful leaves so you'll have interest even after a perennial has bloomed for its typical three- to six-week period.

4. **Roses.** June is primetime for hybrid teas, grandifloras, and floribundas, with a good repeat in September. Shrub types bloom almost nonstop from

June to frost. Shrub roses produce smaller flowers, but lots of them, on plants that are generally more disease-resistant than classic roses. Examples are Knock Out, Flower Carpet, Drift, Easy Elegance, Oso Easy, Simplicity, and some David Austin varieties.

5. **Summer-blooming shrubs.** Hydrangeas are workhorses in summer, especially the summer-blooming panicle types (*Hydrangea paniculata*) and reblooming types of bigleaf hydrangeas (Endless Summer, Forever & Ever series, Let's Dance series, etc.). But many other summer shrubs of assorted sizes bloom for weeks in summer, including crape myrtles, summersweet, butterfly bushes, abelia, spireas, vitex, rose-of-Sharon, and St. John's wort. Many new varieties offer red, burgundy, and variegated leaf color in addition to flowers.

6. **Edibles.** Who says edibles are ugly? Many herbs are colorful enough to grow as ornamentals, especially variegated sages, golden oregano, and purple basil.

Fruit bushes, such as blueberries, currants, and new compact forms of blackberries and raspberries, offer blooms, colorful small fruits, and, in some cases, colorful foliage—especially in fall.

Even vegetable gardens can add summer interest with striking textural plants, such as artichokes, rhubarb, and cardoon, or with colorful leaves of edibles, such as okra, beets, and lettuce. Poke a few attractive edibles into the landscape if you don't have a separate veggie garden.

7. **Water.** This is when your pond, waterfalls, and fountains will reward you most. The sound is peaceful, and water's mere presence has a cooling effect on the landscape.

If you don't want to dig a hole for an in-ground feature, add a plug-in fountain to the deck. Or fill a water-tight container and add a few small aquatic plants and a bubbler.

Summer is when you'll be most glad you added a cooling water feature to the landscape.

Shop for plants in the fall to make sure your landscape has fall interest, as does Kevin Kelly's November front landscape in Pennsylvania.

Fall Interest: Planning Required

In plant-challenged, spring-heavy landscapes, autumn can ho-hum its way out in a lifeless display of monotony instead of flaming out like the glorious ending of a fireworks show. Fall has much potential. It's not just mums and done. It's a season looming with burnt-red fall leaves, bronzing ornamental grasses, ripening berry clusters, and the lingering blooms of late-season perennials.

A good-looking fall landscape takes planning, though, because most of the attraction isn't happening when most people are buying. This is when it pays most to look around and/or go to the garden center to ensure you're adding late-season interest.

Cooler temperatures and rainier days can resurrect baked summer landscapes and open the door to a crescendo of fall splendor—a time when the plant world is capable of delivering some of its most striking color.

Seven Building Blocks for Fall Beauty

1. **Tree foliage.** It's hard to beat the brilliance of maple trees in their fall-foliage glory. Tourists drive hours to see nature's northern fall shows, but plenty of landscape trees can deliver similar color.

   Besides maples large and small, consider dogwoods, stewartias, Persian ironwood, crape myrtles, katsuras, ginkgos, serviceberries, sourwoods, and blackgums.

2. **Shrub foliage.** Smaller woody plants can deliver as much bright fall leaf color as their bigger cousins. Some of the best are fothergilla, Virginia sweetspires, oakleaf hydrangeas, ninebarks, witch hazel, and blueberries (yes, the kind you eat—many turn brilliant red or orange in fall).

   Don't forget those shrubs that offer three or more seasons of foliage color even without a showy turn in fall, such as golden Hinoki false cypresses, blue spruces, variegated weigelas, and dark-leafed ninebarks.

3. **Fall-blooming (or still-blooming) shrubs.** A few shrubs wait until early fall to get around to blooming. Blue mist shrub and fall-blooming camellias are examples. However, many other shrubs bloom a second time in fall or are still blooming from summer. These are the Energizer Bunnies of the woody world, including roses, reblooming hydrangeas, reblooming azaleas, butterfly bushes, and panicle hydrangeas. They just keep going and going and going . . .

4. **Fruits and berries.** A big part of fall interest can come from plants that ripen fruits and berries near the season's end. Some plants, such as viburnums and dogwoods, offer both showy fall fruit *and* changing fall foliage.

   Among the many other attractive fruit-producers are beautyberries, St. John's wort, nandinas, hollies, junipers, hawthorns, cotoneasters, Japanese plum yews, skimmias, aucubas, chokeberries, and pyracanthas.

5. **Fall-blooming perennials.** Mums, sedums, and asters are the big three late-blooming perennials, but others include goldenrod, Japanese anemone, turtleheads, toad lilies, Montauk daisies, and leadwort. Don't overlook perennials that rebloom, especially after a summer "haircut." These include salvias, daylilies, reblooming irises, hardy geraniums, catmint, and scabiosa.

   Many ornamental grasses produce showy seedheads in fall. The pink clouds of muhly grass are particularly showy, but many fountain grasses, maidenhair grasses, and bluestem grasses also produce attractive pink, tan, or bronze seed clusters.

6. **Perennial foliage.** A few perennials have leaves that turn color in fall. Amsonia, with its thready golden foliage, is one of the best. Leadwort turns blood red, some euphorbias take on shades of burgundy and red, and many coral bells and foamy bells shift color in response to cooling temperatures.

7. **Another round of cool-season annuals.** Those same freeze-tolerant annuals that gave you color at the first hint of spring can go back in the ground to replace summer annuals or fill bare spots. These include pansies, violas, snapdragons, dianthus, dusty miller, and nemesia as well as the ornamental cabbage and kale that show up in most garden centers around Labor Day. In the South, many of these can bloom all the way into the following spring.

Amsonia is a perennial flower whose leaves turn golden in fall.

Fruits, such as these produced by Kousa dogwoods, are a key element of a fall landscape.

Winter planters can be made by scavenging clippings from landscape plants.

Winter Interest: The Toughest

Back when winter-long snowcovers were the northern norm, plants and their leafless skeletons were little more than differing forms of white bulging up from the snowy sea. But because warmer winters have yielded at least periodic spells of open ground in most of the United States, the winter landscape is no longer a three-month write-off. Free of a white blanket, a surprising number of plants look good in winter. As with fall, winter interest takes planning.

Seven Strategies for Winter Interest

1. **Evergreens.** Conifers and broad-leaf woody plants that keep their foliage all year anchor the winter landscape. Particularly useful are ones with colorful foliage, such as blue-needled junipers, firs, and spruces; gold-needled pines and false cypresses; and variegated boxwoods, hollies, aucuba, and euonymus. But even plain green ones, such as azaleas, laurels, boxwoods, yews, and arborvitae, add life at a time when most perennials have died to the ground and deciduous plants have dropped their leaves.

2. **Plants with interesting forms.** Not all evergreens are pyramid-shaped uprights. Some have weeping habits, some have spray form, and some are low and spreading. You can even carve many conifers into topiary spirals and pompoms. Some plants have interesting branch structures and actually look best when bare in winter, such as curly willows and the contorted structure of a filbert known as Harry Lauder's walking stick. Japanese maples are particularly showy when leafless in winter.

   Locate attractive specimens where you can see them out a winter window, and consider lighting them with landscape spotlights.

3. **Evergreen perennials.** Not all perennial flowers die back to the ground in fall. As with evergreen shrubs, some hold their leaves most winters and look fairly good when snow isn't covering them.

   Depending on how cold your winters get, choices include liriope, coral bells, foamy bells, hellebores, lamium, candytuft, dianthus, creeping phlox, bergenias, sweet flags, mondo grass, artemisia, and groundcovers, such as ivy, pachysandra, and vinca.

4. **Plants with interesting bark.** When the leaves are off, bark that peels or flakes becomes more engaging. Birch is best known, but other tree-sized "bark stars" include paperbark and coralbark maples, paperbark cherries, Japanese and Korean stewartias, crape myrtles, Kousa dogwoods, yellowwoods, and Persian ironwoods.

   Shrubs with colorful or peeling bark include redtwig and gold-twig dogwoods, ninebarks, and oakleaf hydrangeas.

5. **Winter fruits and flowers.** Some plants hold their fall-ripened fruits throughout part or most of winter, while a few actually flower in winter. Winterberry holly is one of the showiest winter fruiters, usually holding its bright-red or orange pea-sized berries until birds polish them off in late winter. Viburnums, evergreen

hollies, pyracantha, hawthorns, cotoneasters, and nandinas are other woody plants with winter fruits, while many rose varieties produce colorful "hips" that look like berries at the end of stems.

Camellias are showy bloomers in late fall or even at the height of winter in the South. Witch hazel and hellebores often get started in February. And even in the north, snowdrops, winter aconites, and crocus bulbs are often blooming while snow is melting.

6. **Hardscaping.** The nonliving "bones" of a landscape are noticeable most when the plant competition is least. If the landscape is short on "hardscaping," consider adding prominent features, such as stone walls, paver patios, flagstone paths, gazebos, arbors, trellises, and pergolas, or a few smaller eye-grabbers, such as a statuary, benches, fountains, bird feeders, and garage-sale finds.

7. **Winter containers**. Weather-resistant plastic, foam, and concrete pots make it possible to recycle your summer flower pots into winter-interest ones. Scavenge the landscape for such decorative fodder as red-twig dogwood stems, berried sprigs of holly, conifer cuttings, and small bundles of ornamental grass, all of which can be stuck into the potting mix. Or use winter-hardy dwarf conifers in a large container or two.

BELOW: Tree bark becomes more noticeable in winter when leaves drop. One of the most interesting is the peeling, cinnamon-colored bark of paperbark maples.

BOTTOM: Winterberry holly females develop bright red, gold, or orange berry-sized fruits that hold most of winter.

WHAT BLOOMS WHEN

Knowing what blooms when helps with planning an all-season landscape. Bloom times can vary from year to year and even more so from region to region. Here's a month-by-month list of plants by their bloom time in USDA Hardiness Zone 6—the middle range of America's climate and the biggest chunk of US gardening territory. Move up the listed bloom times in warmer areas, and move them back in colder zones.

March

Bulbs: Crocuses, early daffodils, rock-garden irises, snowdrops, winter aconite

Perennials: Hellebores

Trees/Shrubs: Cornelian cherry dogwoods, forsythias, hardy camellias, Oregon grape hollies, some spireas, spicebushes, star magnolias, sweetboxes, witch hazel

April

Bulbs: Crocuses, daffodils, Dutch hyacinths, early tulips, glory-of-the-snow, grape hyacinths, Grecian windflowers, fritillarias, Siberian squills, spring snowflakes, striped squills

Perennials: Barrenwort, bergenias, bleeding heart, bloodroot, candytuft, columbine, creeping phlox, euphorbia, false forget-me-nots, foamflowers, lamium, primroses, pulmonaria, rock cress, Virginia bluebells

Trees/Shrubs: American dogwoods, cherries, crabapples, flowering pears, flowering plums, fothergilla, Japanese andromedas, kerrias, magnolias, PJM rhododendrons, redbuds, serviceberries, viburnums, winter hazel

May

Bulbs: Alliums, camassia, fritillaria, Spanish bluebells, tulips

Perennials: Ajuga, amsonia, bachelor buttons, baptisia, barrenwort, candytuft, catmint, creeping veronica, dianthus, false forget-me-nots, foamy bells, forget-me-knots, fringe-leaf bleeding heart, geum, goats beard, hardy geraniums, Jacob's ladder, lamium, lily-of-the-valley, meadow rue, irises, peonies, salvias, snow-in-summer, sweet woodruff, Solomon's seal, thrift, trillium

Trees/Shrubs: Azaleas, beautybushes, Carolina silverbells, cherry laurels, chokeberries, clematis, coralberry, deutzias, fringe tree, Japanese snowbells, Kousa dogwoods, hawthorns, honeysuckle, horse chestnut, leucothoe, lilacs, magnolias, nandinas, ornamental kiwi vines, red-twig dogwoods, rhododendrons, tree peonies, sweetshrubs, viburnum, weigelas

June

Perennials: Astilbes, baptisia, bellflowers, catmint, coral bells, coreopsis, daylilies, delphinium, dianthus, evening primroses, feather reed grass, filipendula, foxgloves, foxtail lilies, gaillardia, gaura, goats beard, hardy geraniums, hostas, knautia, lady's mantle, lamium, lavender, lupine, penstemon, poppies, red hot poker, rodgersia, rose mallow, scabiosa, shooting star, silene, spiderwort, tiger lilies, verbascum, veronica, yarrows, yellow corydalis, yucca

Trees/Shrubs: Abelia, bush honeysuckle, clematis, elderberries, hydrangeas, Japanese hydrangea vines, Japanese spirea, Japanese tree lilacs, mock oranges, nandinas, ninebarks, potentilla, pyracantha, roses, smoketrees, St. John's wort, sweetbay magnolia, Virginia sweetspire

Most magnolias reach peak bloom in April.

Baptisia is a perennial flower that blooms primarily in June.

Purple coneflowers are a good perennial choice for midsummer flowering.

The blue mist shrub (*Caryopteris*) is one of the latest flowering shrubs to bloom.

Asters are some of the season's last perennial flowers to bloom.

July

Perennials: Agastache, Asiatic and Oriental lilies, astilbes, baby's breath, balloon flowers, bee balm, betony, black-eyed Susans, blackberry lilies, butterfly weed, cimicifuga, coreopsis, crocosmia, daylilies, fountain grass, gaillardia, garden phlox, gaura, goldenrod, hardy geraniums, heliopsis, hollyhocks, hostas, Jupiter's beard, liatris, obedient plant, persicaria, purple coneflowers, veronica, red hot poker, Russian sage, sea hollies, Shasta daisies, silphium, soapwort, stokesia, veronica, veronicastrum

Trees/Shrubs: Abelia, butterfly bushes, clematis, roses, crape myrtles, goldenrain trees, oakleaf hydrangeas, rose-of-Sharon, summersweet, stewartias

August

Perennials: Agastache, asters, betony, black-eyed Susan, cardinal flowers, garden phlox, goldenrod, hardy geraniums, hardy hibiscus, heliopsis, hostas, Japanese anemones, Joe-pye weeds, leadwort, ligularia, liriope, miscanthus, monkshood, perennial sunflower, purple coneflower, reblooming daylilies, Russian sage, sedum, sneezeweed, switchgrass, turtleheads, veronica, yarrow

Trees/Shrubs: Beautyberries, blue mist shrubs, butterfly bushes, clematis, crape myrtles, panicle hydrangeas, rose-of-Sharon, seven son flowers, vitex

September

Bulbs: Dahlias, colchicum, lycoris

Perennials: Agastache, asters, boltonia, catmint, gaillardia, gaura, goldenrod, Japanese anemones, Joe-pye weeds, lavender, leadwort, liriope, mums, reblooming daylilies, reblooming irises, Russian sage, salvias, sedum, toad lily, turtleheads

Trees/Shrubs: blue mist shrubs, butterfly bushes, roses, reblooming hydrangeas, sweet autumn clematis

October

Perennials: Asters, catmint, gaillardia, goldenrod, mums, Nippon and Montauk daisies, salvias, sedum

Trees/Shrubs: Blue mist shrubs, hardy camellia, reblooming hydrangeas, roses

CHAPTER 9
MANAGING WEEDS

By Jessica Walliser

WEED MANAGEMENT CAN CERTAINLY BE AMONG the most disheartening and challenging aspects of gardening. A gardener whose hard work is overrun by unwanted, invasive weeds all too often ends up throwing in the trowel and giving up. But with the right weed-control measures in place, a beautiful, weed-free garden is within every gardener's grasp. The good news is that the most effective weed-management strategies don't require hours and hours of manual labor; they do, however, require careful thought and a major focus on prevention.

The aim of this chapter is to walk you through as many useful weed-management strategies as possible, step by easy step. I start by defining precisely what a weed is, then offer tips for identifying them. But the bulk of this chapter will focus on two concepts: *weed prevention* and *weed control*. I'll skip the obvious cliché about the worth of an ounce of prevention and say instead that the best weed-management techniques start addressing weed problems well before they even start. Because of this, the section on weed prevention is filled to the brim with actionable tips and techniques to keep even the most tenacious weeds from taking over your garden. And in the weed control section, I introduce the many ways you can get a grip on existing weeds in your landscape, without having to resort to synthetic chemical herbicides.

OPPOSITE: A beautiful weed-free garden is easier than you think if you follow the weed-reducing tactics outlined in this chapter.

The truth is that everyone has weeds in their landscape, but the last thing a busy gardener needs to do is waste time and energy fighting weeds with inefficient or inadequate control methods. With the simple, cost-effective weed-reducing tactics presented in this chapter, you'll find smart solutions to even your worst weed woes.

WHAT EXACTLY IS A WEED ANYWAY?

A weed is often simply defined as a plant out of place. But the concept of a weed really should go a bit deeper than that. Weeds are not just misplaced plants; rather, they're plants that cause some type of economic or aesthetic loss to the gardener. Economic loss can come in the form of reduced vegetable yields or the expense and labor involved in managing those weeds, while aesthetic loss is more about how the weed's presence negatively impacts the appearance of your garden.

The extent of economic or aesthetic damage caused by a weed is, of course, relative. The trick is to let your own tolerance be your guide when it comes to the need to manage weeds. It's time to put effort and energy into weed management when you feel their negative impact has reached a critical point that's intolerable to you as the gardener.

Obviously, this critical point will differ from gardener to gardener, and even from area to area. For example, I'm very tolerant of weeds in my lawn and meadow plantings, but I'm far less tolerant of weeds in my vegetable garden, where these rogue plants compete with desired crops for nutrients, water, and light. In some areas of the landscape, a roadside ditch or bank for example, weeds actually provide many benefits. They protect soil from erosion, sequester nutrients, and supply food and habitat to various beneficial insects and pollinators.

The starting point of effective weed management is always choosing your weed battles carefully. Once you determine that control is warranted in a particular garden area, it's time to switch gears and learn precisely who your enemy really is.

Some "weeds" have surprising uses. Dandelions, for example, are edible in salads.

Annual weeds, such as purple deadnettle (left) and oxalis (*Oxalis stricta*) (right) and speedwell, complete their entire life cycle in one year.

STUDY THINE ENEMY

Understanding the life cycle of a particular weed, along with its growth habit and environmental preferences, is the first—and most important—step in preventing and controlling it. Weeds can be grouped into a few different categories based on their life cycles and growth habits. Understanding the nuances of each different category is a useful aid in identifying a particular weed as well as determining the best prevention and control tactics for it.

Annual weeds complete their entire life cycle in a single year. They germinate, grow, flower, and set seed before dying. Some annual weeds germinate in the spring and set seed before fall's first frost (these are called **summer annuals**), while other species germinate in the fall and flower the following spring (these are called **winter annuals**). Annual weeds often produce many, many seeds because the plant is hedging its bets and doing its best to ensure its genes carry on in future generations. Annual weeds are typically shallow rooted and fast growing. Many flower for just a few days or weeks before shedding their seeds. Annual

weeds are among the easiest weeds to prevent and control by employing one or more of the techniques featured later in this chapter. There are, of course, thousands of species of annual weeds in North America, but among the most common are crabgrass (*Digitaria* spp.), purslane (*Portulaca oleracea*), bedstraw (*Galium aparine*), lamb's quarter (*Chenopodium album*), pigweed (*Amaranthus* spp.), speedwell (*Veronica filiformis*), spotted spurge (*Euphorbia maculata*), ragweed (*Ambrosia artemisiifolia*), chickweed (*Stellaria media*), deadnettle (*Lamium purpureum*), henbit (*Lamium amplexicaule*), and smartweed (*Polygonum pensylvanicum*).

Perennial weeds live for three or more years and reproduce by dropping seeds and/or spreading via roots, rhizomes, bulbs, or creeping stems called stolons. Perennial weeds can be a challenge to control, as many are deep-rooted and difficult to dig out, but this chapter contains several effective control methods that are fairly easy to employ. Examples of perennial weeds include wild onions (*Allium vineale*), nutsedge (*Cyperus esculentus*), quackgrass (*Elymus repens*),

Canada thistle (top) and creeping Charlie (bottom) are two perennial weeds that are among the most difficult to control.

Biennial weeds take two years to complete their lifecycle. Both garlic mustard (top) and Queen Anne's lace (bottom) produce only foliage in their first year of growth; flowers don't occur until the second.

creeping Charlie/ground ivy (*Glechoma hederacea*), bindweed (*Convolvulus arvensis*), hawkweed (*Hieracium* spp.), Canada thistles (*Cirsium arvense*), broadleaf plantains (*Plantago major*), dandelions (*Taraxacum officinale*), and creeping buttercups (*Ranunculus repens*), to name just a few.

Biennial weeds are those that complete their life cycle over the course of two years. The first season, they germinate and then produce only a rosette (or low cluster) of leaves. After overwintering, the plant then resumes growth the following spring, flowers, sets seed, and dies. In general, biennial weeds are fairly easy to control, especially if they're targeted during their first year of growth when the plants are still young and not as well-rooted as second-year specimens.

Common examples of biennial weeds are burdock (*Arctium* spp.), Queen Anne's lace (*Daucus carota*), mullien (*Verbascum thapsus*), and garlic mustard (*Alliaria petiolata*).

Determining which one of these categories a particular weed fits into means either carefully observing it for a full year or properly identifying the weed via a printed or digital resource. Thankfully, there are many weed ID websites that provide images and identification keys to help you determine exactly which weed species have made a home in your garden. Many university extension services have online weed identification guides, and they're a great place to start. There are also many print and e-books on the subject of weed identification.

WHAT A WEED'S APPEARANCE SAYS ABOUT ITS NATURE

It's also often possible to puzzle out the best management tactics for a specific weed simply by physically examining the plant itself and looking at its growth habits, without necessarily having to positively ID it. The following are several traits that may indicate you have a problematic weed on your hands.

Flower number. Weeds that produce a large number of flowers will almost always produce a lot of seeds. Eliminating these weeds before the flowers mature into seeds is obviously going to be essential for controlling them. It's worth focusing attention on these weeds early in their growth cycle rather than on those that bear a smaller number of flowers, simply because the former will generate far more progeny.

Seed number and dispersal system. The same goes for weeds whose seedpods contain hundreds or thousands of individual seeds, especially if the seedpods are structured so that the seeds "explode" out of their pods or have "wings" or "fluff" that allow the seeds to travel a great distance from the mother plant on the air. It's absolutely essential that these types of weeds be removed from the garden before the seed is thrown, so it's worth focusing your weed-removal efforts on these weeds over other species that don't throw seeds in the same way.

Weeds with taproots. Weeds with deep taproots (one dominant, long root coming straight down out of the crown of the plant), such as dock (*Rumex obtusifolius*), dandelions, and Queen Anne's lace, are a challenge for an entirely different reason. These weeds seldom spread via their roots, but because the roots extend so deeply into the soil, removing them completely is a difficult task. If even a small portion of the root is left behind, it will re-sprout and cause the weed to return. Most weeds with deep taproots spread primarily via seeds, so removing the flowers and seedpods before the seeds are dispersed is the most critical step in controlling their numbers.

Weeds with runners. Another pair of physical traits that, when present, can tell you a lot about a weed's ability to quickly take over your garden are runners and horizontal plant stems known as stolons that take root along their length to form new plants. Buttercups, creeping Charlie, wild strawberries (*Fragaria virginiana*), and some weedy grasses spread via runners or stolons. These types of weeds can rapidly expand out from the mother plant and cover an entire garden area in short order. When runners or stolons

TOP: Examining a weed's root structure can tell you a lot about how quickly it will spread. Fleshy, horizontal roots often indicate the presence of a weed that's likely to become problematic.

BOTTOM: Weeds that produce seedpods containing many seeds, or seedpods that explode when ripe, are extra challenging to control. This hairy bittercress plant (*Cardamine hirsuta*) will produce thousands of progeny if allowed to set seed.

are noted on a weed, it's important to take action to remove that weed sooner rather than later.

Weeds with spreading roots. As stated earlier, many perennial weeds spread not just by seed, but also by underground roots. The presence of fleshy, underground storage roots (called rhizomes) or roots that extend out from the mother plant in a wide-spreading, horizontal fashion are often indicators of a weed that's very likely to become problematic. For example, several extremely difficult-to-control weeds spread in this fashion, including field bindweed, Canada thistle, mint (*Mentha* spp.), and Japanese knotweed (*Fallopia japonica*). Plants with spreading roots are certainly among the most challenging weeds to manage.

PROACTIVE VERSUS REACTIVE

If all you do to control weeds in your garden is to try to eliminate them after they arrive, you're missing a big opportunity to lessen the negative impact weeds have on your landscape. Hand-pulling, hoeing, and herbicide spraying are all *reactive* methods of weed control, meaning they are actions you take in reaction to the presence of weeds. They're effective, of course, but *proactive* methods are a lot more valuable to time- and energy-starved gardeners. *Proactive* equals prevention and *reactive* equals control.

There's no doubt that the best weed-management strategy puts prevention first and control second. Use a combination of the techniques listed below, picking and choosing those that work best for you. With the right approach and consistent effort, effective weed management requires far less time and energy than you might expect.

THE BEST PROACTIVE METHODS OF WEED PREVENTION

Design the Weeds Out of the Garden

In most situations, the design and layout of your planting beds and gardens influence how many weeds you'll wind up with. Monoculture plantings, especially those with a lot of exposed bare ground in between plants or crop rows, are welcoming environments for weeds. Diverse plantings, on the other hand, with a multitude of plant species or a hearty variety of edible crops, are less inviting to weeds (and insect pests too!). When plants fill different layers of the garden canopy, much like pieces of a 3D puzzle, there's much less room for weeds to move in because of the natural biodiversity these kinds of plantings create.

Weeds can also be designed out of the garden by choosing to include only disease-resistant plants in your landscape (see Chapter 11 for more on disease control). These species can be planted fairly close together, thereby reducing the empty space available for weed growth. Use low-growing plants to outcompete potential weed problems and cover bare soil, and use many different layers of plants, from soil-hugging groundcovers to large trees and everything in between. These layers form a plant matrix to help shade the soil and block sunlight from reaching weed seeds and encouraging them to germinate.

Another excellent way to design the weeds out of a vegetable garden is to not disturb the soil at all and instead go with no-till gardening techniques. Tilling brings weed seeds buried beneath the soil up to the surface where they are exposed to light and warmth and can germinate. No-till methods do not disturb the soil. Instead, planting beds are top-dressed with yearly additions of several inches of organic matter and crops are planted right through it. Over time, this causes a layered, mulching effect and encourages the resident soil life to thrive undisturbed and leaves weed seeds buried well beneath the soil surface. Though no-till techniques are mostly focused on vegetable gardens, it's also a good idea to not disturb the soil in flower and shrub beds either.

LEFT: Filling the garden with many layers, from weed-choking groundcovers to trees, leaves little room for weeds in the landscape.

OPPOSITE: Complex landscapes have fewer weeds due to the matrix of plants they support and their ability to shade out weeds.

Use Mulch

Anything that is applied to the soil surface with the intent of reducing weeds, cutting down on watering, and stabilizing soil temperatures is considered a mulch, and suppressing weeds with a layer of mulch is without a doubt one of the best proactive methods of weed prevention. There are dozens of different types of mulch (see Chapter 7), though some are more effective at controlling weeds than others.

I much prefer to use mulches made from natural materials that will eventually decompose, such as shredded bark, compost, untreated grass clippings, straw, shredded leaves, or pine straw, rather than inorganic mulches that will not break down, such as rocks, shredded rubber, plastic sheeting, or landscape fabric. Not only do natural mulching materials keep weeds at bay, but they also release nutrients to plants as they decompose.

To gain the maximum weed prevention benefits from your mulch, here are a few tips to keep in mind.

Don't over mulch. Regardless of what type of mulch you use, if you pile too much on the soil, you risk inhibiting air exchange with the roots of your plants. About 2 to 4 inches of mulch is sufficient.

Time your application. Always apply mulch early in the season, before annual weed seeds germinate. If you wait too long, newly germinated weed seedlings may poke right up through the layer of mulch. But don't mulch too early either, or the soil could stay waterlogged well into the summer. Wait until the soil dries out a bit, especially in areas with poorly drained, clay-based soil.

Get rid of existing weeds first. Do not pile mulch on top of any weeds already present in your planting beds, especially perennial weeds; always remove them first. A layer of mulch doesn't always smother existing weeds enough to keep them from popping up again as the season progresses.

Use weed-free mulches. Cheap mulch is seldom a good idea. Poor-quality mulch products could contain weed seeds or plant pathogens. Remember that you get what you pay for.

Use straw, not hay. If you opt for straw, make sure you actually use straw. Hay is mixed forage and often contains lots of weed seeds, but straw is the dried stems of farmed grains and is relatively weed free.

There are dozens of different types of mulch, including straw, each with its own merits. Mulch is one of the best proactive methods of weed prevention.

Add More Power to Your Mulch

To really pump up the power of your mulch, add an extra layer of protection with an additional physical barrier. In areas of the landscape where weeds are very problematic, or where you have weeds that spread via underground roots or rhizomes, cover the soil with a layer of unwaxed corrugated cardboard or multiple sheets of newspaper before spreading the natural mulch on top of it. With this extra weed barrier in place, you'll have season-long weed control.

In my own vegetable garden and shrub beds, I always cover the soil with a layer of newspaper 10 sheets thick (any matte newsprint will do, just skip the glossy inserts due to the type of ink they may contain). Then I wet the newspaper down with water from the hose and spread a 2-inch-thick layer of leaf compost on top. When planting time arrives, I simply scoot the mulch aside, cut a slit through the newspaper, and plant away. As long as the mulch you place on top of the newspaper is weed-free, your garden will be too. By the end of the growing season, the beneficial soil microbes will have completely digested the paper, using it as a carbon source to fuel their growth.

Biodegradable paper and film mulches work much the same way. They're spread over the soil surface and pinned into place. You can cover them with a natural mulch, as is done with the newspaper above, or simply leave them exposed. The films are typically made of a corn starch–based material and the biodegradable paper products are made from recycled paper coated in a vegetable resin.

Though geotextile landscape fabrics are common finds at the garden center, I don't recommend using them. These fabrics have to be permeable to allow for water and air exchange with the soil, and the roots of weed seedlings will inevitably find their way down into these tiny perforations, eventually growing into mature weeds that are very difficult to remove. These tiny perforations also often end up trapping the feeder roots of the desired plants the fabric was placed around, leading to potential problems down the line, especially if you ever want to remove the fabric.

Placing several sheets of newspaper beneath your mulch adds an extra layer of weed protection.

ABOVE: Topping involves removing weed flowers before they set seed, cutting down on the seed bank, and preventing future weeds.
BELOW: Corn gluten meal is a granular product that's cast over garden and lawn areas. It prevents weed seeds from germinating.

Top Weeds

Another valuable proactive weed prevention technique is topping. The number of weed seeds present in the soil is known as the "seed bank," and topping is one of the best ways to reduce the number of weed seeds present in the seed bank. Reducing the seed bank in your soil comes down to one simple rule: don't ever let a weed drop seed.

Topping involves removing weed flowers before the seeds are fully mature. It takes far less time to top a weed than it does to completely remove it, and while this technique won't get rid of existing weeds, it prevents many future weeds from arriving. Topping can be done mechanically with a string trimmer or mower or by hand with a scythe, lopper, or pair of pruners. The topped flower stem should be removed from the garden completely, as many weed flowers will continue to turn into seeds even after the flower stalk has been removed from the plant. Whether you're trying to get a grip on annual weeds, such as ragweed, lambs quarters, and pigweed, or perennial weeds, such as burdock and dandelions, topping is an incredibly useful weed-management technique.

Apply Organic Pre-Emergent Herbicides

Though they will not rid your garden of existing weeds, organic pre-emergent herbicides will prevent any new weed seedlings from growing by drying out the emerging plant's initial root. When used correctly, they're a great weed preventative, particularly for annual weeds. They're also a source of nitrogen.

Organic pre-emergent herbicide products are made from corn gluten meal, a byproduct of the corn milling process. The granules are distributed over the surface of the

soil or mulch, forming an invisible barrier to weed growth. Be aware, however, that corn gluten meal kills the initial root of *all* seedlings, so do not use it where you intend to grow any plants from seed.

The timing of weed seed germination is based on soil and air temperatures as well as the type of weed in question, so it's important to apply corn gluten at the right time. The product only remains effective for five to six weeks after application, so if you put it on at the wrong time, you'll miss your window of opportunity for preventing weeds.

If you're trying to prevent summer annual weeds whose seeds germinate in the spring, such as crabgrass, purslane, prostrate spurge (*Euphorbia supine/E. prostrata*), and pigweed, corn gluten meal is typically applied in the early spring, when the soil temperature reaches about 50°F 4 inches beneath the surface (which is usually around the same time the forsythias are mid-bloom and the redbud trees start to flower).

If you're trying to prevent winter annual weeds whose seeds germinate in the late summer or fall, such as bittercress, deadnettle, henbit, and chickweed, or perennial weeds whose seeds germinate in fall, apply the corn gluten meal in the late summer, as soon as daytime temperatures start to wane (in my Pennsylvania garden, that's typically around the first week of September).

The best weed control is obtained when applying the corn gluten meal twice a year, once in the spring and again in the early autumn.

The more diligent you are when using these products, the better. Each year you use them, the results are greatly improved. A study at Iowa State University found that a huge reduction in weeds occurs with two to three years of use, and five years of use often results in 100 percent control of new weed seed germination.

There are many different brand names for these products, including Concern Weed Prevention and Espoma Organic Weed Preventer. I do not recommend using pre-emergent herbicides made from synthetic chemicals, such as those found in weed and feeds and other granular or spray products. I'm an organic gardener and do not consider these products either safe or necessary, especially when corn gluten meal works so beautifully.

Crabgrass is one of the weeds that's easiest to control with yearly applications of corn gluten meal. Each year you apply these products, the more effective they are.

Carefully inspect all potted plants before buying them. If you don't, you could be introducing a new weed to your garden.

Buy "Clean" Plants

A surprising number of weeds come into the garden as hitch-hikers. Use caution when purchasing plants from local plant sales or digging them out of a friend's garden. You could inadvertently introduce an unwanted weed issue. You should also pay careful attention to plants you buy at nurseries and garden centers. If there are weeds growing in the pot, don't buy the plant unless you're okay with taking the risk.

Be Smart about Soil Additions

Accidental weed introductions may also occur when soil amendments, topsoil, and mulches are contaminated with weed seeds or root pieces. Only purchase these products in sealed bags or from reputable bulk suppliers. High-quality soil amendments and mulches should be weed free and they should smell earthy, not foul. Bulk topsoil can come from various sources, including farms, construction sites, and other areas. Always use extreme caution when adding topsoil to your garden. If you can find steam-sterilized or pasteurized topsoil, it will be pathogen- and weed-seed-free, but it also will be devoid of beneficial soil microbes.

Monitor Your Compost

If you make your own compost (see Chapter 7 for more on this topic), the most critical weed control tip is to carefully monitor your compost pile and its ingredients. Do not add any weeds that have gone to seed in the pile unless you plan to turn the pile at least once a week. If you add ingredients to your pile but do not turn the pile regularly to introduce oxygen to the microbes, the pile will probably not reach the 140 to 160°F necessary to kill most weed seeds. To ensure there are few, if any, viable weed seeds in your finished compost, turn it regularly and make sure the 140 to 160°F temperature is maintained for at least 10 to 15 days.

Try Soil Solarization

One final weed prevention tool I'd like to share is soil solarization. Soil solarization involves using high temperatures to kill most weed seeds found within the top few inches of the soil. To solarize the soil, cover a freshly irrigated area of bare soil with a clear plastic tarp for four to eight weeks during the hot summer, making sure the edges of the plastic are pinned down tightly or buried. The radiant energy from

Clear plastic will heat up the soil, killing any weed seeds.

the sun is trapped in the soil, heating the top few inches to between 100 and 140°F, depending on how much direct sun the site receives. Soil solarization also kills many common soilborne pathogens and pests.

Solarization will not kill weed seeds much below a depth of about 6 inches, so don't disturb the soil after the solarization process is complete. If you till or cultivate, you risk bringing viable seeds up to the surface where they'll germinate. Solarization controls many common weed seeds, especially annuals, but some species are more resistant to high temperatures than others.

One minor downside to soil solarization—other than having a big sheet of plastic in your yard for a month or two—is the temporary damage it can do to populations of non-target soil organisms. Beneficial fungi, bacteria, and certain insect species within the top few inches of soil may also be killed during the solarization process, but most will move further down the soil profile to get away from the heat before it harms them. Those that do survive will quickly recolonize the area. Soil solarization causes little, if any, long-term damage to their populations.

THE BEST REACTIVE METHODS OF WEED CONTROL

Even with these proactive weed prevention strategies in place, gardeners may find themselves having to control mature weeds from time to time. Here are some useful and effective methods of getting rid of unwanted weeds after they've taken hold.

Hand-Pull Weeds

Though it can be time consuming, removing existing weeds by hand is among the most surefire methods of weed control. Invest in a good hand weeder, such as a Japanese digging knife (called a "hori hori"), dandelion digger, or sharp trowel, to grub up individual weeds by the root. Or, if you prefer to stay upright while weeding, use an upright weeder, such as the Fiskars Stand-Up Weeder or another long-handled weeding tool.

Hand weeding is typically not seen as an appealing gardening task, but it's quite satisfying to pull up an entire weed with its root system fully intact. To ensure the greatest chance

While hand weeding isn't considered fun by most gardeners, it is satisfying, especially when you bring up an entire root system. A good weeding tool helps.

If you'd like to avoid bending over while you weed, invest in an upright weeder.

Hand cultivation with a hoe is a great way to cut weed seedlings off at their base, reducing the number of weeds that reach maturity.

of success, always hand weed after rain or irrigation. Soft soil makes pulling weeds a lot easier, though some weeds are always easier to pull than others, regardless of the moisture content in the soil. Try to remove as much of the root system as possible to keep the weed from growing back.

Dispose of weeds properly. Don't toss weeds that have gone to seed onto the compost pile, unless you plan to monitor the pile's temperature to ensure it gets hot enough to kill the seeds (see previous section). Also, do not add weeds that spread by runners, stolons, rhizomes, or branching roots to the compost pile. Root pieces of these plants can easily survive home compost piles that do not reach high enough temperatures.

Weeds with seeds or invasive, spreading roots should be disposed of in another way. At my house, I have a separate "junk" compost pile where I toss these types of weeds and let them naturally decompose, but I never spread the resulting compost on my gardens. Instead, I just let it sit in the pile, and I continue to add more "junk" materials to the top. Another option is to take the weeds to a collection place designated by your city. You can also burn pulled weeds, but

be very careful that pulled poison ivy doesn't find its way into the burn pile too; inhaling poison ivy–laced smoke can be very problematic. Another option is to send any seeded or invasive weeds to the landfill, though this should be a last resort.

Till and Cultivate

Mechanical tilling and hand cultivation are two other effective ways to remove existing weeds, especially while they're young. Turning newly germinated weed seedlings into the soil or cutting them off at the base by hand with a hoe or clawed cultivator reduces the number of weeds that reach maturity. It's particularly effective in between rows in the veggie garden and around established perennials in flower beds. Though using a power tiller can break down good soil structure and disturb the roots of desired perennials, trees, and shrubs, a light mechanical tilling can be helpful in large vegetable gardens where many weed seedlings are present.

However, cultivating or tilling areas where established perennial weeds are present is never a good idea. Tilling and cultivating chop up the roots of perennial weeds, essentially creating thousands of tiny root cuttings. Each of these root pieces can go on to form a whole new plant. Never till perennial weeds that spread by rhizomes, such as Canada thistle, quackgrass, field bindweed, or knotweed.

Flame Weeding

Portable propane-fueled weed torches, commonly known as "flamers," fry weeds in a single pass, using intense heat to blast apart their cell walls. Flaming is not only really fun, it's also very effective. It works particularly well on broadleaf weeds, due to the ability of the heat to kill their exposed growing points. It's less effective on grassy weeds whose growing points are located very low on the plant or even below the soil surface.

Flaming large established weeds will definitely knock them back, but it takes a lot more fuel to kill the weed entirely, making this technique most effective against young, tender weeds. It's especially useful for organic gardeners trying to battle weeds along fence rows or in the cracks of a patio or driveway.

Tarping

Though it's similar in some ways to the solarization weed prevention technique described previously, tarping uses a large plastic tarp to get a grip on existing weeds rather than prevent new ones. It should only be used on the most pernicious and invasive weeds, those that scoff at every other weed management tactic. I've used tarping to kill a stand of Japanese knotweed even after other techniques failed.

Mechanical tilling between vegetable rows can help eliminate small weeds, but never till an area where perennial weeds are present. Chopping up their roots can easily generate more plants.

Use a flame weeder to torch weeds along fence lines, in between crop rows, and in sidewalk and driveway cracks.

The tarping process begins by cutting down all top growth of the weed to ground level. Carefully dispose of all the severed shoots in the trash or by burning them. Then spread a heavy-duty, extra-large, dark-colored tarp over the entire area, being sure to surround all sides of the weed patch by 18 inches or more. If the area is large, duct tape two or more tarps together.

After the tarp is in place, dig a 6- to 8-inch-deep trench around the entire area and bury the margin of the tarp in the trench all the way around. This effectively blocks all sunlight from the area. Leave the tarp in place for at least a full year, carefully and quickly duct taping any holes or tears that should occur. The absence of sunlight means the absence of photosynthesis and the eventual starvation of the weed's root system. Do not disturb the area after the tarp is removed; you don't want to bring any buried seeds up to the surface. Instead, as soon as the tarp is lifted, cover the area with sheets of corrugated cardboard and a few inches of mulch.

Be on the lookout for any new growth. If any should occur, either tarp the whole area again or use a smaller tarp just over the section where the new growth occurred.

Use Post-Emergent Organic Herbicides as a Last Resort

Though they should be on the very bottom of your list of weed control tools, herbicides are a valuable weapon against weeds. Turning to synthetic chemical herbicides is a personal decision for gardeners, and one not to be taken lightly. If you choose to use them, be sure to follow all label instructions, including safety measures and application rates.

The good news is that there are many organic herbicide alternatives on today's market too, many of which are effective against common weeds. They're a useful replacement for synthetic chemical–based herbicides, and are more widely available than ever before.

Most organic spray herbicides contain a combination of citric acid, clove oil, acetic acid, citrus oil, and other ingredients. They readily kill annual weeds and grasses, though repeat applications may be necessary for tough perennial weeds.

Keep in mind that, like their synthetic counterparts, these herbicides are nonselective and will damage any plants with which they come in contact. The acids contained in these products are very aggressive and can harm human tissue too, so be sure to protect yourself by following all label instructions and wearing eye and skin protection when spraying them. There are many brand names but the most common include Avenger, BurnOut, and AllDown.

A newer class of natural herbicides based on chelated iron target broadleaved weeds only, leaving grasses unharmed.

There are many organic herbicides on today's market. Read the ingredient list and application instructions carefully before use.

A Word of Caution Regarding Poisonous Weeds

When it comes to weeds that cause allergic reactions, such as poison ivy, oak, or sumac, wild parsnips, and others, extreme caution must be used when trying to rid your landscape of these plants. While hand removal is the best way to ensure their complete removal, doing so comes with great risk. When your skin comes in direct contact with these and other rash-inducing plants, the results can be both painful and long lasting. Herbicides are somewhat effective against these weeds, but in some cases, the irritating oils are still present in the plant tissue even after the plant is dead.

When I remove a poisonous plant from my own landscape, I don a full poison ivy suit, which consists of a rubber rain coat and rain pants, rubber boots, and chemical-resistant gloves dedicated only to this particular job; I don't use them for anything else. I dig up the offending plant (using a dedicated poison ivy shovel) and then pull a thick garbage bag up over my arm. I pick up the freshly dug plant with the bagged hand and then flip the bag down over the plant like I'm picking up a pile of dog poop. Once the weed is fully enclosed in the bag, I tie the bag closed and toss it in the trash. Then I hang my poison ivy suit back up in the shed and head inside to wash up with an oil-cutting soap and a stiff wash cloth.

There's no doubt that the best weed-management strategy puts prevention first and control second. Use a combination of the techniques listed above, picking and choosing those that work best for you. With the right approach and consistent effort, effective weed management requires far less time and energy than you might expect.

There are a number of plants that can cause a severe allergic reaction in those who come in contact with the plant's foliage. Poison ivy (*Toxicodendron radicans*) (right), wild parsnip (*Pastinaca sativa*), giant hogweed (*Heracleum mantegazzianum*), and stinging nettles (*Urtica dioica*) (left) are just a few such plants.

In addition to these kinds of organic contact herbicides, a newer group of natural herbicides has recently been brought to market. Natural herbicides based on chelated iron (FeHEDTA) kill only broadleaved weeds; they do not harm grasses, making them a good choice for managing weeds in lawns. There are a few different brand names of iron-based natural herbicides, including Iron X! from Gardens Alive!, Fiesta Turf Weed Killer, and Natria Lawn Weed Control.

If you spend any amount of time online, I'm sure you've come across various recipes for homemade herbicide concoctions, often involving salt, vinegar, soap, or other household items. I strongly recommend against using these homespun weed controls, as they can be very harmful to soil health. They may kick weeds back a bit, but they seldom kill them completely, and they can contaminate your soil and harm beneficial soil life. Not to mention that these products have not been tested for their safety or effectiveness.

CHAPTER 10
CONTROLLING PESTS AND INSECTS

By Jessica Walliser

HEALTHY GARDENS ARE NATURAL HABITATS, FULL of not just plants but also a whole host of other creatures. From fungi and flies to mice and monarchs, a healthy garden is alive with thousands of different organisms. Yes, some of these organisms are "nicer" to our plants than others, but the fact is that gardens are not merely a place for green things to grow—they are also complex ecosystems where layers of organisms interact in an interconnected web. As gardeners, we have a tremendous responsibility to understand and nurture that web, because our own actions play a vital role in the well-being of the many creatures that share our gardens with us.

For many, many years, farmers and gardeners have focused primarily on battling the creatures we perceive as pests because they nibble our plants' leaves, chew through their blossoms, or cripple their roots. No group of creatures has felt our wrath as much as insects, but it's important to remember that the vast majority of insects we encounter in our gardens are helpful rather than harmful. They break down organic matter to feed our plants, pollinate our crops, and, most of the

OPPOSITE: Most of the insects you find in your garden are not harmful. This caterpillar may be munching on dill, but in a few weeks, it will turn into an important pollinator, the Eastern black swallowtail butterfly.

time, simply go about their business without bringing any harm to us or our plants. In fact, of the million or so identified insect species on this planet, less than one percent are classified as agricultural or human pests. That means the remaining insect species are either benign or beneficial to the plants living in our landscape.

Because of this, your first reaction upon seeing an insect in your garden should not be to stomp on it or run for the spray can. Instead, investigate the insect and watch what it's doing in your landscape. If it's not bringing harm (which is true of most insects), just ignore it. But if you do discover it's having a negative impact on the health of your plants, it's time to dive a little deeper and determine if any action is necessary.

This is the point at which this chapter will prove the most helpful. It's designed to hand you all the tools necessary to determine whether or not a particular critter is friend or foe. You'll learn how to properly identify pests and discover ways you can keep them from becoming problematic in the first place. From there, we'll talk about controlling problem insects through good garden design, proper plant care, encouraging beneficial predatory insects, and a handful of other means. I'll also share some of my favorite organic product controls to be used as a last resort.

The final section of the chapter is dedicated to some of the non-insect pests that occasionally feed on our garden plants.

WHAT IS A GARDEN PEST?

A garden pest is defined as a weed, pathogen, insect, or animal that causes a significant negative impact on the health or aesthetics of a plant. In Chapter 9 you were introduced to weeds and learned many different ways to safely manage them. In Chapter 11, we'll delve into plant pathogens and discuss how to manage fungal, bacterial, and viral diseases. This chapter is dedicated to insects and other animals. Let's begin with insects.

ABOVE: Not all garden pests are insects. Several mammals, such as deer, groundhogs, and rabbits, can also be problematic for gardeners.

OPPOSITE: Gardens are complex ecosystems with many layers of organisms living in them. It's important to remember that while some of these organisms are harmful to our plants, the vast majority of them are not.

Aesthetic damage is often not harmful to the health of your plants; it just detracts from their appearance. In most cases, some amount of aesthetic damage should be tolerated by the gardener.

Determining whether or not a pest is worth controlling involves considering your personal tolerance, the extent of the damage, and the number of pests present on the plant.

In order for an insect to be deemed a pest, it has to cause a significant amount of economic or aesthetic damage to a plant. Yes, a lot of insects eat plants, but most of them do not cause significant damage. And, in most cases, the harm these insects cause is not life-threatening; it just makes the plant look not so hot for a short time. It's surprisingly rare for a pest insect to outright kill its host plant; after all, it's not in an insect's best interest to eliminate its food source and the food source of future generations.

Exactly what amount of economic or aesthetic damage is deemed "significant" depends on the tolerance of each particular gardener. Once you come to realize that most leaf-munching insects are not out to kill your plants, your tolerance for their damage should naturally go up. Obviously, if you're a farmer who needs to grow near-perfect crops for your livelihood, your tolerance of pest damage that cuts into your bottom line will be far less than Joe Homeowner who's just growing a garden to help beautify his outdoor living space.

Pest numbers also matter. One teeny tiny aphid is not a pest because the damage it causes is minimal, but hundreds of aphids can cause a far more significant amount of damage, and the gardener may need to step in with a management strategy. On the other hand, one tomato hornworm can nibble an entire tomato plant to the nub, so implementing a few management tactics is certainly called for, even when there's just one hornworm present.

All this means is that deciding whether or not a particular pest is worth the time, money, and effort to control is best determined by careful consideration of your personal tolerance, the type of damage caused, and the number of pests present. Every gardener's opinion on when it's time to step in will vary, but I encourage you to not step in too soon, because not only are properly cared for plants very forgiving, but also, as you'll come to learn later in the chapter, many pest issues are naturally managed by beneficial predatory insects.

HOW TO IDENTIFY PESTS IN YOUR GARDEN

Another essential step in determining whether anti-pest action is required is to make sure you've properly identified the pest and that you understand its life cycle and the extent of damage it can cause. For example, some pests have life cycles that only last a few weeks, while others only feed on plants for a short period of their lives, so taking action against a pest in one of these two groups isn't worth the time and effort because the pest will be gone before they can cause much damage. On the opposite end of the spectrum are the insects that are capable of producing multiple, overlapping generations within a single growing season. Their populations can explode in short order, causing a great amount of damage in a relatively short period of time. The only way to know how much a pest's life cycle influences the amount of damage it can potentially cause is to properly identify and learn about that pest before you decide to take any action. There are several different ways to do this.

1. **By physical description.** This identification method considers the insect's size, shape, coloration, leg count, wing count, and other physical attributes. It's a useful method if you have access to a good insect ID book or website where you can compare photos to the live insect in your garden.

2. **By type of damage.** Often the insect itself isn't actually present on the plant; instead we just come across the damage. Identifying insects by the damage they cause is easier than it might seem. Many insects

have very distinctive feeding patterns and the damage they leave behind is unmistakable. This method of identification often goes hand in hand with the next method, because when you find a particular type of damage on a particular host plant, it helps narrow down the possibilities even further.

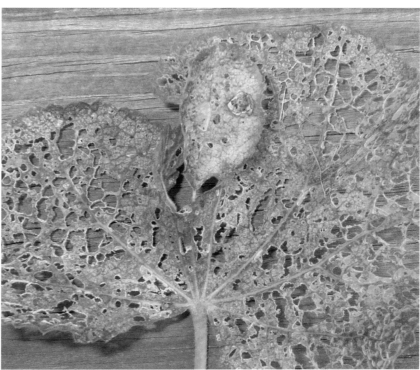

TOP: Identifying insects, such as this blister beetle, by their physical traits is one way to determine who is nibbling on your plants. Use a good insect ID book or website to help with the sleuthing.

BOTTOM: Some pests have very distinctive damage that makes identifying them easy. Hibiscus sawfly larvae are responsible for this hole-filled leaf.

3. **By host plant.** In many instances, a leaf-munching insect pest only dines on a select few species or families of plants. Some insect pests are even so specialized that they can only consume one species of host plant (think asparagus beetles, holly leaf miners, and rose sawflies, to name just a few). Matching up the plant species with the insects that commonly feed on it is just another key to unlocking the identity of a pest.

Sometimes just one of these three methods is all you'll need to properly identify the pest. Other times, it may require using a combination of two or three of them.

To confirm the identity of the pest, you should then consult a good pest insect identification book or website. Here are some of my favorites.

Books

Garden Insects of North America: The Ultimate Guide to Backyard Bugs by Dr. Whitney Cranshaw
Good Bug Bad Bug: Who's Who, What They Do, and How to Manage Them Organically by Jessica Walliser
National Audubon Society Field Guide to Insects and Spiders: North America by the National Audubon Society

Kaufman Field Guide to Insects of North America by Eric R. Eaton and Kenn Kaufman

Websites

www.bugguide.net
www.insectidentification.org
www.knowyourinsects.org
www.whatsthatbug.com

For non-insect garden pests, you can use the same three methods. If you can't see the animal eating your garden long enough to get a physical description (perhaps they dine at night?), look at how they feed on the plants and what plants they're consuming. You can also look for footprints in and around the garden. Or, if you don't see any footprints, sprinkle a coating of all-purpose flour around the nibbled plants and see whose footprints are in the dust the following morning. The pest animal management info in the last section of this chapter will help with this sleuthing too.

Once you've properly identified the culprit and read up on its feeding habits and life cycle, it's time to look into ways to prevent and control it.

When it comes to identifying mammalian pests, look for footprints in and around the garden. These hard to see tracks are from rabbits feeding on young kale plants.

Whenever possible, select naturally resistant plant varieties. For example, butternut-type squashes are more resistant to squash bugs than other varieties.

PEST-MANAGEMENT STRATEGIES

Just as with weed management (Chapter 9), the silver bullet of effective pest management is prevention. Because of this, the first three steps in this section on managing pests focus on prevention. The last three steps feature effective control measures to implement should the pests decide to show up despite your best stab at prevention.

This method of pest management is so successful because it works *with* nature instead of against it. It encourages you to examine how pests interact with plants and how human actions can play an important role in reducing pest damage, without harming non-target insects and other creatures living in your landscape.

Three Steps to Pest Prevention

1. Design the Pest Out of the Garden

The first, and most critical, step in preventing garden pests involves the design of your garden. Consider how variety selection, plant placement, and plant health influence pest damage. Your goal should be to create and maintain a garden full of "happy" plants that are adept at minimizing pest damage through their own natural immune response. There are many different pieces of the design puzzle that influence how this happens, but here are a few key items to keep in mind.

- **Always choose pest-resistant varieties.** If 'H19 Little Leaf' and 'Saladin' cucumbers are more resistant to cucumber beetles than other varieties, then that's what you should be planting. Stop basing your plant selections purely on eye appeal or taste. There are plenty of excellent varieties of fruits and veggies that are not only attractive and flavorful, but also naturally resistant to pests.

- **Right plant, right place.** Each species of plant has differing environmental preferences, and when we place a plant in the conditions where it's most likely to thrive, the result is a healthier plant that's better able to fight off pests and diseases. Put shade-loving plants in the shade and sun-lovers in the sun. Stressed-out plants are a welcome mat for pests and diseases.

- **Give plenty of room to grow.** When plants are overcrowded, they're competing for light, water, and nutrients, which can easily lead to the stress-filled

conditions that invite pests. Plus, plants that are spaced too closely make it easier for pests to hop from one plant to the next.

- **Design for diversity.** Complex landscapes filled with many different species of plants layered together in a pleasing way are havens for the beneficial insect, bird, amphibian, and reptilian species that help us control pests. Don't include just a select few species of plants in your garden—include dozens of them.

2. Examine Your Own Actions

Take a good hard look at what *you're* doing in the garden and how it might be influencing pest numbers. Many times, gardeners inadvertently invite pests into the garden by not caring for their plants properly.

There are many ways in which your actions in the garden impact pest populations.

- **Overfertilization.** Many pest insects are attracted to the succulent, green foliage of an overfertilized plant. In most cases, if you maintain healthy soil (see Chapter 2), supplemental fertilization isn't necessary; only fertilize if a soil test recommends it.

- **Poor pruning practices.** Pruning plants at the wrong time or with dull equipment can often invite pests. Know when it's the correct time to prune each plant and keep your equipment clean, sharp, and in tiptop shape. Each plant is genetically programmed to reach a certain height and width and allowing it to grow into its natural shape and form means you'll have a healthier plant.

- **Watering woes.** Lots of pests and diseases thrive in wet conditions. Because of this, limit evening watering and instead focus your irrigation efforts during the morning hours so the foliage has time to dry off before nightfall.

When designing your garden, give plants plenty of room to grow. This cuts down on competition and decreases the stressful conditions that attract pests.

Design your garden to include a wide variety of plants. Complex landscapes host more beneficial insects and other animals that can naturally reduce pest numbers.

• **Improper garden hygiene.** Many pests overwinter in garden debris, but so do the pollinators and the beneficial insects that help us naturally control pests. Gardeners have been told for a very long time to cut the garden down to the ground at the end of each growing season, rip out annual plants and vegetable crops, and rake up every last leaf and twig to put the garden to bed "clean" for the winter. Now we know that, in most cases, this is a practice that does not help us achieve a healthier garden. Instead, it throws the balance of "good" and "bad" insects off kilter. But because some pests do overwinter in the garden, how do we provide a safe haven for the good bugs without encouraging the bad? If you know a particular plant hosted a pest or disease, that plant gets cut down in the fall, but the rest of the plants can stay intact, allowing us to maintain a steady population of beneficial insects from year to year.

3. Use the Pest's Life Cycle against It

Once a pest has been properly identified, research its life cycle to see when it might be the most vulnerable. For example, pests are often easier to control during their larval stage because they don't have wings and aren't as mobile as they are when they're adults. It's far easier to target a cabbageworm caterpillar or Japanese beetle grubs than it is to target the highly mobile adult insect.

You should also consider a pest's life cycle when timing your planting tasks. If a certain pest insect is active for only a short time of the year, delay planting susceptible crops for a few weeks so the life cycles of the pest and the plant are not in sync with each other. Sometimes just holding off on planting cucumber, squash, or melon seeds by two weeks is enough to prevent future issues with squash vine borers, cucumber beetles, and squash bugs.

TOP LEFT: Growing cucumbers and other vining crops vertically can also help limit pests by keeping the developing fruits off the ground and away from soil-dwelling insects.

TOP RIGHT: Delay planting beans by 2 or 3 weeks so their life cycle falls out of sync with the Mexican bean beetles that love to feast on them. If the newly emerged beetles don't find host plants in your garden upon "waking" in the spring, they'll go elsewhere.

LEFT: Pest insects may be more vulnerable to control measures while in their larval stage. Japanese beetle grubs are fairly stationary within the soil, so targeting them instead of a highly mobile adult beetle is smart.

10

Three Steps to Pest Control

1. Utilize Physical and Mechanical Control Measures

If you've done everything you can to prevent pest issues by following the preceding three steps but still end up with a troublesome insect issue in the garden, turn first to physical and mechanical control techniques. Many times garden pests can be handled with a little physical intervention rather than by reaching for a product control. Here are some of the ones I find the most useful:

• **Handpick pests.** For some pests, the easiest way to be rid of them is to manually remove them from plants and drop them into a jar of soapy water. While this is effective for larger pests, it's a lot more challenging for small pests such as aphids and mites. In these cases, knock them off your plants with a sharp stream of water from the hose. Once dislodged, they'll quickly perish or be eaten by beneficial insects at the ground level. To make handpicking highly visible pest eggs off of plants a lot easier, wrap a piece of tape around your palm, sticky side out. Then press the sticky surface of the tape onto the egg cluster to remove all the eggs at once.

ABOVE: Picking pest insects off of a plant by hand is a tedious chore, but it's incredibly effective, especially for larger pests.

TOP RIGHT: Floating row covers are an excellent physical barrier to pests. Cover plants with the fabric in early spring and leave it in place until harvest, or until the plants come into flower if it's a crop that needs to be pollinated.

BOTTOM RIGHT: Another physical barrier is a foil strip positioned around the base of summer squash plants to deter the egg-laying activities of female squash vine borers.

• **Erect a barrier.** Eliminate damage by putting some kind of tangible barrier between the plant and the pest. Cover vegetables with floating row cover to keep pests such as Colorado potato beetles, asparagus beetles, and many others off plants. Just remember to remove the cover when plants come into flower if the crop requires pollination. Other physical barriers include putting toilet paper tubes around young seedlings to protect them from girdling cutworms or wrapping aluminum foil strips around the base of zucchini plants to keep squash vine borers from laying eggs where the stem meets the soil.

Yellow cards coated in non-drying glue are a great way to trap many flying pests. Place them just above plant tops. Pest insects are attracted to them, while beneficials and pollinators are not.

- **Use traps and lures.** For certain pests, it's possible to get a grip on their numbers by setting up commercial or homemade traps and lures. In the orchard, there are traps for coddling moths and apple maggots. In the vegetable or flower garden, you can trap slugs in shallow saucers of beer. Even yellow sticky cards placed above plant tops are useful for trapping hopping flea beetles, cucumber beetles, and many other pests. One word of caution, however: Avoid Japanese beetle bag traps because they've been known to attract more beetles than they trap. If you're going to use one, place it several hundred feet from the garden.

If you've done your research and still can't find a mechanical or physical control that solves your problem, look next to biological controls.

2. Turn to Biological Controls

Biological controls use one living organism to combat another. In this case, we're using a beneficial insect, bacteria, or nematode (microscopic roundworms) to limit pests. Thankfully, there are tens of thousands of good bugs that dine on common garden pests. There are also many different biopesticides and species of nematodes you can use to target specific pests.

Beneficial Insects

It's a bug-eat-bug world out there, and there are many insects that relish consuming the pests that plague your garden. Beneficial predatory insects, such as ladybugs, lacewings, assassin bugs, and many others, catch and consume garden pests day and night. Parasitoidal beneficial insects, such as parasitic wasps and tachinid flies, use many species of garden pests as hosts for their developing young. These good bugs should be encouraged and fostered because when you have enough of them around, they naturally keep pest numbers in check and create a well-balanced garden ecosystem.

To encourage beneficial insects to take up residence in your garden, create a safe haven for them.

- Stop using synthetic chemical pesticides, which can kill the good bugs just as quickly as the pests.
- Provide beneficials with plenty of nectar. Most of these insects don't just need the protein found in their prey; they also need the carbohydrates found

There are over 400 species of ladybugs in North America and they're just one small portion of the thousands of different pest-eating beneficial insects you can find in your garden.

in nectar. Plants with small flowers are the best nectar sources for these insects. Include plenty of flowering plants in the carrot family (Apiaceae), the daisy family (Asteraceae), and the mint family (Lamiaceae) in your garden; these plants are among the most helpful to beneficial insects.

- Give them a year-round habitat. Don't clean up every last fallen leaf; instead, leave a good bit of garden debris so they can take shelter until spring.

Beneficial insects can also be purchased for release into the garden, but this is not a practice I—or many other experts—recommend. Some species of beneficial insects purchased at the garden center (Chinese praying mantis egg cases, for example) are not native to the North American continent and they don't belong here any more than Japanese beetles do. Other beneficials are wild-collected, ladybugs in particular, and when they're harvested with backpack vacuums, it impacts the number of insects left in the habitat from which they were collected. It can also introduce diseases and other pathogens to native populations when these wild-collected insects are relocated to your garden. If you're going to introduce lacewing larvae, mealybug destroyers, or any other species of beneficial insects, make sure they are insectary reared. But, rather than introducing purchased beneficials, it's much better, of course, to build and foster a hearty population of existing beneficial insects in your garden by doing the three things I mention above.

Biopesticides
There are also many products on the market that are derived from other living organisms, namely bacteria, to

This hornworm has fallen victim to a parasitic wasp who has used it as a host for her young. A new generation of parasitic wasps are now pupating in cocoons attached to the hornworm's body.

Imported cabbageworms are one of many caterpillar pests that are easily controlled with Bt-based pesticides.

help us control garden pests. They're effective, safe to use, and don't bring harm to non-target insects or soil life. Here are four biopesticides I've found to be very useful.

- ***Bacillus thuringiensis* (Bt).** Bacillus thuringiensis is a naturally occurring bacterium that's used to control caterpillars. It's safe for humans and non-target insects, though it will kill all types of caterpillars, so care should be taken to not get Bt-based products on plants hosting butterfly larvae.

There are two primary strains of Bt for use in a garden setting.

1. ***Bacillus thuringiensis* var. *kurstaki*.** Works against all caterpillars. Works best on young caterpillars but is harmless to non-target creatures. It degrades quickly in sunlight. Brand names include DiPel, Thuricide, Monterey Bt, and Garden Safe Bt Caterpillar Killer, to name a few.

2. ***Bacillus thuringiensis* var. *israelensis*.** Works against mosquitos, black flies, and fungus gnat larvae in wet areas, including marshes, ponds, birdbaths, rain barrels, and other standing water. Once ingested, it kills 100% of the larvae of these insects but will not harm fish, humans, pets, or other wildlife. It's most commonly found as donut-shaped mosquito dunks that are dropped into the water.

- **Spinosad:** Spinosad-based products have become a great tool in the arsenal of many gardeners, and with good reason. These products (brand names include Captain Jack's Deadbug Brew, Entrust, and Monterey Garden Insect Spray) are made from a very unique fermented soil-dwelling bacterium called *Saccharopolyspora spinosa*. They work most effectively when ingested by the pest, so insects with piercing-sucking mouth parts aren't very susceptible, but a wide range of leaf-munching insect pests are, including Colorado potato beetles and Japanese beetles.

Spinosad-based products have a low toxicity to beneficial insects. However, spinosad is toxic to foraging bees, so it's absolutely essential that you apply the spray when no bees are active; early morning or evening is best.

- ***Nosema locustae*.** Products based on this biopesticide are made from protozoan that affect primarily grasshoppers. It's typically applied to the

Leaf-chewing insects, such as these viburnum leaf beetles, are controlled with spinosad-based products.

garden as a bait premixed with wheat bran flakes. Once young grasshoppers ingest these products, they stop feeding and eventually die, and when they do so, the pathogen spreads and infects other hoppers. Brand names include Semaspore and Nolo Bait.

- **Milky spore:** Milky spore disease is caused by a bacterium, *Paenibacillus popilliae*, and it infects only Japanese beetle larvae. Milky spore is available as a granular or powderized product that's spread over turfgrass that's infested with Japanese beetle grubs. The extent of control is dependent on soil conditions, the number of grubs present, and other factors.

Nematodes

Nematodes are naturally occurring microscopic roundworms that are found throughout the world. There are many different species; some are harmful to plants while others are not. The nematode species that act as biological controls for certain pest insects are not the same species that feed on plant roots. Instead, these beneficial nematodes live in the soil and enter pests and infect them with a deadly bacteria. The nematodes continue to reproduce within the body of the dead insect, multiplying until they exit the insect and search for a new host.

There are several different species of beneficial nematodes that can be purposefully introduced to garden environments to help control specific pests. Some of these species are mobile and move through the soil, seeking out host insects. Other species are stationary and work best against insects that don't move around too much in the soil profile.

Beneficial nematodes are living organisms that should be stored and applied with care. Typically kept under refrigeration until use and applied in cooler morning temperatures, nematodes are often mixed with water and applied via a pump sprayer, watering can, or hose end sprayer.

Because most beneficial nematodes do not survive freezing temperatures, it's best to apply them on a yearly basis when the weather warms in the spring.

Depending on the nematode species, they can be used to control various lawn grubs, black vine weevil larvae, and many others.

3. **Apply an Appropriate Natural Pest-Control Product**

If preventative techniques fail you, you can't find an appropriate physical or mechanical control, and no biological controls have proven to be effective, then and only then is it time to turn to an alternative product control. Though all the products I recommend here are natural, it's very important to carefully follow all label instructions (labels are the law) and know that these pesticides may have hazards associated with them even though they are natural.

- **Insecticidal soap.** Made from potassium salts of fatty acids, these products must come in direct contact with the insect. Easy to use, and with low toxicity to humans and other mammals, insecticidal soaps work against all soft-bodied insects, including mites, aphids, whiteflies, mealybugs, different insect larvae, and many others. Be cautious because these products may also harm larval beneficial insects and beneficial insect eggs if direct contact is made.

- **Horticultural oil.** These products can be petroleum or vegetable based. They work by smothering insects and insect eggs by clogging their breathing pores. They must come in direct contact with the pests but they can be used against a broad array of pest insects, including young caterpillars, scale crawlers, and many others. Heavier oil products are known as dormant oils and should be used only on woody trees and shrubs during the winter to smother overwintering pest insects.

- **Botanical oils.** Several different products fit into this category, including those based on citrus oil, garlic oil, hot peppers, and various herbs. Most of these products work as both deterrents and contact poisons. They're effective against a broad range of insects, so be sure to check the label of each product for a list of targeted pests.

- **Neem.** Neem-based pesticides are made from a tropical tree known as the neem tree (*Azadirachta*

Microscopic roundworms known as nematodes are excellent predators of many soil-dwelling pests. They're typically mixed with water and applied to garden soil or turfgrass.

Natural pesticides derived from botanical oils can be an effective control against certain pests. Many work as both repellents and contact poisons.

indica). They act as insect repellents, feeding deterrents, and toxins. They also block insect development. Neem products are contact poisons, but they also have some systemic action as well, meaning they remain effective for some time after the application is made. Neem is useful against many pests, including Japanese, cucumber, and other beetle species, as well as various caterpillars, weevils, and many other pests.

- **Pyrethrins.** Made from a species of chrysanthemum, this contact poison causes immediate death to any insects exposed to it. It's extremely toxic to bees and other beneficial insects, and because of this, it's only recommended as a pesticide of last resort. Some humans and other mammals may have an adverse reaction to pyrethrins as well. Available as both a dust and a spray, pyrethrins are labeled for use against a broad range of insect pests.

There are many commercial brands of deer repellent on the market. Their effectiveness is based on the product itself, the herd's feeding habits, and also on the regularity of the product's application.

- **Kaolin clay.** Kaolin clay is used primarily on tree fruits as a pest deterrent. A wetable powder that's mixed with water and sprayed onto plants, kaolin clay acts as a barrier between the pest and the host plant. Once dry, it leaves a coating of fine dust over all plant surfaces, which irritates and repels pests, though the coating easily washes off of apples and other fruits after harvest. Repeat applications are necessary to protect plants for long periods of time.
- **Iron phosphate baits.** These slug and snail baits are an excellent alternative to chemical slug baits that are toxic to dogs, cats, and other animals. Made from a naturally occurring mineral, iron phosphate baits act as a stomach poison for land-dwelling mollusks such as slugs and snails but will not harm mammals or worms and other soil creatures. The pellets are sprinkled around favorite plants and soon after ingesting them, the slug or snail stops feeding. Death follows soon after.

NON-INSECT GARDEN PESTS

If your garden is plagued by fur-covered pests, it's a whole different ballgame. Here's the skinny on some common garden interlopers and a few ways you can effectively keep them out of your veggie patch and flower beds.

Deer

If deer are regular visitors to your landscape, use these tips to keep them from feasting on your plants.

- **Plant only deer-resistant plants.** This should always be your first line of defense. Deer dislike plants with fuzzy leaves, spines, and heavily fragranced foliage. Herbs and members of the mint family, including bee balm, nepeta, salvias, and others, are safe bets. Your local nursery may also have a list of deer-resistant plants for your area. In the vegetable garden, stick with cucumbers, onions, garlic, squash, eggplants, and tomatillos, as the deer typically dislike them.
- **Use spray deterrents.** There are many effective deer repellents and deterrents on the market, but how well they work is almost completely dependent on how they are used. If you want great results, you have to be religious about using them. You can't

Fencing deer out of the garden is the best way to keep them away from prized plants, but make sure the fence is a minimum of 8 feet tall, as deer are agile jumpers.

spray once and then forget about it. Set a weekly reminder on your cell phone so you don't forget.

Most deer repellent sprays use a combination of odor and taste deterrents and, as a result, they smell pretty bad until they dry. Regardless of which product you choose, you must be consistent about applying it because it will eventually wash off.

Commercially made repellent sprays can be made from dried blood, garlic, soaps, putrefied eggs, or a combination of ingredients. Several studies have found that egg-based products tend to be the most effective.

There are also many granular, hanging, and clip-on deer repellent products that claim to be effective in sending the deer packing, but the results are often mixed. Don't be afraid to experiment with these products, but use them only in a small area first to see how well they perform.

- **Put up a fence.** Fencing deer out is one of the best ways to keep them from nibbling on your garden. Though it's expensive, erecting a deer fence is worth it, especially if you live in a region with a very heavy deer population. Fences should be a minimum of eight feet tall, and stockade fences tend to work better than those the deer can see through because they don't like to jump over something unless they can see what's on the other side.

Electric fencing is another option, though you must check local zoning laws to make sure they're legal before installing one. You'll have to inspect the fence regularly to make sure it isn't grounded by overgrown vegetation.

You can also use "invisible" deer netting to fence deer out of your garden. This black mesh netting is often attached to wooden 4×4s, though it too must be at least eight feet tall to keep the deer from jumping over it.

Live traps like this one are a great way to remove nuisance groundhogs from the garden. Just be sure to contact your municipal animal control *before* you trap any animals to find out what to do with them once they've been trapped.

Fencing individual plants is another option and one that's far less expensive than fencing an entire property. Use black mesh deer netting to cover favorite plants and protect them from the deer.

- **Scare the deer away.** While clattering pie pans and strips of aluminum foil hanging in the garden will do nothing to deter deer, there is one scare tactic that works: a motion-activated sprinkler. These gadgets have been very useful in my own garden because when they sense motion, they deliver a sharp burst of water in the direction of the movement, scaring the wits out of the deer. The range of the sprinkler's aim can be adjusted on most models to a fairly targeted area, making them ideal for protecting everything from vegetable gardens to shrub and flower beds.

Be aware, however, that motion-activated sprinklers have their limits. Because they're hooked up to the hose, you can't use them in the winter when the hose will freeze, and you'll need more than one of them to protect a large garden or property. If you want the sprinkler to work at night, you'll need to buy a brand with an infrared sensor, and battery-powered options may work better than solar-powered ones, especially on cloudy days.

Groundhogs

Groundhogs are probably the biggest headache a gardener can face. I have no doubt they've made many of us want to go vigilante. Groundhogs are proficient diggers and agile climbers; we've even seen them sitting in our apple trees munching on our apples!

- **Use fencing.** Excluding groundhogs from your garden without resorting to bullets does require a bit of finesse, but it's doable. Fully enclosing your garden with plastic netting won't work because a groundhog can chew right through it. If you decide to fence in your garden, use metal fencing, such as chicken wire or galvanized cattle fencing. Bury the bottom edge of the fence a foot below the ground and do not secure the top 18 inches of the fence to the post. When the groundhog tries to dig under the fence, the buried wire will stop it, and when it tries to climb, the unattached top edge of the fencing will flop down and hopefully knock the groundhog to the ground.

- **Employ spray deterrents.** Some spray repellents are labeled for use against groundhogs too. Check the shelves of your local nursery to see if they have any on hand. As with deer repellents, be religious about using them.
- **Live trap.** A better bet is using a live trap to capture the groundhog. These humane traps are metal and have a trip plate that closes the trap's end(s) when the animal steps on it. Make sure to select the appropriate-size trap and bait it properly. I've found the best bait for groundhogs to be marshmallows (who knew?), very ripe cantaloupe, or peanut-butter-covered apple slices. Set the trap somewhere you've seen the groundhog, and leave a Hansel and Gretel–style trail of small pieces of bait outside the trap to lead them into it. Then put bigger chunks of bait inside the trap, right on the trip plate.

Rabbits are frequent visitors to gardens, regularly nibbling on the lowest leaves of their favorite plants.

Groundhogs are only active during the day, so *always* close the trap at night. If you don't, you'll have an angry skunk, possum, or raccoon on your hands first thing the next morning. Check the trap several times throughout the day. If you do not want to trap the groundhog yourself, there are critter control companies that will come to your home and do it for you.

Rabbits

Rabbits are frequent visitors to gardens and, occasionally, you may find one munching on your prized plants. Though selecting rabbit-resistant plants should always be your first battle tactic, there are other non-lethal measures you can turn to.

- **Employ a repellent.** There are many commercial animal repellents labeled for use against rabbits. Granular repellants are sprinkled around the perimeter of the garden, forming a scent barrier of sorts. These repellents are not supposed to come in contact with the plants themselves, so keep them on the ground, not on plants. Spray repellents are another option for ornamental plants. Often based on hot peppers, egg solids, and other odorous and distasteful ingredients, they work much like deer repellents.
- **Fence in your garden.** The easiest way to keep rabbits out of a garden is to install a fence around the perimeter. It only has to be two feet high because rabbits won't jump very high, but you'll want to bury the base of the fence by a few inches to keep the rabbits from burrowing beneath it. To keep out baby bunnies, be sure the holes in the fence are no bigger than two inches square. Chicken wire or box wire work quite well for this task.
- **Block off individual plants.** You can also beat the bunnies by installing small blockades around each of their favorite plants. I use a foot-tall collar of galvanized hardware cloth placed around the base of each plant to keep them away from their favorites. Cut the sheet of hardware cloth and bend it into a ring that's about three or four inches wider than the width of the plant. Fasten it closed with a couple of plastic zip ties.

CHAPTER 11
CONTROLLING DISEASES

By Jessica Walliser

PLANTS ARE LIVING ORGANISMS THAT ARE, IN MANY ways, at the mercy of their environment. Because of this, plants have evolved a stunning array of ways to defend themselves from pests and diseases. Some plants have foliage that's filled with pest-deterring chemical compounds, while others have hairs, spines, or a waxy coating on their leaves to stifle leaf-marring fungal diseases. Many plants even produce volatile chemicals they release into the air to signal beneficial predatory and parasitic insects, inviting them to come to the plant's aid and consume whatever pests are munching on the plant's foliage. But even with this complex defense system in place, plants sometimes fall victim to pests and pathogens.

From blight on tomatoes and powdery mildew on bee balm to brown rot on peaches and botrytis on geraniums, there are numerous plant diseases that can strike your garden throughout the growing season, and understanding them is one of the biggest keys to growing a healthy garden. Though plant pathology is a complicated affair with many nuances involving the complex relationship between the plant, the pathogen, and the environment, most home gardeners are able to manage common plant diseases without having to delve too deeply into this intricate science. Instead, the focus of home gardeners should be on growing healthy, naturally disease-resistant plants and employing various techniques aimed at preventing pathogens from taking hold in the first place; this chapter will focus on precisely that.

OPPOSITE: Raised beds allow plants to be closely inspected and easily treated or removed when they show problems.

Plant pathogens can be bacterial or fungal or they can be viruses, such as the tobacco mosaic virus affecting this tomato plant.

MEET THE PATHOGENS

Most plant diseases are biotic, meaning they are caused by another living organism and can spread from one plant to another. Though there are other causes of biotic diseases, the three primary plant-disease-causing agents are fungi, bacteria, and viruses. There are thousands of different plant diseases caused by these three agents, with each one affecting plants in a different way.

Fungal Pathogens

Fungal pathogens are a diverse crew that cause a number of different symptoms and negative effects on plant health but they do have a few things in common. Unlike plants, fungi can't make their own food through photosynthesis, so instead, they get their nutrition from either the decomposition process (whereby their food comes from something dead) or by robbing nutrients from another living organism (whereby their food comes from living tissue). In the first group, these decomposing fungi use decaying organic matter as a food source and typically aren't harmful to plant health. The second group of fungi, however, act as parasites, obtaining nutrition from living plant tissue; the members of this group are the ones that can prove harmful to plants.

These harmful fungal pathogens can enter plants through wounds, plant pores, or even by using their thread-like structure to needle into healthy plant tissue. Once inside, these pathogenic fungi can cause a number of plant diseases, with each disease being specific to the exact species of fungi involved.

Just as many plants reproduce by seeds, fungi reproduce by producing spores. Depending on the species of fungi, these spores can be dispersed in air, in water, and/or on objects, making some fungal pathogens fast spreading and infectious.

Bacterial Pathogens

The many species of bacteria responsible for plant diseases often act as parasites too, drawing nutrition from their plant hosts, but they can also continue to live without a suitable host plant to infect, sometimes sitting in the soil, on plant debris, or inside the digestive tract of vector insects for long periods of time.

Disease-causing bacteria can enter plants through natural openings or via natural, insect-, or man-made wounds in the tissue.

Viral Pathogens

Essentially, viruses alter the metabolism of plant cells and direct them to generate more of the virus instead of healthy plant tissue. Because of this, oddly distorted and/or discolored growth is one of the most common symptoms of a viral infection.

Pathogenic viruses often come into a plant through the feeding action of an insect but they can also be transferred from plant to plant via human actions, such as pruning and propagation. Some viruses can even be transmitted by human hands as you work within a population of plants.

Viruses can be contained in seeds, bulbs, and all plant parts. They can even be in pollen. This means that plants that are infected with a confirmed virus should be destroyed immediately to prevent the spread of the viral pathogen to healthy plants. Some viruses are actually used intentionally to generate unique plant forms and foliage variegation, such as striped tulips and variegated flowering maples (*Abutilon* spp.).

Like human viruses, there is no cure for plant viruses. In humans, most viruses are prevented through the use of vaccines; in plants, viruses are prevented by purchasing only "clean" seeds and plants and immediately disposing of any virus-infected plants before the pathogen can spread. Controlling any insects that transmit the virus is another helpful way to prevent their spread. However, plant viruses are best prevented by planting naturally resistant varieties. For example, there are a number of cucumber varieties resistant to cucumber mosaic virus. Carefully read seed packets and catalogs before making purchases because a list of disease-resistance is often noted in the text. Only plant certified virus-free seed potatoes, strawberries, grapes, fruit trees, and other crops.

In home gardens with a hearty variety of plant species present—and where the gardener is sure to purchase only certified virus-free plants—these viruses are not typically a major threat, and because they aren't "curable," I have not included any of the plant diseases caused by viruses in the list of common plant diseases discussed later in this chapter.

HOW DISEASE PATHOGENS AFFECT PLANTS

Each different plant pathogen affects its host in a different way. Some are asymptomatic (meaning they show no symptoms), while others can kill an entire plant in short order. In general, however, plants infected with a pathogen are negatively impacted in one or more of the following ways.

Plant pathogens can

- divert the carbohydrates made via photosynthesis from fueling plant growth to fueling more pathogen growth,
- inhibit plant reproduction by affecting flower and fruit production,
- impact the plant's hardiness by inhibiting the storage of winter food reserves,
- reduce the rate of photosynthesis, thereby impacting the amount of food available for generating more plant growth,
- stifle nutrient absorption from the soil,
- negatively impact a plant's ability to draw water from the soil,
- disrupt the plant's vascular tissue and restrict the movement of nutrients and water within the plant,
- cause significant aesthetic damage,
- reduce yields of fruiting plants and leaf crops, and
- negatively impact the storage life of harvested fruits and vegetables infected with a pathogen.

Diseases such as fusarium wilt are more than an aesthetic issue; they can easily kill an entire plant. Other pathogens are less destructive, causing only marred foliage but not affecting production or yields.

The first step in growing a disease-free garden is understanding how pathogens can be prevented and how they spread. Diseases such as rose rosette are complicated organisms; choosing resistant plant varieties should always be your first line of defense.

Though some plant diseases can cause a wide variety of damaging issues, others cause far less significant injury. In fact, in some cases, a plant can live with a pathogen for many years with little to no ill effects. In other cases, the disease can bring a dramatic death. Because of this, it's best to arm yourself with the know-how to put preventative measures in place; you won't have to battle a pathogen, of course, if it never strikes in the first place.

THE THREE-STEP DISEASE-PREVENTION PLAN

The good news is that, if you utilize a few preventative measures, you'll greatly reduce your risk of encountering plant pathogens in your garden. This three-step system will enable you to take better control of your garden's health and keep diseases out of the garden's ecosystem as much as possible.

Step 1: Plan for Resistance

You might be surprised to learn that plants have an immune response, though it's quite different from our own. Unlike us, plants don't have specialized cells that travel throughout their tissues attacking pathogens like our white blood cells do. Instead, most plant cells have the built-in ability to fight off diseases by suppressing pathogen growth with assorted antimicrobial chemicals, proteins, and enzymes. In some situations, infected plants can even signal neighboring plants by emitting a volatile chemical that tells the neighboring plants to begin to activate their own defense systems.

But just because plants have this built-in immune response doesn't mean they're always able to fight off the pathogen. Many pathogens bypass this defense system by tricking plant cells into hosting them. And, just like humans, each plant shows a different level of immunity to a particular pathogen, even among the same species of plant. Plant breeders seek out disease resistance in a population of plants and selectively breed for that trait. Over time, the result is a specific variety of a plant that's resistant to a given pathogen while still being productive and beautiful.

There are disease-resistant varieties of almost every edible and ornamental plant you might want to include in your garden. Choosing plants with known disease resistance is an absolute must for smart gardeners.

But how do you know which varieties of a particular plant are the most disease resistant? Thankfully, plant breeders aren't shy and you can readily find that information in most seed catalogs and numerous online sources. When perusing seed catalogs and reading seed packets, you should keep a sharp eye out for letter codes that indicate which pathogens a variety is resistant to. For example, when looking for a good tomato variety, the letter *V* indicates a resistance to verticillium wilt (a bacterial disease I describe later in this chapter, along with many others), *T* means resistance to tobacco mosaic virus, *F* indicates resistance to fusarium wilt, *LB* is late blight, and so on. There are letter codes that note disease resistance for most fruits and vegetables, including beans, beets, carrots, corn, cucumbers, eggplant, lettuce, melons, onions, peas, peppers, pumpkins, potatoes, squash, spinach, and many others. Don't pick vegetable varieties just for their flavor or good looks; pick them for their disease resistance too.

The same goes for ornamental plants. Seek out disease resistance whenever possible. If you aren't sure whether a specific plant is prone to disease, a 10-minute Google search will tell you all you need to know.

To design the pathogen out of the garden, seek out plant varieties with a natural resistance to fungal diseases, such as powdery mildew, seen above.

Ornamental plants can be selected for disease resistance too. Some hollyhock varieties are more prone to developing rust than others.

11

GRAFT

Step 2: Control Environmental Conditions

The second step in preventing diseases in your garden involves understanding how environmental conditions affect disease prevalence, and learning how to manipulate the garden environment to make it less welcoming to pathogens. In this step, we're essentially keeping the pathogen out of the garden by designing the space and arranging our plants in a way that improves their health and reduces the risk of disease.

Most diseases caused by fungal pathogens are more likely to strike and proliferate during wet weather. Fungal spores require moisture to thrive, so one relatively easy way to keep fungal diseases at bay is to keep plant foliage as dry as possible. While you can't control the weather, you can promote good air circulation, which enables leaves and stems to dry more quickly after rains, by spacing plants properly. Don't crowd plants, and make sure each one has more than enough room to grow. Spacing plants properly also improves their health by reducing competition stress. Give each plant plenty of access to light, water, and nutrients. Proper spacing can also slow the spread of pests and diseases; when plants are smushed close together, it's easier for a pest to hop from one plant to another or for spores to splash from one leaf to another.

Irrigate plants from the bottom whenever possible, targeting water directly on their root zone while keeping foliage dry, and prune out any crossing branches to improve air flow through fruit trees, tomatoes, and other disease-prone plants.

Proper weed management is also important (see Chapter 9). When weeds crowd desired plants, it reduces air circulation and raises the humidity of the air around your garden plants, possibly promoting fungal diseases.

ABOVE: Some phlox varieties are more susceptible to powdery mildew than others but giving plants plenty of room and improving the air circulation around them cuts down on the pathogen as well.

OPPOSITE: Grafted plants, such as this tomato, are often selected for improved disease resistance. Two tomato varieties are grafted together to incorporate both disease-resistance and tasty fruits into a single plant.

Step 3: Alter Human Actions

This step involves all the maintenance tasks a gardener can perform to limit the chances of disease occurrence. The healthier our plants are, the greater their ability to resist disease. Our own actions in the garden are a huge contributing factor in the vigor or susceptibility of our plants.

Here are some positive actions gardeners can take to prevent diseases in the landscape:

- Many diseases are more likely to develop when a plant is stressed and not thriving. Weak plants are more susceptible to diseases, so test your garden soil to make sure your plants have all the nutrients they need (but don't overfertilize!), and ensure they have ample water throughout the growing season.

- Mulch your garden immediately after you plant it. Because many fungal diseases can live in the soil, putting a protective layer of mulch between the plant and the soil keeps the spores from splashing up onto the foliage when it rains. For the best results, put mulch down over the soil immediately after planting, even before you water the plants in. This is of particular importance in the tomato patch where early blight and septoria leaf spot can easily spread to plants via spores in the soil. Right after planting, cover the soil with shredded leaves, straw, untreated grass clippings, high-quality compost, or another type of mulch.

- Good sanitation is key. Fungal spores can easily overwinter on plant debris and fallen leaves. If you know a plant was affected by a disease, make sure you clean up all the debris from that plant at the end of the growing season and throw it into the garbage or burn it.

- Diseases can also overwinter on infected fruits, so if you're a fruit grower, make sure you remove any fallen fruit or fruit left clinging to the branches and dispose of it as mentioned above.

- Properly clean and maintain your gardening equipment. Because many pathogens can live on digging and cutting tools and can spread from plant

Gardeners should look carefully at their own actions when trying to determine how and why a disease spreads. Never work with wet foliage, as fungal spores can easily be transferred from one plant to another on water droplets.

Staking and trellising also helps deter pathogens by keeping the plants up off the ground. Mulching soon after planting also keeps soilborne pathogens from spreading.

Diseases can easily spread from one leaf to another. Be sure to remove any damaged foliage as soon as you spot it, tossing it into the garbage or burn pile, not your compost pile.

to plant via pruning, sanitize all pruners, saws, and other equipment with a spray disinfectant or a 10-percent bleach solution each time you use them. Throughout the gardening season, each time you use equipment to prune a plant that's affected by a disease, whether it's black spot on your roses or septoria leaf spot on tomatoes, that piece of equipment should be disinfected before being used on another plant.

- If you're a container gardener who was faced with diseases last season, completely empty the potting mix in all your containers and sanitize the pots with a 10-percent bleach solution. Dispose of the old potting soil and replace it with new potting mix prior to planting next spring.

- Water plants in the morning, whenever possible, to allow enough time for the foliage to completely dry before nightfall.

- Don't overfertilize plants. Succulent, tender foliage is more susceptible to certain fungal attacks.

- Avoid working in the garden when the foliage is wet. Fungal spores can spread from plant to plant on water droplets clinging to your clothes or skin.

- Immediately pick off any diseased foliage you find, but don't toss these infected leaves onto the compost pile. Most home compost piles don't reach a high enough temperature to kill fungal spores unless you're religious about the ingredients you use and turning the pile weekly.

- Carefully inspect all newly purchased plants for signs of disease before introducing them to your garden. Purchase plants from a good, local nursery, and avoid buying any that may be hosting a disease.

- Crop rotation is another key to disease prevention, especially in the vegetable garden. Even if your garden is small, moving the plants over a few feet from where they were the previous season can make a difference. Don't follow a plant from a certain family with another plant from the same family for two subsequent growing seasons.

As always, prevention is key, but even when you follow all three steps to a *T*, there will still be an occasional disease occurrence, especially during years with a lot of rainfall or years where a pathogen was accidentally introduced to your garden from nursery stock or another source. When this happens, tackle the pathogen by following these four steps:

1. Properly identify it.
2. Implement ways to stop its spread.
3. Treat infected plants with a control product or remove the plant completely.
4. Put preventative measures in place to keep it out of next year's garden.

The following profiles of common plant pathogens walk you through each of these four steps for each different disease. In each profile, effective product controls are listed. Use them only as a last resort.

13 COMMON PLANT PATHOGENS

Basil Downy Mildew (*Peronospora belbahrii*)

Susceptible Plants: Basil

Identification: The fungus easily spreads via air currents, infected seeds, and plant tissue, making it extremely difficult to control. Early symptoms appear as mottling between the leaf veins on the upper leaf surface. On the

Early signs of basil downy mildew include tiny purplish-grey spores on the undersides of the leaves.

Bacterial wilt exhibits as wilted and drying leaves but will eventually kill the entire plant. All members of the cucurbit family are at risk, including melons.

leaf undersides, you'll see tiny purplish-grey spores. Eventually, leaves develop dark-brown irregular splotches and powdery, dark-grey spore clusters on leaf undersides. Plant death follows soon after. This disease does not live in the soil.

Prevention: Plant only basil varieties with known resistance, including 'Red Leaf', Thai, Lemon, 'Spice', and 'Red Rubin'. Purchase plants from local growers who use certified disease-free basil seeds whenever possible. Properly space basil plants to improve air circulation.

Control: If used before the onset of symptoms or immediately after noticing them, some organic fungicides, including bicarbonate-based products and *Bacillus subtilis*, are helpful in combating this disease. Remove and discard any plants with a suspected infestation immediately.

Bacterial Wilt (*Erwinia tracheiphila*)

Susceptible Plants: All members of the cucurbit family are affected, with cucumbers and muskmelons being the most susceptible and pumpkins, squash, and watermelons being the least susceptible.

Identification: The first sign of infection is often wilted and drying leaves. Eventually, the entire vine wilts and dies. For confirmation of infection, cut a wilted stem off at the base and touch the cut with your fingertip. If thin, white, thread-like strands come out of the cut vine when you pull your finger away slowly, bacterial wilt is to blame.

Prevention: Plant only bacterial wilt-resistant varieties. Cucumber choices include 'County Fair', 'Salad Bush', 'Saladin', and 'Marketmore 76'. Because bacterial wilt is spread by cucumber beetles, the key to preventing it is to keep the beetles off the plants. Cover young vines with a floating row cover (see Chapter 10) and leave it in place until the plants flower. Then, remove the cover to give pollinators access to the flowers. You can also trap the beetles by placing yellow sticky cards above plant tops. See Chapter 10 for more info on controlling cucumber beetles.

Control: Once a plant is infected with bacterial wilt, there is no method of control. Pull up and destroy diseased plants as soon as possible.

Black Spot (*Diplocarpon rosae*)

Susceptible Plants: Roses

Identification: This fungal disease appears as dark spots on rose leaves. Once infected, the leaves turn yellow and fall off. Eventually, the plant may become completely defoliated. Black spot is a devastating disease for rose growers.

Prevention: There are many types of roses with a natural resistance to black spot, including the Knock Out, Earth-Kind, and Easy Elegance roses. Remove infected leaves as soon as the black spots appear and toss them into the garbage or burn them. Water roses only at ground level to keep the foliage dry. Black spot easily overwinters on fallen foliage. Clean up all dropped rose leaves every autumn.

Control: Bicarbonate-based fungicides, Neem oil, and *Bacillus subtilis* both prevent and manage black spot infections.

Botrytis or Gray Mold (*Botrytis* spp.)

Susceptible Plants: Thousands of different plant species can be affected by botrytis, but geraniums, strawberries, grapes, chrysanthemums, roses, dahlias, and peonies are among the most susceptible.

Black spot is a common pathogen on roses. Your first line of defense is always planting resistant varieties. Bicarbonate-based fungicides also work well to prevent this disease.

Black spot is a common pathogen on roses. Your first line of defense is always planting resistant varieties. Bicarbonate-based fungicides also work well to prevent this disease.

ABOVE: Botrytis is a fungal disease that affects many plants. It appears as white or gray splotches with fuzzy spores clearly visible.

RIGHT: Cercospora leaf spot creates small, round lesions on foliage. Eventually the lesions develop a grey fuzz. When severe, the plant may face defoliation.

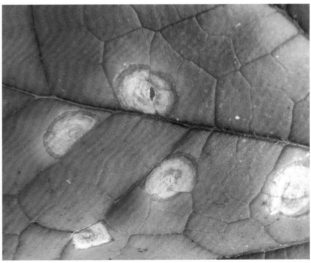

Identification: Because it affects a broad range of plants, botrytis is very common in greenhouses. It's fast growing and fast spreading and often enters via an injury site or pruning cut. Appearing first as white or gray splotches with fuzzy spores clearly visible, botrytis can affect leaves, stems, flowers, fruits, and buds. The fungal spores easily spread by water, wind, or physical contact. Eventually the infected plant tissue turns slimy and rots away.

Prevention: The best way to prevent the spread of botrytis is to remove and dispose of any infected tissue. Sanitize all pruning equipment after working on a plant with botrytis and sanitize all containers that housed an infected plant before planting something else in them. Spores of this fungus overwinter in the soil and on stem and leaf tissue but it can also overwinter on infected fruit left clinging to branches. Remove and discard all infected berries and fruits (called "mummies") at the end of the growing season.

Control: Effective controls include copper-based fungicides, *Bacillus subtilis*, and bicarbonate products, though good sanitation is definitely key to controlling this disease.

Cercospora Leaf Spot (*Cercospora* spp.)

Susceptible Plants: Because there are many different species of this fungal pathogen, it also affects many different plants. Common hosts include figs, hydrangeas, eggplants, okra, carrots, roses, peppers, beans, and beets.

Identification: This fungal disease starts as small, circular yellow lesions on the lower foliage of a plant. These lesions eventually develop a soft grey fuzz at the center and a dark-brown ring around the exterior. Sometimes concentric rings appear, leading this pathogen to sometimes be called "frog eyes." In severe infestations, defoliation may occur. Fruit size and production may be reduced as well.

Prevention: Cercospora leaf spot survives the winter in plant debris and when spring arrives, the spores are spread by wind, rain, people, and animals. Sanitation is key to controlling cercospora leaf spot. Clean up all diseased plant debris at the end of the season and sanitize pruning equipment before every use.

Control: Cercospora leaf spot is largely an aesthetic issue for home gardeners and fungicide use isn't typically necessary.

Early Blight (*Alternaria solani*)

Susceptible Plants: Members of the nightshade family, including tomatoes, potatoes, eggplants, and peppers.

Identification: A very common fungus, early blight first appears as bullseye-shaped brown spots on the lower leaves of a plant. Often the tissue around the spots turns yellow. Eventually, infected leaves fall off. In most cases, the fruit will continue to ripen, even as the disease symptoms progress up the plant.

Prevention: The early blight pathogen lives in the soil, and once a garden shows signs of early blight, it's there to stay because the organism easily overwinters in the soil. To prevent future early blight infections, mulch susceptible plants immediately after planting with a layer of shredded leaves, straw, or another mulch. This prevents the spores from splashing from the soil up onto the lower leaves. Space and prune plants properly to provide adequate air circulation, and remove and dispose of infected leaves as quickly as possible to keep the spores from spreading. Fortunately, most tomatoes will continue to produce even with moderately severe cases of early blight.

Control: Organic fungicides based on *Bacillus subtilis*, bicarbonates, and copper are effective in preventing and managing this disease.

Early blight is a very common fungal disease that most tomato growers have faced at one time or another. It usually affects lower leaves first and progresses up the plant.

At first, fusarium wilt causes a single branch to wilt. As the disease progresses, branch dieback expands, eventually causing the entire plant to collapse.

Fusarium Wilt (*Fusarium oxysporum*)

Susceptible Plants: Fusarium wilt is problematic for many different plants, including tomatoes, eggplants, potatoes, legumes, cucumbers, and melons, as well as some ornamental plants. This pathogen is typically more common in warm Southern climates.

Identification: Early signs of fusarium wilt include drooping leaf stems. Sometimes an entire branch may wilt, often starting with the lower portion of the plant and progressing upwards until the entire plant collapses. To confirm an infection, cut the main stem and look for dark streaks running lengthwise through the stem. Occasionally, dark, sunken cankers are seen at the base of the plant.

Prevention: The fungus that causes fusarium wilt lives in the soil and can survive for many years. It's spread by water, gardening equipment, humans, and plant debris. Plant only resistant varieties. Remove infected plants immediately and disinfect stakes and tomato cages at the end of the growing season.

Control: Once fusarium wilt occurs, there's little you can do to control the current year's infection. Instead, focus on preventing the pathogen in future years. Soil solarization will help kill the fungal spores in the top few inches of soil (see Chapter 9 for more on this technique). Practice crop rotation and do not plant other members of the same plant family in that same planting area for at least four years after the infection. You can also use a biological fungicidal drench on the soil (look for one based on the bacteria *Streptomyces griseoviridis* called Mycostop or a granular one based on the fungus *Trichoderma virens* called Soil Guard). These products may help prevent the infection from colonizing the roots of future crops.

Late blight is one of the most destructive diseases of tomatoes and potatoes. It's fast spreading and can turn entire plants black and slimy.

Late Blight (*Phytophthora infestans*)

Susceptible Plants: Tomatoes and potatoes.

Identification: Late blight is among the most destructive diseases of tomatoes and potatoes. Thankfully, it's not very common, especially in the North where it doesn't survive winter's freezing temperatures without a host plant. Late blight is caused by a fungus and it creates irregularly shaped splotches that are slimy and water soaked. Often, the splotches occur on the topmost leaves and stems first. Eventually, entire stems rot on the vine, turning black and slimy. There may also be patches of white spores on the leaf undersides. In the North, the pathogen overwinters in buried potato tubers. In the South, it easily survives the winter.

Prevention: The spores of this disease are fast spreading, moving on the wind for miles. If you live in the northern half of the continent, do not purchase potatoes or tomatoes that were grown in the South, as you may inadvertently introduce late blight spores to your garden. This is not a common pathogen, but if late blight is reported in your area, there is little you can do to prevent the disease because the spores spread so rapidly. Plant only locally grown plants to help keep the pathogen out of your area.

Control: Once late blight strikes, there is little you can do. Tear out the plants, put them in a garbage bag, and throw them out to keep the disease from spreading. Organic fungicides based on *Bacillus subtilis* are somewhat effective in preventing this disease.

Some varieties of bee balm are more susceptible to powdery mildew than others. Always choose resistant varieties whenever possible.

There are many plants affected by different rust organisms. The species that affects daylilies isn't as destructive as those that infect edible crops, such as grains, coffee, and apples.

Powdery Mildew (many species)

Susceptible Plants: Many common plants are prone to powdery mildew infections, including lilacs, phlox, bee balm, cucumbers, grapes, squash, and melons.

Identification: Powdery mildew infections are caused by several different species of fungal organisms. Because these fungi live on the leaf surface, powdery mildew is largely an aesthetic issue. Signs of a powdery mildew infection appear as powdery white spots on the leaves and stems, most often on the lower leaves first, that make the plant look as if it were dusted with talcum powder.

Prevention: Aside from choosing resistant varieties, keep the leaves as dry as possible when watering plants and space plants properly to allow for adequate air circulation. Powdery mildew is mostly an aesthetic issue, so there's no need to go to extreme measures to save an infected plant.

Control: Organic fungicides based on *Bacillus subtilis*, Neem oil, and bicarbonates help keep powdery mildew in check.

Rusts (many species)

Susceptible Plants: Most rust diseases are plant specific, meaning they only affect a single species, or related group, of plants. Though rusts attack many agricultural crops, including soybeans, grains, cotton, and coffee, there are also many susceptible ornamental plants, including daylilies, geraniums, hollyhocks, roses, mums, and asters. Certain tree species often fall victim to rusts as well, including apples, pines, hemlocks, and birches. Some rusts also affect turfgrass, though they seldom cause significant damage.

Identification: This group of fungal plant pathogens are among the most destructive, affecting a broad range of plants. Thankfully, the rusts most commonly encountered by home gardeners cause primarily aesthetic damage, rather than the economic damage caused by rusts that strike agricultural crops. Rusts are interesting fungi, as some of them require multiple hosts to survive, spending part of their life cycle on one species of plant and the rest of it on another. Most rusts cause rust-colored or orange pustules on the leaf undersides, stems, fruits, or needles of infected plants. They're quite distinctive in appearance and can cause leaf distortion and defoliation.

Prevention: Rust spores require moisture to infect host plants, making good air circulation essential. Also, choose resistant plant species whenever possible. Carefully remove and dispose of any rust-infected leaves or stems to prevent further spread of the spores. Clean up infected plant debris at the end of the gardening season.

Control: Though certain fungicides, such as Neem oil, bicarbonates, and *Bacillus subtilis*, are useful as preventatives, they often aren't necessary for ornamental plants where the damage is primarily aesthetic.

Septoria Leaf Spot (*Septoria lycopersici*)

Susceptible Plants: Tomatoes and ground cherries (*Physalis pruinosa* and *P. peruviana*). Another species of septoria leaf spot attacks 'Goldsturm' rudbeckia.

Identification: Appearing as tiny, round splotches on the leaves, this fungal disease typically starts on the lowest leaves first. The spots have dark-brown edges and lighter centers and there are usually many spots on each leaf. Infected leaves eventually turn yellow and then brown and fall off.

Prevention: Remove diseased plants at the end of the season to prevent the spores from overwintering in the garden. Cut off and destroy infected leaves as soon as you spot them and disinfect pruning equipment before moving to another plant.

Control: Organic fungicides based on copper or *Bacillus subtilis* are effective against septoria leaf spot, especially when used as a preventative measure.

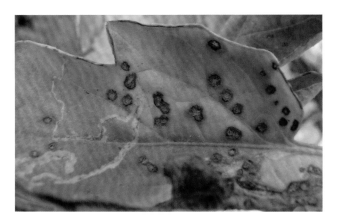

Southern Bacterial Wilt (*Ralstonia solanacearum*)

Susceptible Plants: This bacterial pathogen affects a huge number of plants, including almost 200 different species. Susceptible plants include geraniums, impatiens, mums, zinnias, tomatoes, salvias, petunias, eggplants, verbenas, and many other bedding and vegetable plants.

Identification: Unfortunately, once present, Southern bacterial wilt spreads like wildfire. It's soil borne but the pathogen can travel by soil, water, plant debris, and even on clothes, tools, and skin. It's naturally found in tropical

LEFT: Septoria leaf spot creates tiny, round splotches on the leaves, typically starting with the lowest leaves first. It's mostly an aesthetic issue.

BELOW: Southern bacterial wilt is an incredibly destructive bacterial pathogen. It affects a wide range of plants, and once present, it's tough to get rid of because it can survive for long periods in the soil and on plant debris.

The soilborne pathogen responsible for verticillium wilt blocks the transport of water and nutrients within an infected plant. Often, symptoms progress slowly until the entire plant yellows and withers.

11

regions and greenhouses but it can arrive in the garden via infected plants that were purchased from other areas. Initial symptoms include the wilting of just a few leaves on a plant, while the rest of the foliage appears healthy. Over time, more and more leaves wilt and turn yellow until all the leaves succumb, though the stem remains upright. Slimy ooze threads out of the cut stems, and when they're placed in water, milky streams of bacteria ooze out of the cut.

Prevention: Bacterial wilt is soil borne and can survive for long periods in the soil on roots and plant debris. Like many other diseases, it favors high temperatures and high humidity. The best way to prevent this disease is to purchase and plant only locally grown plants or grow your own plants from seed.

Control: There is no cure for this disease. Once confirmed, infected plants must immediately be removed and discarded in the trash.

Verticillium Wilt (*Verticillium* spp.)

Susceptible Plants: Hundreds of species of vegetables, herbs, flowers, and woody trees and shrubs can be affected by verticillium wilt.

Identification: This fungal disease is caused by several soilborne pathogens. When present in a plant, they block the vascular tissue in the plant and cause the leaves and stems to wilt. Symptoms progress slowly, often one stem at a time. Eventually, the entire plant yellows and withers. To confirm diagnosis, cut through the main stem of the plant and look for dark-brown discoloration inside. Verticillium wilt is most problematic in late summer.

Prevention: Verticillium fungi can survive for many years in the soil and on plants. They thrive in slightly cooler summer temperatures (between 70 and 80°F). Plant only resistant plant varieties.

Control: Once verticillium wilt occurs, there's little you can do to control the current year's infection. Instead, focus on preventing the pathogen in future years. Soil solarization will help kill the fungal spores in the top few inches of soil (see Chapter 9 for more on this technique). Practice crop rotation and do not plant other members of the same plant family in that same planting area for at least four years after the infection.

CHAPTER 12
PROPAGATING

By Dr. Jacqueline A. Soule

PLANT PROPAGATION IS A FANCY WAY TO SAY "making more plants." Plants do this all the time, entirely unaided by humans. They have an astonishing assortment of ways to make more of themselves, including through seeds, stolons, bulbs, rhizomes, offsets, divisions, and more. As gardeners, we take advantage of the fact that the genes of every living thing demand reproduction and an increase in population.

Plants make more of themselves in two major ways—sexually and asexually.

Sexual propagation of plants happens with flowers. There are a number of precise botanical terms but it boils down to male pollen carried by animals, such as bees, or blown by wind to the female ovules. When the pollen fertilizes the ovule, sexual reproduction occurs and the plant turns the ovule into a seed with the newly shared genes.

Asexual propagation happens when plants make more of themselves without sharing their genes with another plant. Also called vegetative propagation, there are a variety of methods by which the parent plant can create genetic clones of itself.

As gardeners, we don't have to rely only on nature's process to propagate plants. There are many ways we can do this using seeds, cuttings, and other processes.

OPPOSITE: Melons are among the plants that sprout easily when sown directly into garden soil.

SEED PROPAGATION

In nature, plants make seeds to help spread their genes. These seeds are spread generally by physical forces, such as wind, water, and gravity. Many plants depend on animals to disperse their seed.

Seeds dispersed by animals typically have hooks or sticky seed coats that cling to fur or feathers. These are mostly from plants considered either wildflowers or weeds. Seeds may also be carried internally in animals, such as the seeds of raspberry or mesquite that are eaten and then eliminated in a new location. Because large seeds such as nuts do not survive being eaten, the plants from them reproduce when animals forget where they've stashed some of the nuts.

Some seeds require soaking on a damp paper towel to dissolve the germination-inhibiting chemicals that are naturally present in the seed coat.

Seed Treatment

Seeds of some plants require scarification—a treatment of the seed coat—to germinate. Think of the seed coat as something the mama plant wraps her seed child in to

ABOVE: Some plants are treasured for their showy seedpods, which are more decorative than their flowers.

OPPOSITE: Many specialty gardens are a combination of perennials propagated by root division and colorful annuals propagated by planting new or gathered seeds each year.

protect it before sending it out in the world. The coat is constructed to help ensure that the seed germinates under ideal survival conditions months or sometimes years later. Gardeners planting seeds often want to speed the scarification process by weakening, opening, or otherwise altering the coat of a seed. Scarification is done mechanically, thermally, or chemically.

Mechanical scarification. Several both desert- and stream-dwelling species use this method. The tough seed coats are naturally tumbled along in (flash) floods, grinding against sand and gravel. For home gardening, you can rub the tough seed on sandpaper.

Thermal scarification. This occurs with temperate plants when seeds require either the cold of winter or the heat of a fire before germination. To germinate seeds of temperate plants at home, you may have to keep the seeds in the refrigerator, or even a freezer, for a set amount of time prior to germination.

Chemical scarification. It sounds daunting until you realize the chemical is generally good old H_2O—in other words, water. Water is needed to dissolve the germination-retarding chemicals that are naturally in the seed coat. At home, this is done by folding seeds inside a damp paper towel and soaking them overnight. In nature, chemical scarification occurs when seeds are eaten and passed through the intestinal tract of animals.

How to Save Seed

It's easy to save the seeds of annuals, wildflowers, vegetables, and herbs. The key is to collect the seed just as it matures and before it starts to drop or once the fleshy fruit is fully ripe. You especially want to keep an eye on pods that dry and shatter open to disperse seed.

Gathering Seeds

Stalks of shattering pods. Snip off the stalks and invert them into large paper bags. Fold the bags shut. Now when seedpods shatter, the seeds are trapped in the bag for next year's sowing. Arugula, radish, and columbine are best treated this way.

Seedheads. Often these seedheads simply break off in your hand. Hold a container beneath them as you break them off. Some seed is most easily harvested on the spot by shaking the flower stalks over an old bed sheet. The corners of the sheet can be held up to transfer the seed into an appropriate container. Carrot, sunflower, and penstemon can be treated this way.

Seeds in fleshy fruit. Spread the seed on a sheet of absorbent paper, such as a paper towel or blotting paper. Leave the paper open and allow the paper to dry fully before folding it up for storage. Tomato, strawberry, and persimmon are best treated this way.

Caring for Seeds

Drying. Seed should only be stored when it's entirely dry. If they were in pods, once they are out, dry them further. Place them in a single layer deep in a paper bag, in a terracotta saucer, or (if they are large enough) on window screen. This helps them dry without fungus growing on them.

Exception: Seeds should only be dried if they are typically dried in nature. For example, oak seeds (acorns) will die if allowed to dry out. Most tropical plant seeds, such as avocado or citrus, will not germinate if allowed to fully dry out.

Cleaning. For future sowing, you don't need to clean the seed, although purists prefer to. For seed you will use as a herb (such as coriander or dill seed), you do need to clean the seed. Kitchen colanders and strainers can be used to allow the chaff to fall through and the seed remain behind.

Storing. Store seeds in glass jars or envelopes, making sure to label each accurately, including the date. Seed ages and eventually becomes nonviable. Some seed will be able to germinate decades (or even centuries) later, while some will only last two or three years.

Store your saved seed so that pests, such as flour moths or carpet beetles, can't infest it. Place them in envelopes or glass jars (use glass jars with tight-fitting lids for herb seeds). To help repel pests, place small pieces of untreated cedar in the seed jars or near any envelopes with seeds.

ASEXUAL PROPAGATION

Many species of plants readily propagate themselves through asexual or vegetative propagation. Growers take advantage of this to produce numerous plants for sale in a short amount of time. People also use methods that plants do not use, such as grafting (more on that later).

Plants have meristem cells (read more about them in Chapter 6) located throughout them. Think of meristem as "bud" tissue that can grow into whatever the plants need to survive—roots, stems, leaves, flowers, scar tissue, or entire new plants. We take advantage of meristems when we propagate plants, growing roots and shoots where there were none before—and ultimately entirely new plants.

There are eight main techniques for vegetative propagation you can use: using storage organs, dividing crowns, using offsets, using stolons, taking cuttings, ground layering, air layering, and grafting.

OPPOSITE: Many succulents produce "baby" offshoots that are easily propagated simply by severing them from the parent plant and transferring them to new pots or garden locations.

With good growing conditions, bulbs propagate (multiply) and must be divided so that the patch remains healthy and blooms better.

Storage Organs

A number of plants wait out times of adversity with underground storage organs. They may wait out icy-cold winters if they are daffodils or they may wait out drought in their native lands if they are cyclamen or ginger. When times are right, they sprout and grow, storing energy for the next time of adversity. If they have an extra good growth season, they make more energy than they can store in one storage organ, so they propagate and make some more storage organs.

Humans will water and fertilize plants to ensure they grow well and then, in the case of potatoes, onions, and the like, we harvest and eat these extra storage devices. In the case of tulips, gladiolus, and other garden flowers, growers divide the clumps and sell them for our gardens. The storage organs are grouped into bulbs, corms, rhizomes, and tubers.

Bulbs and Corms

Bulbs (such as tulips and daffodils) and corms (such as crocuses and freesia) are somewhat globe-like storage structures with a flattened base where the roots emerge and a pointy tip on the opposite end where shoots emerge. Over time, a clump of bulbs or corms will become crowded and flower less and less due to the crowded conditions. If this happens, they have propagated prolifically, and now it's time for you to divide your plants, generally every two to four years.

To divide bulbs and corms, wait until flowering is done for the year. If you are going to move the divisions to a new place in your garden, you can work when the leaves are still green; otherwise, wait until all greenery has died back for the year. When you dig up your plants, you will find that each bulb has two or three smaller bulbs attached, perhaps held next to the parent with papery scales. These young bulbs need to be gently snapped off. Young corms will be attached beneath the globe, along the ring of root tissue, sometimes tipped and growing sideways. Gently snap them off the parent. These are now ready for planting in a new area, storage, or trading and sharing with friends and neighbors. Plant with the pointy end up.

BELOW: Potatoes are tubers that can be cut into sections, allowed to dry for a day or two to form calluses, and then planted. Be sure each section planted has at least one bud.

BOTTOM: Rhizomes grow horizontally in the soil, sending up leaves in several different areas at once. Each of these growing green shoots with their fleshy rhizome can be cut off and planted.

Rhizomes

Rhizomes are storage stems found in a number of plants, including iris, canna, and ginger. They're not planted pointy end up. Instead they are laid in the soil with the storage stem placed horizontally. The plant grows this stem tissue horizontally through the soil, reaching for newer fertile areas in all directions and sending leafy shoots skyward every so often. Over time, the rearward portion of the stem dies, leaving a bald patch in the garden.

With growth, the rhizomes become large with many branches or "fingers." They will flower less prolifically if the clump is overly crowded. Like with bulbs and corms, you will need to divide them every two to four years. Divide the rhizome after flowering is done for the year. Dig it up and snap or cut off the fingers at the narrow necks. Avoid cutting through wide areas of the rhizome, as you can over-divide the plant and kill it. Ideally, dry the divided rhizomes in a shady place for a few days before replanting. This allows the plant time to form callus (scar) tissue over the wound, which helps prevent rot.

Tubers

Tubers are storage stems. They include potatoes, dahlias, daylilies, oxalis, and many other plants. Like rhizomes, many tubers can be cut into smaller sections and planted when you wish to propagate the plant. With the common potato, a piece of stem with two or three buds (called "eyes") can easily grow an entire new plant with many more tubers attached.

12

Many tubers are not so forgiving when divided. Ornamental plants, such as dahlias and some daylilies, have tubers that must be carefully taken from the parent tuber at the narrowest spot with minimal wounding. Tropical tubers, including sweet potatoes (in the morning glory family) and true yams (Dioscorea family), tend to rot if cut, so instead they are encouraged to produce "slips," rooted sprouts growing out of the tuber, which are slipped off and planted.

Crown Division

Crown division is a propagation term that indicates we are doing a little more than simply dividing storage organs. The crown is where the roots meet the shoots. Plants that grow in dense clumps need occasional crown division because the center can get cramped and may start to die in the middle. Crown division removes any dead parts of the plant and offers the plant a chance to spread out and grow healthier foliage and roots. Crown division is typically done for herbaceous perennial plants, such as hostas, liriope, ornamental grass, perennial poppies, sedges, and Shasta daisies.

The timing for doing crown division depends mostly on where you live. In climates with hot summers and mild winters, divide in autumn. In climates with icy winters, divide in spring. If you live somewhere in between, do crown division in the growing season that occurs after flowering is done.

To do crown division, dig up the plant by digging all the way around the plant clump at the drip line. This ensures that you will get as many of the nutrient-providing roots as possible. Also dig well under the plant. Use two shovels or garden forks to lift it out of the soil.

Rinse the soil off the roots and carefully pull apart the plant with your hands, if possible. If you can't do that (some plants, such as ornamental grasses, are too tough to pull apart by hand), then cut apart the clump with a sharp straight spade, axe, or machete. Each divided section of the plant must have at least one bud for the plant to grow new foliage.

You can then plant each section.

Offsets

Offsets are essentially clones of a main plant that are connected to the main plant by a runner called a stolon. A number of plants produce offsets, including agaves, aloes, artichokes, bromeliads, and on through the alphabet. Onion family members typically produce offsets called "bulbils."

In nature, storms or the feet of passing animals may break off the offsets and help distribute them to a new location. Thus, in theory at least, you could simply break the "daughter" offsets off the mother plant and scatter them around the garden. Yet in nature, many such scattered offsets fail. So, if you want to propagate plants with offsets, you need to pot them. Take the offsets off the parent with a clean, sharp blade (pruners or a knife). Lightly dust the open wound with rooting hormone and place the offset in rooting media or potting soil. Keep moist but not waterlogged until the offset has produced roots and can be planted in the garden.

ABOVE: Offsets are easily propagated because their role in nature is to break off from the parent plant and find a new home.

OPPOSITE: Plants that grow in dense clumps, such as ornamental grasses, require periodic crown division where the roots meet the shoots.

Propagating **219**

Rooting Media

Some plants root well in water, but others will drown, so some type of rooting media is needed. These are the most common ones used alone or in combination:

Peat moss is the remains of marsh or bog vegetation that has been preserved underwater in a partially decomposed state. It has been used by gardeners for years but is no longer considered "green" due to the slow rate at which peat bogs regenerate. Sphagnum peat moss is recommended for rooting because it holds moisture well, has ample air space, and tends to discourage fungal growth.

Coir fibers come from coconut hulls and are increasingly available and generally replacing peat moss. Coir retains water and nutrients without becoming waterlogged. It is considered rot-resistant, and is a byproduct of the coconut oil industry.

Vermiculite is a sterile, lightweight medium produced by heating a type of clay to 2,000°F. Vermiculite is available in four particle sizes. Use the larger-sized particles because they provide better aeration.

Perlite is produced from a type of volcanic rock that is crushed, screened, and then heated to approximately 1,400°F. The result is a very lightweight, porous material. Its principal value in propagation mixtures is aeration. It does not hold water and nutrients as well as vermiculite.

Sand is small, weathered rock particles. It is heavy and has no nutrient value. Sand occurs in different grades; sharp builders sand is best for propagation. Fine sands, such as pool filter sand, are not recommended. Pour boiling water over sand to sterilize it before you use it—builders sand may contain pathogens and weed seeds.

Milled bark, particularly pine bark, is a renewable byproduct of the lumber industry. It is often used as a rooting medium. Milled pine bark is lightweight and holds nutrients well while providing excellent drainage and aeration.

A blend of sand and perlite makes an excellent rooting mixture for succulents because the sand helps hold the cuttings upright while the perlite ensures drainage and aeration.

When stolon tips sense adequate light, they will produce an offset rather than more stem tissue.

Tip for Success: Less Is More with Rooting Hormone

Rooting hormone powder stimulates root growth, but use it with care. Too much of it can cause a plant *not* to root! If you use rooting hormone when propagating plants, a light dusting of the powder will do.

Although the cost of rooting hormone may seem high, it is worth it. Because a little bit goes a long way, a single jar often lasts for years.

Stolons

Stolons are stem tissue that can be underground or aboveground. We just learned that they produce offsets. Strawberries have aboveground stolons, while many lawn grasses have underground stolons. Plants send stolons off seeking an area of adequate sunlight in which to start an offset. Science shows us that the meristem cells at the tip of the stolon can sense the amount of light received and will start to form an offset when the light is sufficient. Generally, this is when they are out of the shadow of the parent plant.

If the stolon has not produced an offset for you to propagate, it is easy to stimulate the plant to make some. Simply expose the tips of the stolons to light by trimming a few leaves off the parent plant, or move soil to expose underground stolons.

A number of trees have roots that function much like stolons: aspens, apples, jujubes, willows, and many others will grow sprouts off the root if there is sufficient light seeping through the soil. This is most annoying if you are trying to maintain a lawn, but it's a great way to dig up a rooted fruit tree. Note that if your fruit tree is a grafted one, the new tree is from the root stock and you might not wish to use it. (More on this topic later in this chapter.)

12

ABOVE: Cuttings of most garden plants are best taken while they are actively growing, not flowering and not dormant.

BOTTOM LEFT: Remove leaves from three to five nodes.

BOTTOM CENTER: A light dusting of rooting hormone stimulates the production of roots in stem tissue.

BOTTOM RIGHT: Cuttings being rooted need filtered light, not direct sunlight.

Cuttings

You can also propagate plants by taking cuttings of different parts. What portion of the plant you will be propagating from depends on the species. Stem cuttings are the most common but there are also root, leaf, and cane cuttings. You may have seen it done. Prune a piece of pathos (a common houseplant) and plunk it in a jar of water. This works for a number of species, especially many houseplants, but jars of water are a disaster for succulents and woody perennials, resulting in a stinky rotten mess.

For cuttings in general, choose a cool, non-windy day to take them, to avoid excessive drying, and take them from plants that are not in bloom or producing fruit. Use a clean, sharp, cutting tool and clean it with a rag dipped in alcohol when you go from one plant to the next. You can take many cuttings at once; carry them with you in a box or dry bucket and avoid bruising tissues if you can.

Once the cuttings are taken, remove the leaves from the three to five lowermost nodes. If immersed in rooting media, those lower leaves will rot and you don't want that in your little plant nursery! The nodes you expose to the potting media have the meristem that will form roots. After the leaves are removed, lightly powder the cut area with rooting hormone, and then place the cuttings in rooting media. Keep moist but not soaking wet for two to six weeks for most species.

Types of Cuttings

Softwood, or green tip cuttings, are cuttings of the stem that are placed directly into rooting media. This is the most common form of cutting, and is often used for the propagation of herbs and perennial flowers, lightly woody shrubs, such as autumn sages or lilacs, and many houseplants. Softwood cuttings are best taken in the spring in areas of cold winters and in the fall in areas of mild winters.

Hardwood cuttings are generally used in commercial propagation of deciduous shrubs and trees, including currants, gooseberries, grapes, and willows. Hardwood cuttings are most commonly taken during the cold winter months, when the plant is dormant.

Cane cuttings are stem cuttings of plants that form canes, such as bamboo, sanseveria, and many tropical houseplants.

Leaf cuttings and petiole cuttings are made from the leaves of plants that are succulent or fleshy, especially those from tropical regions, such as rex begonias, sanseveria, and African violets.

How to Take Cuttings of Succulents

Many species of succulents can be propagated from stem cuttings. Simply use a clean, sharp knife or pair of clippers. If your plants are in humid conditions where rot is a factor, be sure to sterilize your tools.

To propagate succulents, including most members of the euphorbia and cactus families, lay stem cuttings on a screen or set them upright in a dry container for a week or so, until you can see the thickened callus over the cut area. Place them in a well-drained rooting media, such as perlite, vermiculite, or sand. Peat moss and coir retain too much moisture, and can lead to rot.

Many succulents, such as crassula, echeveria, kalanchoe, and sansevieria, can be grown from leaf cuttings. Remove the leaf and allow it to dry for a few days, and then place in rooting media with the stem end touching but not buried in the media. Christmas cactus should also be propagated this way, although the leaf-looking structure you are propagating is technically stem tissue.

Succulent plants need to form callus tissue to resist rotting during rooting. Although they may look callused after a day, let them sit for a week in a shaded area. They have stored water, so they can take it.

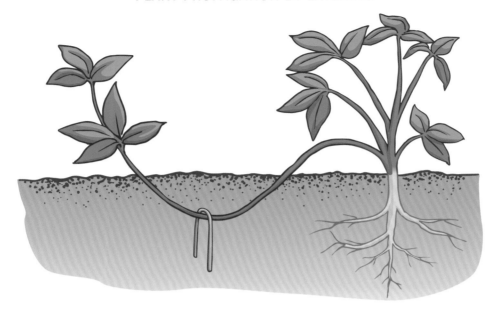

Ground layering induces stem tissue to grow roots where there were none before. This newly rooted plant can then be cut off the parent and planted elsewhere.

Root cuttings are used to propagate plants that naturally produce suckers from their roots, such as raspberries and many perennials, including marsh marigolds, Oriental poppies, and California tree poppies. In a sense, these are simply small divisions of the roots, approximately 2 to 4 inches long and ⅛ inch in diameter. The cuttings need to be stored in a cool area over winter to form calluses and then planted in spring in a horizontal position, about 2 inches deep, preferably in a loose, sandy soil.

Ground Layering

In many cases you can persuade a plant to grow roots on a stem or branch simply by allowing the stem to come in good contact with the ground. Ground layering has a high success rate because you are rooting first, *then* cutting, rather than cutting and then trying to induce rooting in traumatized tissue.

The simplest technique is to lay a stem or branch (still attached to the parent plant) on the ground and place a weight on it to hold it down. You can enhance the chance of rooting by lightly wounding the stem where the roots are to form. Enhance it further by placing the stem in a rooting media that provides aeration and a constant supply of moisture.

Simple layering is done by burying part of the stem, leaving 6 to 12 inches of stem above the soil. It can be done in early spring using a dormant branch or in late summer using some first-year wood. Periodically check for adequate moisture and for the formation of roots. It may take one or more seasons before the layer is rooted and ready for removal. Plants propagated by simple layering include autumn sages, azaleas, boxwoods, climbing roses, forsythias, honeysuckle, jujube, lonicera, perennial marigolds, plums, rhododendrons, rosemary, salvias, and wax myrtles.

Tip layering is almost the same as simple layering, but instead you bury the tip of the stem. Be sure it is a current season's shoot. The tip will curve upward to emerge from the soil and form roots at the tip you buried. Cut off the new layer at least two or three seasons later. Raspberries and blackberries are traditionally propagated this way.

Compound or serpentine layering is similar to simple layering, but you make more than one hole and bury the stem in multiple places. This method works well for plants producing vine-like growth, such as clematis, grapes, passionflowers, and wisteria. It is also an excellent way to propagate many species of groundcover.

Mound layering (or stool layering) takes a year and is useful with heavy-stemmed, closely branched shrubs. In the dormant season, cut the plant back to 1 to 3 inches above the soil surface. Dormant buds will produce new shoots in the spring. Mound soil over these new shoots several times as they grow. Roots will develop at the bases of the young shoots. You can cut and replant these layers in the following dormant season. Mound layering works well on cotoneasters, daphnes, magnolias, quince, spirea, and Texas ranger.

Air Layering

Air layering works well with plants that do not root well from cuttings or ground layering, including azaleas, camellias, figs, hollies, magnolias, and houseplants such as rubber trees. Be patient; it can take up to two years for the plant to grow roots.

You need a sharp knife, peat moss or coconut coir, plastic wrap, aluminum foil, thin sewing elastic or long rubber bands, and, optionally, rooting hormone.

Moisten your rooting media but don't wet it. Squeeze the media; it's good to use when no more excess water runs out. Select the branch you wish to propagate from and come down from the tip at least 12 inches. This distance ensures you are far enough from the leader producing its growth-inhibiting compounds.

Cut through the bark with two parallel cuts 1½ inches apart. Don't cut through the branch! Just cut deeply enough so the bark can be peeled off. At this point, lightly dust the exposed wood with rooting hormone. Next, wrap all the way around the wound with a 2-inch-thick layer of moist media. Be sure the media entirely covers the wounded area. Now cover this with plastic wrap to form an airtight pouch. This is easiest to do if you have placed the media in the plastic wrap first.

Secure the plastic wrap to the branch with the elastic. Elastic holds the rooting media firmly in place yet allows the plant to grow. If you don't have an extra pair of hands to help, you can use twist ties to hold the plastic wrap in place while you tie on the elastic. Roots grow best in the dark, so cover the plastic wrap with aluminum foil. The foil also reflects sunlight and keeps the rooting area from getting too hot.

This method takes lots of time. Every so often, remove the aluminum foil to see if roots have grown to the edge of the plastic. Once you have ample roots, you can cut this rooted plant off the mother plant and plant your new plant.

Air layering takes patience but it may be the only way to share plants that don't propagate well by other means, such as azaleas, camellias, or citrus.

CHAPTER 13
HARVESTING EDIBLES

By Charlie Nardozzi

SUPPOSE YOU'VE WORKED HARD IN YOUR VEGETABLE, herb, and fruit garden. You planted, weeded, watered, and fertilized your plants and crops. Now it's payoff time. Proper harvesting is often a technique gardeners overlook because they're so focused on the growing part of the equation, but the timing and way you harvest is important too.

Harvesting your vegetables, herbs, and fruits at the right time means you'll be picking them when they have the highest nutritional content. Plus, timing your harvest so you're ready to either cook, eat, or process your produce will ensure the nutrients won't be lost.

But mostly, we want to harvest at the right time to get the best flavor. If you harvest some fruits too early, they won't be at their peak sweetness and flavor. If you pick some vegetables too late, they might be tough and chewy. Timing is everything. In this chapter, I'll help you determine the best time to harvest and the best way to do it for more than 50 common vegetables, herbs, and fruits. So, let's get picking!

OPPOSITE: Harvesting your produce at the right time will make your basket full of fresh produce taste as good as it looks.

HARVESTING VEGETABLES

One of the keys to harvesting is remembering that many vegetables taste great when harvested on the young side. I'm always encouraging gardeners to pick early and often in their vegetable patch. Vegetables such as zucchini, summer squash, cucumbers, beans, beets, and carrots are best when picked young. Their texture is more tender and their flavor mild and inviting. I'll often harvest zucchini and summer squash with their flowers still attached, carrots once they color up but before they get woody, and beets when they're the size of a small chicken egg.

Another reason to harvest veggies on the young side is that picking will stimulate the plant to produce more fruits. A vegetable plant's mission in life is to reproduce and make mature seeds. If you keep harvesting vegetables, such as zucchini, summer squash, cucumbers, peas, and beans, before they fully mature their seeds, the plants

Harvest zucchini fruits small, even with the flower still attached, for the most tender texture and best flavor. Cut at the stem, don't twist.

Pick bush beans when the leaves are dry. Harvest before the bean seeds inside the pods start to swell.

will continue to grow more fruits. So, by picking when the fruits are small, you'll stimulate more fruiting throughout the season.

Some vegetables do taste best when allowed to mature to their full ripeness. Sweet peppers taste okay when green, but they're sweet and delicious when matured to red, orange, yellow, or whatever the ultimate color is for that variety. Sweet corn, cantaloupe, and watermelon taste bland when harvested too early.

Some vegetables will continue maturing after you harvest them. If tomatoes, pumpkins, and winter squash are harvested once they're fully grown, they will continue to turn color and mature to a sweet flavor provided you bring them into a warm, dry location. That's great for gardeners growing veggies in a short-season, cold-climate area.

The best time of day to pick is usually the morning (especially for herbs) when the weather is cool. This is when the flavor is at its peak. Avoid harvesting vegetables that wilt easily, such as lettuce, during the heat of the day. Also, avoid harvesting beans when the foliage is wet so you don't spread disease. When harvesting root crops, such as carrots, beets, and parsnips, moisten the soil—if it's not wet already—to make it easier to pull your roots from the ground without breaking them.

Finally, when harvesting vegetables for storage, pick at the right time for peak flavor and process the vegetables quickly, either freezing, canning, or drying them for storage. For many vegetables, the longer the harvested produce hangs around, the fewer nutrients and flavor it will have when processed.

When and How to Harvest Vegetables

Here are 30 of the most popular vegetables, with detailed information on when and how to harvest them for best flavor. Of course, use this information as a guide and don't be shy about taste-testing produce in the garden to see if it's ready to eat. (I often taste-test so many of our peas that there aren't many left for the kitchen table.) Also, check the variety you're growing. Some varieties, such as some kohlrabi, are meant to be harvested when large, so you should have an idea what to expect before you pick. Bring a sharp knife, a basket, and bags into the garden to gather your produce.

VEGETABLE	WHEN AND HOW TO HARVEST
Asparagus	With your hands, snap off spears at ground level with when they're 6 to 9 inches long and at least the diameter of a pencil. Start harvesting when plants are 3 years old. Harvest for 3 to 6 weeks each spring as long as the spears are still thick in diameter
Beans (snap)	Start hand harvesting 2 to 3 weeks after blooming before the bean seeds form in the pods. To avoid spreading disease, don't harvest when the leaves are wet.
Beets	Pull when the beet roots are 1 to 3 inches wide. Don't forget to harvest and eat the beet greens as well.
Broccoli	With a knife, cut the flower heads when they're still tight and compact, before the yellow flowers begins to open. Once the flowers open, the flavor turns bitter. Continue harvesting side shoots all summer.
Brussels sprouts	Snap sprouts off the stem by hand or cut them off with a knife when the sprouts are 1 inch in diameter.

In spring, snap off asparagus spears that are wider than a pencil in diameter.

Harvest side shoots of broccoli by removing the whole shoot. This will encourage other large side shoots to keep growing.

VEGETABLE	WHEN AND HOW TO HARVEST
Cabbage	Cut the head at the soil line with a knife when the heads are firm when squeezed.
Cantaloupe	Lift with your hands and harvest when the fruit slips off the vine easily. Sniff for a sweet smell on the blossom end as well.
Carrots	Pull when the tops of the roots are 1 inch wide and have colored up.
Cauliflower	Cut with a knife below the head when the head is white or the mature color but before the florets in the head turn rice-like.
Corn (sweet)	Pull off the stalk by hand when the silks are brown and dry. Check the kernels in the corn ear tip to see if they're mature. The kernels should be milky and still plump when you pierce one with your fingernail.
Cucumbers	Cut with a knife when slicing types are 6 inches long and pickling types are 2 to 3 inches long.
Eggplants	Cut with a knife any time the skin color turns glossy but before the skin is dull. Use gloves when harvesting because eggplant can have thorns on the stems.
Kohlrabi	Harvest the whole plant by hand when the kohlrabi is 2 to 3 inches wide.

When harvesting corn, look for the brown, dried silks on corn ears and check for firmness when you squeeze the ear.

Harvest carrots any time after they form edible roots. Brush off the soil around the carrot top base to see the width of the roots.

Harvest cabbage heads once they are firm when squeezed.

VEGETABLE	WHEN AND HOW TO HARVEST
Lettuce and greens	Harvest any time enough leaves form for a meal and are still tender. Harvest individual leaves by hand or with scissors or let the head mature and cut it with a knife at the soil line.
Onions	Pull onions for storage when one-third of the tops have naturally fallen over and the necks near the bulb are dry. Pull onions for fresh eating any time after the bulbs form.
Parsnips	Pull once the roots form. For the sweetest flavor, wait to harvest until after a few fall frosts or even until late winter.
Peanut	Pull the entire plant once the leaves turn yellow but before a frost. Hand pick the peanuts off the roots.
Peas	Handpick when the pods are tender and before the seeds inside the pod mature. Harvest flat-podded snow peas any time after the pods have formed.
Peppers	Harvest peppers once they reach full size for that variety. Let them grow to their mature color for the sweetest flavor. Harvest with a pruner or knife so you don't damage the plant.
Potatoes	Dig with a shovel or iron fork once the vines die back. Harvest new potatoes when the plant flowers by carefully hand digging around the base of the plant and stealing a few young tubers.
Pumpkins	Cut with a knife once the shell has hardened, there are signs of a color change, and before a frost. Pumpkins will continue to ripen and change color after harvest. Leave a 6-inch-long piece of the stem on the fruit when harvesting so they will last longer in storage.

Harvest potatoes once the tops have died back. Dig carefully so you don't damage the tubers. Eat any damaged tubers first because they won't store well.

Pumpkins can be harvested when they first begin to change color; their color will continue to deepen after picking.

VEGETABLE	WHEN AND HOW TO HARVEST
Radishes	Pull whenever roots are up to 1 inch wide.
Rutabagas	Pull whenever roots reach 3 to 5 inches in diameter.
Spinach	Handpick individual leaves once they form and are tender or harvest whole heads with a knife, cutting it at the soil line.
Squash (summer/ zucchini)	Cut with a knife when 6 to 8 inches long.
Squash (winter)	Cut with a knife once the shell has hardened and the fruit reaches the mature color for that type. Leave a 6-inch-long piece of the stem attached to the fruit when harvesting so they last longer in storage
Sweet potatoes	Dig with a shovel or iron fork once they're big enough for a meal but before a frost.
Tomatoes	Handpick when fully colored for that variety. Tomatoes will continue to color up and mature after harvest if placed in a warm, dry place out of direct sunlight.
Turnips	Pull when the roots are 2 to 4 inches in diameter.
Watermelon	Cut with a knife when the tendril closest to the fruit browns and dries, when the belly turns yellow, and when you hear a dull sound when you thump the fruit.

Pick tomatoes when they have achieved the proper color for their variety.

Watermelons will tell you when they're ripe—thumping the rind will produce a dull sound.

HARVESTING HERBS

What would a vegetable garden be without some fresh herbs? Herbs give your tomato sauce a rich flavor, balance the zing in your salsa, and add zip to your pickles. If you're into cooking and exploring recipes with your fresh veggies, you have to grow herbs too.

Not only are herbs essential to cooking and eating, but they're also beautiful and useful plants in the landscape. Some herbs, such as thyme and mint, can spread as groundcovers in your garden. Many herbs flower, attracting bees and beneficial insects to your yard. And herbs can be used fresh, dried, frozen, or canned to add a taste of your garden to winter cooking.

Knowing the type of herb you're growing is important in knowing when to harvest it. Herbs can be annuals (basil), biennials (parsley), or perennials (mint). Annual herbs should be stripped clean of leaves by the fall because they will die anyway. Biennial herbs can be moved indoors so you can enjoy them in early winter before they send up a flower stalk and die in the spring. Perennial herbs come back every year. They should, for the most part, be harvested up until one month before a frost so they can go dormant for winter.

Herbs are grown for their leaves, flowers, or stems. Knowing which you'll use will help you in harvesting. When harvesting leaves, never remove more than one-third of them at any one time so you don't shock the plant. Snip stems with a knife or hand pruner so you don't harm the plant. Harvest seeds as they mature by shaking the mature seedhead over a bag.

Like vegetables, herbs have the best flavor when harvested in the cool of the morning, preferably on a sunny day after the dew has dried. Their essential oil content is highest then and the oils haven't started to evaporate, which they do in the heat of the day. Harvest leaves and stems before the herb starts to flower. That's when they also have the highest oil content.

ABOVE: Harvest leaves of parsley whenever you need some.

OPPOSITE: Cut off basil stems when harvesting to encourage more growth of stems and leaves.

When and How to Harvest Herbs

Harvest herbs as needed for cooking or to process and have for winter use. Bring a sharp knife, hand pruner, bags, and basket into the garden. Harvested leaves dry out quickly, so place them in plastic bags as you harvest. If harvesting for drying, wash the stems and let them dry in a well-ventilated room out of direct sunlight; once dry, store them in glass jars. If harvesting for freezing, wash the stem or leaves, pat them dry, and place in freezer bags. You might even consider processing herbs into vinegars, pestos, and oils for future use.

Here's how and when to harvest 13 of the most popular culinary herbs for the best flavor.

HERB	WHEN AND HOW TO HARVEST
Basil	Once the flower buds form, but before they open, pick individual leaves or whole stems (for processing big batches). Snip off any remaining flowers to encourage more leaf growth.
Chives	With scissors, cut chive leaves as needed 6 weeks after planting or in early spring as this perennial starts to grow. Cut the plant back multiple times during the summer to encourage fresh, young chive leaves to form.
Cilantro/coriander	Before the plant flowers, use scissors to harvest young plants to 2 inches above the soil line for the leaves. For coriander, let the plant flower and set seeds. Collect seeds before they drop off the plant.
Dill	Pinch off leaves 8 weeks after planting for fresh use. For dill seeds, let the plant flower and set seeds, collecting them before they drop to the ground.
Lavender	Harvest stems for cooking before the flower buds open. With a pruner, cut whole stems and use fresh, or dry them in an airy place. For flowers, wait until the blooms open to cut stems.

After dill flowers have died but before the seeds turn brown, place a paper bag over the head to catch the maturing seeds.

Cut lavender flowers in the morning, when the fragrant oils are highest in the plant.

HERB	WHEN AND HOW TO HARVEST
Lemon balm	With a knife or scissors, harvest individual leaves for tea or whole stems for cooking or drying. Harvest once this perennial plant starts growing in spring but before blossoms open, or after seedlings get established from a spring planting.
Mint	Handpick leaves and whole stems as needed throughout the growing season.
Oregano	Pinch individual leaves or short stems as needed for fresh use before flowers form (usually 6 weeks after planting).
Parsley	Handpick outer leaves as you need them. For drying or freezing, cut the whole plant to the ground in early summer. It will regrow later this season.
Rosemary	With a pruner or scissors, harvest 6- to 8-inch-long stems 6 weeks after planting, or on mature plants, for best flavor, any time before flowering.
Sage	Handpick leaves any time once the plant is established, or on mature plants. Don't harvest more than one-half of this perennial plant the first year to encourage it to get established.
Tarragon	Using scissors, harvest fresh shoots of French tarragon in early summer for best flavor, before the shoots get woody. Tarragon can lose some of its flavor if dried.
Thyme	With scissors, harvest leaves or sprigs of this perennial herb all summer. The younger sprigs have the best flavor, especially when harvested before flowering.

Harvest cilantro leaves when young for greens or let it flower and set seed. The brown seed is called coriander.

With a pruner, cut off fragrant, young thyme stems for cooking. Harvesting also encourages growth of more stems.

13

HARVESTING FRUITS

Fruits and berries are rewarding shrubs and trees to grow in your yard, if you have the room. Luckily, newer varieties of many of our favorite fruits and berries have been created that are dwarf and they fit not only in the yard but in containers too.

The key to harvesting fruits and berries at the right time is knowing your varieties. For example, some blueberries will ripen early in the season while others wait until late summer to mature. By knowing roughly when your fruits should be maturing, you'll be ready to jump on the harvest. Check with the local extension service in your state to get guidance on when certain types of fruits are expected to ripen in your area.

Most home gardeners will grow just a few berries and fruits in their yard. The best way to know when the fruits are at peak sweetness is to do a smell and taste test. You can almost smell the sweetness of some fruits, such as peaches and strawberries. You can also look at the fruit's skin color change. Some are obvious, such as strawberries, raspberries, and blackberries. When they are the desired color, start eating. Other fruits, though, can be tricky: blueberries, cherries, plums, gooseberries, and table grapes may look like they're ready to harvest, but their sugars may not have totally developed. That's where the taste test comes in. Munch on a few fruits each day to tell when they are becoming sweet enough to harvest. Then there are fruits, such as pears, that are intentionally picked early while still firm and allowed to ripen indoors.

Harvesting berries is easy because you simply pluck them off the plant. Another indication they are fully ripe is when the fruits come off the plant easily, without much effort.

Harvesting tree fruits can take a little more care. While you may not need a hand pruner or knife to harvest them, being gentle is important because fruits can easily bruise if dropped. For both berries and tree fruits, watch the birds to know when they're ripe. Birds have an uncanny ability to know when it's time to swoop down and start their harvest of your fruits.

Here are 10 common fruits and berries and guidance on when and how to harvest them.

13

ABOVE: Taste-test a number grapes around the cluster to determine when to harvest. Grapes on the outside of the cluster will ripen faster than grapes on the inside.
OPPOSITE: Lift and twist apples on the tree to tell if they're ripe. When ready for harvesting, they should come off the tree easily.

When and How to Harvest Fruits

Bring a bucket, basket, or tray, and hand pruner into the garden when getting ready to harvest. Soft fruits, such as raspberries, cherries, and strawberries, can rot easily if damaged during harvesting, so don't stack these fruits deeply in your container. For tree fruits growing on tall trees, consider purchasing a pole harvester or harvesting ladder to reach fruits in the upper branches. Avoid climbing in trees to harvest so you don't break any branches. For large harvests, invite friends and family over to join in the fun and share the bounty.

FRUIT	WHEN AND HOW TO HARVEST
Apples	Know your variety to know roughly when it should be ready to harvest. Watch for color to change to the mature color for that variety. Gently lift and twist the fruit. If it comes off the tree easily, it's ready to harvest. When some fruits start naturally dropping, that's also a sign to start harvesting. Fruits on the outside of the tree will ripen before those on the interior.
Blackberries and raspberries	Harvest these brambles in summer or fall, depending on the variety. Wait until blackberries turn deep black and raspberries turn red, purple, or yellow, depending on the variety, before starting to hand-pick them. Use the taste test to know if they're sweet. Harvest 2 to 3 times a week as the berries ripen. When ripe, they should gently drop off the canes with a slight tug. Don't pick brambles when the fruits are wet or they will get mushy fast.
Blueberries	Blueberry harvest can vary by a few months in summer, depending on the variety. Know if you have an early, mid-, or late-season variety. Once the berries turn blue, wait a few more days for peak sweetness. Use the taste test. When ripe, the berries should easily drop off the plant when touched.
Cherries	Cherries ripen in the summer, but don't rush to pick them once they turn red. Cherries' sugar content rises significantly the last few days of ripening. Use the taste test. Ripe tart cherries should drop off the tree easily when tugged. Sweet cherries may not. If you won't eat them right away, harvest leaving the stem attached to the fruit. If processing the cherries, don't worry about keeping the stem attached.

FRUIT	WHEN AND HOW TO HARVEST
Currants and gooseberries	Wait until currants and gooseberries are the mature color for that variety; then taste-test them to know when to harvest. If harvesting for jams, pick on the early side, when pectin levels are highest. When ripe, gooseberries also will be soft when gently squeezed. Like cherries, they will be sweetest if left on the plant a few days after turning their mature color.
Grapes	Table grapes may need 1 to 3 weeks after turning their mature color to be ready to harvest. Wine grapes will need to be tested with a hygrometer to know when they are sweet enough to harvest. Table grapes are easy. Taste-test a number of grapes from around the clusters to know if the whole cluster is ripe. With a scissors or pruner, cut clusters of grapes after taste-testing them to see if they're sweet. Grapes that were shaded by foliage may ripen a little later.
Peaches	Wait to hand harvest peaches and nectarines until the green undertone of the skin is gone, when they develop a sweet aroma, and when the fruits give a little when gently squeezed. Fruits on the top and outside of the tree will ripen sooner than fruits on the interior of the tree.
Pears	Unlike most other fruits, pears will ripen from the inside out, so if you wait for the outside flesh to be ripe, the inside will be mushy and rotting. Harvest when the fruits are firm and mature but not ripe, and let them ripen off the tree. To know when to harvest, in late summer, lift the pear fruit and turn it horizontally while it's still attached to the tree. When mature, it will easily slip off the branch.
Plums	Harvest plums in summer when the fruit has a little give when squeezed. When you twist and raise the fruit, it should easily come off the tree.
Strawberries	Strawberries are ripe 4 to 6 weeks after flowering, when the fruits are fully red-colored all around. To harvest, pinch off the stem with your thumb and pointing finger, or use scissors. Try to keep the cap of the strawberries intact, especially if you won't be eating them for a few days. They will last longer if stored in the refrigerator.

OPPOSITE LEFT: Harvest pears when they are large and still firm. They taste best when brought indoors to complete ripening, preferably in a cool environment.

OPPOSITE RIGHT: Blueberries should be harvested after they color up completely and have a sweet flavor. Fruits should easily come off the plant when fully ripe.

LEFT: Peaches are mature when the background color of the skin turns from green to tan.

CHAPTER 14
GARDENING WITH NATIVE PLANTS

By Lynn Steiner

THIS CHAPTER IS ALL ABOUT CELEBRATING THE native plants of North America and learning how to enjoy them in your own garden. Many native plants, including flowers, grasses, shrubs, and trees, make great garden plants. You will learn which natives are suitable for traditional gardens and how to effectively and acceptably use them in your garden. The end result will be a beautiful landscape that reflects a sense of our natural plant communities, provides habitat for native fauna, and provides you with a garden abuzz and aflutter with pollinators, hummingbirds, birds, and many other happy creatures.

Gardening with native plants isn't really all that different from traditional gardening. There are native plants that will work in almost any landscape situation, from wet, boggy soils to arid, sandy soils; heavy, cool shade to full sun conditions; and formal style to naturalistic settings. North America is home to a wide variety of indigenous plants—and many, such as black-eyed Susans, maidenhair fern, and viburnums, are garden plants that you already know and grow. By bringing these plants into your landscape, you are helping to preserve our natural plant heritage, something that becomes more important every day as we continually lose our natural plant communities to human activities.

OPPOSITE: Native plants have a lot to offer the landscape, including habitat for wildlife and lower maintenance. Best of all, they are beautiful!

WHAT IS A NATIVE PLANT?

A general definition of a "native plant" is any plant that grew in North America naturally without human intervention and was here before European settlement. Unlike most introduced plants, a native plant fully integrates into a biotic community and has complex relationships with local plants and animals in that community. It depends on the organisms with which it has evolved, and the other organisms depend on it, creating a true web of life. This natural system of checks and balances ensures that native plants and insects seldom grow out of control in their natural habitats.

Wildflower—a plant that grows wild in areas—is a term that's often confused with native plants. But wildflowers include introduced plants that have escaped cultivation and grow wild. Examples are tawny daylily, dame's rocket, and ox-eye daisy, common roadside plants that are not native to any area of the United States.

REASONS TO USE NATIVE PLANTS

There are many reasons to use native plants, some more tangible than others. For many gardeners, the initial attraction comes from native plants' reputation of being lower maintenance. For the most part, this is true—provided native plants are given landscape situations that match their cultural requirements. Because they have evolved and adapted to their surroundings over thousands of years, native plants are better adapted to local climatic conditions and better able to resist the effects of native insects and diseases. Their reduced maintenance results in less dependence on fossil fuels and reduced noise pollution from lawn mowers and other types of equipment.

Attracting Wildlife

Native plants are very important to native insects, birds, and other wildlife, which are critical to the health of humans and the planet. A native landscape can be a good substitute for the natural habitats that are being destroyed at a rapid

Consult a good reference book or check out your state's department of natural resources website to find out what plants are native in your area. Visit a local botanic garden that features native plants to see them in a garden setting.

rate. This is often in great contrast to how most gardeners think, but it is time to plant a garden that is attractive to insects, birds, and other types of wildlife rather than repellant to them.

Avoiding Invasives

Many introduced garden plants have the potential to become invasive and weedy when grown in conditions without the natural checks and balances that keep them under control. When a native species moves into a natural area from a garden bed, it usually just becomes a part of the ecosystem. When an alien species move in, it often grows faster and reproduces more successfully. The result is a monoculture that displaces native species and provides little or no habitat for native fauna. Buckthorn, vinca vines, and garlic mustard are prime examples of garden plants gone bad.

Sense of Place

Gardening with native plants will help you create a sense of place rather than just a cookie-cutter landscape. Your yard will be unique among the long line of mown grass and clipped shrubs in your neighborhood. You will get an enormous sense of satisfaction helping re-establish what once grew naturally in your area. You will see an increase in wildlife, including birds, butterflies, and pollinating insects, making your garden a livelier place.

Connection with Nature

A less tangible—but possibly more important—side of using native plants is the connection you make with nature. Gardening with natives instills an understanding of our natural world—its cycles, changes, and history. Communing with nature has a positive, healing effect on human beings. Learning how to work with nature instead of against it will do wonders for your spiritual health. By observing native plants throughout the year, a gardener gains insight into seasonal rhythms and life cycles.

These bees are enjoying the nectar of a smooth blue aster flower.

Landscape interest comes from more than just beautiful flowers. The showy seedpods of white baneberry are just as pretty as any flower.

MISCONCEPTIONS ABOUT NATIVE PLANTS

Despite the increased interest in and promotion of native plants, many people still hesitate to use them for one reason or another. It's time to dispel some common misconceptions about gardening with native plants.

Not Showy Enough

Some people have the mistaken idea that native plants are colorless and dull. Once you learn about the wide variety of natives and how to use them properly, you will discover that they have much to offer—not only colorful flowers but also interesting textures, colorful fruits, and year-round interest. They may not all be as bright and showy as a lot of introduced plants, but their subtle beauty can be just as effective in landscaping.

Native Plant Interactions: Monarchs and Milkweeds

Many native plants have very specific relationships with insects. A prime example is the important relationship between monarch butterfly caterpillars and members of the milkweed family. Without milkweeds, there would be no monarchs. Female monarchs lay eggs under the leaves, caterpillars eat the leaves and flowers, and the adults feed on the nectar of milkweeds.

Acquiring Native Plants

Do not buy plants that were collected in the wild. You want to purchase plants that were "nursery propagated," not just "nursery grown." Reputable nurseries will readily volunteer information on the origin of their plants, so if a plant seller is being evasive or ambiguous, be wary. Here are some additional tips:

- Do not dig plants from their native habitats unless the plants are facing imminent destruction from development.
- If you have permission to collect seeds from a stand of native plants, take only what you need. Collect only a few seeds from several plants in the stand; never take all the seeds from one plant.
- Do not collect underground plant parts. Collecting must never endanger a plant population.
- Be aware of which plants are endangered in your area, because in many states it is illegal to gather, take, buy, or sell them.

Source of Allergens

Unfortunately, native plants often have a reputation of being the source of allergies. Goldenrods are especially burdened by this misconception because they bloom at the same time as ragweed. The truth is, most native plants are insect pollinated rather than wind pollinated. Kentucky blue grass has the potential to produce more allergens than any native plant.

Weedy

Native plants are sometimes described as weedy, but most are no weedier or invasive than other garden plants. Any plant can become invasive if it is given the right conditions—a site more conducive to rampant growth than its preferred habitat and a lack of the native insect predators that help keep it in check.

Too Messy

Some people think native-plant landscapes are messy. Well, nature is "messy." It's full of fallen logs, recycling plant parts, and plants that weave together rather than lay out in straight lines. Once you understand and appreciate this, native plants will no longer appear unattractive. There are many things you can do to make a native landscape look neater, such as incorporating small patches of lawn grasses, creating paths and neat edges, and cutting back certain plants when they are done blooming.

Hard to Find

Some people avoid native plants because they think they are hard to find in the nursery trade. Once you learn which plants are native, you will be surprised how many are available at local nurseries. In every part of the country, you will find nurseries that specialize in native plants, and many of them sell online.

OPPOSITE: Goldenrod gets a bad rap because it blooms about the same time as ragweed, a major source of allergens. But as this photo shows, these plants are avidly pollinated by insects, not by wind.

NATIVES IN GARDENS AND LANDSCAPES

There are basically three ways to use native plants in a landscape: doing a restoration, creating a habitat garden, and integrating them into your established gardens.

require quite a bit of time and effort in plant eradication and site preparation. They also usually require at least an acre to create an effective plant community. Get help from a professional company specializing in native-plant restorations before you begin such an endeavor.

Restoration

Recreating or restoring a prairie or woodland with plants that are indigenous to your region is a wonderful way to support natural ecosystems. Unfortunately, it is not practical for most homeowners. Because our landscapes have been altered so much by human activity, restorations

Habitat Gardens

People who have a strong interest in growing native plants will get immense pleasure from the creation of habitat gardens within their landscape. A well-functioning habitat garden should be based on a natural plant community, preferably one that would have been found in your area.

To restore or recreate a prairie, you need full sun and a minimum of about an acre to be able to fully realize this plant community. While this is a wonderful way to use native plants, it's not always practical for homeowners.

Use these communities as a starting point when choosing plants for your own garden. Obviously, plants that evolved in the same conditions as in your landscape will do well in your gardens. However, it is still important to base your final plant selections on your existing conditions. If you live within a forested area but have a yard without any trees, you will not be able to replicate that shady woodland habitat. You will need to stick with plants that evolved in sunnier habitats.

An effective habitat garden should include all, or almost all, native plants, and should be allowed to evolve and grow in a naturalistic way, ultimately forming a working community. Start by assessing the different areas of your landscape and determining which native habitats would be best suited to the conditions. If you are tired of fighting with grass under large shade trees, remove the grass and begin creating a woodland garden. If you have a large open lawn area in full sun that is just a drain on your lawn mower and your time, consider a prairie or meadow garden. By establishing large areas of native-plant communities, you will help preserve natural ecosystems that once flourished in your area and have an attractive, easy-to-tend garden filled with plants with similar cultural requirements.

Integration

For most gardeners, though, the most practical way to use native plants is to integrate natives with nonnative, traditional landscape plants that have proven to be noninvasive and adaptable to your area. You may already be doing this without realizing it. If your mixed border includes blazing star, butterfly weed, or black-eyed Susan, or if your shade garden is home to wild ginger, dogwoods, or maidenhair fern, you are already well on your way to using native plants. Once you see which natives work well for your site, you can replace more nonnative plants, increasing the value your landscape offers our native fauna.

TOP: Don't be afraid to integrate native plants into your established gardens. The plants will all get along just fine!

LEFT: A savanna grassland habitat garden replaces turfgrass in this landscape, providing habitat for many types of birds, butterflies, and small animals.

A native landscape can come under great scrutiny from skeptical neighbors, so it's important that your gardens be well tended and cared for. This front-yard garden employs several strategies to keep it look well kept: a small area of turfgrass, a limited number of species, and an effective hardscape. The are no straight lines in nature, so any time you incorporate them into your landscape, you are sending the signal that this a tended garden.

CREATING A WELL-TENDED NATIVE LANDSCAPE

Even with all the benefits of using native plants, there are still people who have a hard time appreciating them in traditional landscape settings. If this describes your situation, or if you just like a more traditional-looking landscape, there are several things you can do to help your native landscape look more tended and cared for.

Traditional Design and Planting

While most natives adapt best to naturalistic designs, they can be used in formal settings as well. You'll just have to put a little more thought into plant selection and planting design. Start by using traditional planting and design methods. Plant in groups of three, five, or seven plants, as this is more typical of nonnative landscapes. In small spaces, limit the number of species and maybe consider a simple planting of one species, such as a contained bed devoted to little bluestem or prairie dropseed. Include some areas of visual calm where the eye can rest momentarily from stimulation. Small patches of green lawns, a small grouping of green- or silver-foliage plants, or a simple green deciduous or evergreen shrub all create spots of calm.

Drifts and Repetition

There is a misconception that natural landscapes are chaotic and lack perceptible patterns. In relatively undisturbed, naturally evolving landscapes, patterns are ever-present—not in the form of orchard-like grids of trees, but in the subtle arrangements of plants. Nature tends to mass similar forms together and accent them with contrasting forms. Take a cue and plant in drifts, or groupings, of color rather than in

This grouping includes several cultivars of native plants: 'Little Joe' Joe-pye weed, 'Ruby Dwarf' Helen's flower, and 'Little Lemon' goldenrod.

straight rows. Drifts can consist of several of the same plants, which have the added advantage of being extra attractive to pollinating insects, or single plants of similar colors from several different species. For a sense of unity, repeat a few specific plant groupings or color schemes at intervals throughout the landscape. Take a cue from nature and use contrast sparingly to give your garden a natural look.

Consider Cultivars

Whenever possible, plant the pure species or, better yet, your local genotypes, to ensure that the flowers, bloom times, and plant shapes match the requirements of their respective pollinators. However, in more traditional landscapes in cities and suburbs, cultivars may be better choices. (Read more about species and cultivars in Chapter 1.) The main reasons for considering cultivars of native flowers and grasses are that they are more compact and therefore less likely to get floppy (requiring staking) or offer greater resistance to diseases. Many are also less aggressive than the species in garden settings, and some are hardier.

When it comes to using native shrubs in traditional landscapes, cultivars are often a better choice. Most native shrubs tend to be suckering, spreading plants that can get quite tall in their natural settings. The nursery industry has introduced cultivars of many native shrubs that have more compact growth habits, smaller overall height, better flowering and fruiting, and improved disease resistance.

Proper Maintenance

In addition to design considerations, there are also some maintenance techniques you can employ to help give your landscape a more tended and cared-for look. Where appropriate, consider using "upscale" mulches such as cocoa-bean hulls or shredded bark. Mulching has the added benefits of reducing weeds, which helps the landscape look neater, and reducing the need to water.

Dealing with Municipal Laws and Neighbors

Homeowners who decide to grow a lot of natives—especially in their front yard—are often confronted with an array of laws, regulations, requirements, and sometimes outright hostility. Most of these issues are simply due to ignorance. There are several things you can do to prepare yourself for neighborhood opposition.

Learn your local laws and ordinances. Chances are you will be able to stay well within them by putting some thought into your landscape before you plant. If they don't allow for the use of native plants, go through the proper channels to try to obtain a variance or get an ordinance changed.

Education is key. Take every chance you can get to teach your neighbors about this intricate plant community. Anytime you see a neighbor outside, invite them over to look at a flower or butterfly in your yard. Encourage them to walk through your landscape so they can see some of the important details that may be missed from the outside.

Once your landscape is planted, **be attentive and keep up with the necessary maintenance.** Let your neighbors know by your presence and activities that your yard is being cared for and not neglected.

Be sensitive to the people around you and approach any conflict calmly and reasonably. Many of your neighbors may have lived in their homes for decades and are used to a certain look and feel in their neighborhood. An attitude of self-righteousness and arrogance will only make things worse.

Although it's not something usually advocated because of their benefits to wildlife, consider cutting back at least some of your taller plants in fall. This won't harm the plants. The truth is, many native plants, especially grasses, turn brown in winter, and not everyone finds this attractive in the front yard.

Add Ornaments

One of the misconceptions about native-plant landscapes is that they are boring. Unfortunately, people sometimes take native plant design a little too seriously and think they can't use funky garden accents. Not true! There's no reason you can't incorporate any of the garden accents you'd use in a regular landscape. Native-plant landscapes can include sculptures, sundials, gazing balls, fountains, and feeders, houses, and baths for birds, just like any other garden. It's your garden and you should include things that make you happy.

As with all gardens, keep in mind that these items are meant to be accents. They should be used with discretion and carefully placed rather than just plopped down in the garden. Select sculptural pieces that can be nestled into the garden and surrounded by plants, as if they were growing up out of the ground rather than sitting on a concrete pedestal.

If you are trying to recreate a truly natural-looking garden, limit your accent pieces to well-placed natural materials, such as rocks and logs. Take cues from nature and try to place them as if they had been left there. Moss-covered logs should look like they were once part of a tall forest tree that fell to the ground years ago. Rocks should be buried one-half to two-thirds underground, as if a glacier placed them eons ago, rather than set on the surface.

DECIDING WHAT TO GROW

When choosing which natives to grow, it is usually best to start with what is native in your area. There are many resources; a good place to start is the Ladybird Johnson Wildflower Center website (www.wildflower.org). They have a searchable database of North American native plants. You can find out which plants have been native to your state and also narrow your search by plant type, growing conditions, and plant characteristics. They also have a Recommended Species page that lists plants by state and a list of suppliers in each state. Another good resource is the USDA Plants Database (www.plants.usda.gov). Their searchable database provides a list of plants native to your state and even fine tunes it to what's native at a county level.

You can certainly also include plants that are native to other areas of North America, providing they are hardy, well suited to your site, and available. Just make sure they are not potentially invasive in your area of the country. A good resource to check for this is www.invasiveplantatlas.org.

OPPOSITE: Rocks blend nicely into native-plant landscapes, but they should be carefully placed to appear natural.

Boulevard and Strip Gardens

Boulevard strips are those narrow areas between the sidewalk and the street (sometimes they're called "hell strips"). From a gardening standpoint, they offer extended opportunities for space-starved urban gardeners. From an environmental standpoint, they can be very effective at keeping grass clippings out of the street and storm sewers.

Boulevards are among the most challenging spots to grow and maintain plants. The soil is usually compacted and low in fertility and often gets bombarded with road salt in cold climates. They are usually hot, dry, and sunny—unpleasant conditions for tending—and often the garden hose doesn't reach that far, creating maintenance issues.

Many native prairie plants, with their ability to withstand hot, dry, and often sunny conditions, are good choices for boulevards. Stick with low-growing, clumping plants. Stay away from prolific self-seeders, because even a couple extra plants can make this small space look weedy. Any plant growing over a foot in height will probably need to be cut back in fall. Plan on cutting back any remaining plants in spring and raking off the debris.

Native plants that are great choices for boulevard gardens include prairie alumroot, nodding onion, and pussytoes.

Native Flowers and Ferns

Many native flowers are well suited to garden and landscape use. Their showy blooms, various sizes and forms, and interesting leaves bring color, interest, and texture to a landscape. Many are attractive to butterflies, birds, and bees, and some are good for cutting. Others are more functional, offering erosion control on a slope or attractive ways to deal with a low area in the lawn or dry shade under large trees.

Some you may already know and grow; monarda, butterfly weed, Joe-pye weed, asters, and black-eyed Susans are all commonly grown in perennial beds and mixed borders, and maidenhair fern, bloodroot, and blue phlox are common in shade gardens. Although some flowers can be used as single specimen plants, most flowers look best in groups of three, five, or seven or more, as they are in nature.

Some native flowers are ephemeral in nature, meaning they are up early in spring, bloom, set seed, and then go dormant before summer's heat. While they are very welcome

Native ferns adapt well to shady landscape situations, where their foliage provides interesting textural contrast and adds visual buoyancy, lightening the garden with a wide assortment of shapes and varying shades of green.

Many native flowers are already common garden plants, including garden phlox, black-eyed Susan, and blanket flower.

sights in early spring, keep in mind that they'll leave bare spots in the garden. They should be planted with plants, such as wild ginger, ferns, and coral bells, that will cover the bare ground when the ephemerals "disappear." Be careful not to dig up dormant clumps of spring ephemerals. If you will be cultivating that area of the garden, you may want to mark them in late spring so you don't disturb their roots in summer or fall.

Native ferns are typically used in shade gardens, where they are excellent background plantings, fillers, blenders, groundcovers, or even focal points. Although the small fiddleheads appear fairly early in spring, the leaves do not fully mature for quite a while. This growth pattern makes ferns good companions for early flowering ephemerals. Some ferns can be used in foundation plantings and some of the sun-tolerant types can be used in mixed borders. They look good around water gardens and some of the smaller types can be used in shady rock gardens. They can also be used to create a soft boundary between one section of a garden and another.

Native grasses really shine in the fall garden, where they provide color, contrast, and movement. Many continue to add color and texture well into the winter months.

Grasses

Native grasses are very adaptable, growing in poorer soils than most garden plants and, once established, requiring very little care beyond annual cutting back. They rarely need watering or fertilizing and are seldom bothered by insects, diseases, or deer. Grasses come in a wide range of heights, colors, and textures and offer more than one season of interest. They also bring movement and sound to the landscape, two elements lacking in most plants. Most grasses are tolerant of wind and can be used in open, exposed areas where other plants would be damaged.

Native grass flowers can be lacy panicles, stiff brushes, or waving plumes, often with beautiful fall color. Most grasses flower from late summer into fall, but some flower earlier. They can be used as accent or specimen plants, groundcovers, and screens. Many of the clump-forming types also mix well in perennial borders. Most grasses, especially those with delicate, airy seedheads, look best against a dark background, and should be placed where they can catch morning or evening light. Native grasses have a pure, abstract quality that blends well with modern architectures, and their shapes, colors, and textures contrast nicely with wood, stone, and other hard structural surfaces. Some people choose to create entire gardens of grasses. Beyond their landscape value, many are valuable sources of food and cover for birds and the mature seedheads are prized for dried arrangements.

Consider Sedges

Sedges are grasslike plants, but they're not true grasses. They can be distinguished from grasses by their solid, three-angled flower stems (grasses have round, hollow flower stems). Most sedges form dense, compact clumps of bright-green foliage. Many make nice landscape plants, and can be used like grasses. Some are even quite shade tolerant.

Pennsylvania sedge (*Carex pensylvanica*) is a flowering grass that is native to much of North America and used as a landscape plant in zones 3 to 8. It is an excellent choice for shady locations.

or multiple stems. Small trees are often used as specimen plantings, where the beauty of their flowers, bark, and foliage can really shine. They are good choices for providing shade in small yards where traditional shade trees grow too big. Small trees are important for adding height to entry and patio gardens, and many make nice lawn trees in small yards. Most large shrubs can be pruned into small trees, adding another dimension to their landscape use.

Native Shrubs That Can Be Pruned as Small Trees

- *Acer circinatum* (vine maples)
- *Acer glabrum* (Rocky Mountain maples)
- *Aesculus pavia* (red buckeyes)
- *Amelanchier* spp. (serviceberries)
- *Betula occidentalis* (Western birches)
- *Carpinus caroliniana* (American hornbeams)
- *Chilopsis linearis* (desert willows)
- *Chionanthus virginicus* (fringe trees)
- *Cornus* spp. (dogwoods)
- *Cotinus obovatus* (American smoketrees)
- *Dirca* spp. (leatherwoods)
- *Hamamelis virginiana* (witch hazel)
- *Hydrangea paniculata* (panicle hydrangeas, 'Grandiflora' or 'Tardiva')
- *Illicium floridanum* (anise)
- *Kalmia latifolia* (mountain laurels)
- *Photinia pyrifolia* 'Brilliantissima' (red chokeberries)
- *Prunus nigra* (Canada plums)
- *Ptelea trifoliata* (hop trees)
- *Rhus typhina* (staghorn sumacs)
- *Stewartia* spp. (stewartias)
- *Styrax* spp. (snowbells)
- *Viburnum lentago* (nannyberries)
- *Viburnum prunifolium* (black haws)

Shrubs and Small Trees

Many small- to medium-sized native shrubs work well in the mixed border, where they complement herbaceous perennials and provide season-long interest. Many shrubs have fruits that provide winter interest as well as attract birds and other wildlife. In shade and woodland gardens, shrubs and small trees provide that middle layer that ties together full-sized shade trees and the flowers and groundcovers growing beneath them. Evergreen shrubs are great for providing year-round interest, either as part of a border, in foundation plantings, or as well-grown specimen plants. Shrubs are valuable for hedges and massing, and some can even be used as large-scale groundcovers.

Small trees are trees that usually stay under 25 feet tall or large shrubs that can be easily pruned to a single stem

Trees

Large trees are valued for their beauty as well as for the shade they provide, but they have a lot more to offer landscapes. They provide structure with their weight and form. The overhead leafy canopy of a spreading tree frames the elements and the view below it. Trees are home to many types of birds and also provide habitat for butterflies and beneficial insects. Many provide beautiful fall color when their foliage turns shades of red, yellow, and orange. And don't forget the

14

benefits at eye level, especially in the dormant season: many trees have bark with interesting texture and color.

CARING FOR NATIVE PLANTS

For many people, the initial appeal of using natives comes from their desire for "no maintenance." While native plants are certainly not maintenance free, once established, they usually require much less in the way of watering, fertilizing, and grooming than traditional landscape plants. A long-term goal of creating a native-plant landscape is often to create a sustainable community that requires little or no effort on your part. This is in great contrast to a traditional landscape or garden, where human intervention is constant and necessary to keep things looking as planned. However, if you want a "garden," you will still need to perform some regular maintenance. Fortunately, most of the required tasks come under the heading of "desirable" for most people who enjoy tending plants.

With native plants, the need to water and fertilize is all but eliminated once they are established, and the use of pesticides to kill insects or diseases should never be on the maintenance list. Once you eliminate the nasty tasks of spraying, watering, and fertilizing, you can spend your time tending the plants and improving the overall design of your gardens. If you go one step further and use native plantings to replace areas of traditional lawn, you will reduce your need for weekly mowing and all the other maintenance issues that come with growing turfgrasses.

When developing a maintenance plan for your native landscape, keep in mind the things that make a garden look unattractive and untended. These include an excess of weeds; floppy plants; unhealthy or browned plants; large areas without pathways, ornaments, or other aspects of a hardscape; large areas of nondescript green foliage with little or no color from flowers or foliage; plants with a lot of insect or disease damage; plants that have been eaten back by deer or other herbivores; wilting plants; and bare soil where plants have gone dormant and nothing has filled in. Anything you can do to minimize these things will help your gardens look better and be healthier.

Redbud is a native tree that has showy deep-pink flowers in early spring.

Controlling Plant Height

Many native perennials get too tall for formal landscape settings. Staking is a popular solution, but it takes a lot of time and needs to be done within a specific window of time.

A technique to reduce the height of late-summer and fall-blooming perennials is to cut them back in mid-spring. To do this, prune back plants to 6 to 10 inches, or by about half. This may seem ruthless at the time, but the plants will soon bounce back and you won't even be able to tell the cuts were made. Your reward will be a compact, often heavier blooming plant that won't require staking. It may bloom a few days or a week later, but this can also be used to your advantage. By pruning back only the plants in the front of a grouping, you will get an extended bloom time.

Native Perennials That Can Be Cut Back in Spring

- *Agastache* spp. (anise hyssops)
- *Boltonia asteroides* (boltonias)
- *Chelone* spp. (turtleheads)
- *Echinacea* spp. (purple coneflowers)
- *Eutrochium* spp. (Joe-pye weeds)
- *Helenium* spp. (sneezeweeds)
- *Heliopsis helianthoides* (oxeyes)
- *Lobelia* spp. (cardinal flowers, lobelias)
- *Monarda* spp. (bee balm)
- *Phlox maculata* (wild sweet William)
- *Phlox paniculata* (garden phlox)
- *Physostegia virginiana* (obedient plants)
- *Rudbeckia* spp. (black-eyed Susans, coneflowers)
- *Salvia azurea* (azure sage)
- *Solidago* spp. (goldenrods)
- *Symphyotrichum* spp. (asters)
- *Tradescantia* spp. (spiderworts)
- *Verbena* spp. (vervains)
- *Vernonia* spp. (ironweeds)

To reduce the height of late-summer blooming perennials such as sneezeweed, cut plants back in spring.

Deadhead to Increase Bloom

Almost every gardener wants more flowers, and a common complaint against using native plants is that they don't bloom as long as many exotics. The best solution for this is to plant a wider variety of plants with an extended range of bloom times. You can also plan to do some deadheading, or removing of spent flowers before they go to seed. Cut back to the next set of leaves to encourage new buds to open. Many native perennials will have an extended bloom time if you deadhead them regularly. These include black-eyed Susans, blanket flowers, bluets, hairy false goldenasters, obedient plants, oxeyes, prairie coneflowers, spiderworts, tickseeds, and wild sweet William.

Remove Excess Seedlings

Many native plants are heavy reseeders. They needed this adaptation to make sure they were able to reproduce in the highly competitive native-plant communities in which they evolved; only a small percentage of seeds would survive to germinate and grow into mature plants. But in gardens, where competition is less and the soil is rich and water is usually plentiful, a high percentage of seeds germinate and grow into plants. These extra plants turn into weeds in your garden.

It is important that you learn what plants are heavy seeders and then plan to deadhead them or weed out unwanted seedlings each spring. This list includes bee balm, black-eyed Susans, goldenrods, hairy false goldenasters, prairie coneflowers, rattlesnake master, sneezeweeds, spiderworts, tickseeds, and wild petunias.

Remove Spent Flowers

Many plants have flowers that turn into showy seedheads that offer winter interest or seeds for birds. It is nice to allow these flowers to remain whenever possible, but some plants have flowers that turn brown after flowering and detract from the more-attractive foliage. By removing spent flowers you will get a nicer-looking plant for the remainder of the gardening season. Consider removing spent flowers from coral bells, hoary vervain, obedient plants, queen of the prairie, spiderworts, wild petunias, and yarrows.

Cut Back

Some plants don't really have showy seedheads and can be gently cut back after flowering to improve their shape and overall appearance in the late-summer garden. These include blue stars, harebell, hoary vervain, large-flowered tickseed, obedient plant, purple poppy mallows, and spiderworts.

It is nice to leave the foliage on grass plants over winter so both you and the birds can enjoy the flowers. Cut back plants in late winter before new growth begins. If you only have a few plants, use a pair of hand pruners or hedge shears. A string trimmer can be used if you have a large number of grasses to cut back. If practical, burning is also effective.

Learn to identify seedlings of prolific seeders and pull them out as soon as they are spotted to help prevent these plants from become weedy. These are volunteer snap dragon seedlings.

CHAPTER 15
WATER-WISE GARDENING

By Lynn Steiner

THERE ARE MANY REASONS TO BE SMART ABOUT water use. Changes to global climate make it more challenging for gardeners in many ways, but perhaps fluctuating rainfall amounts present the greatest challenge. Arid places of the country are experiencing longer dry spells, but areas that usually have reliable rainfall are experiencing drought as well. And when the rain does come, it often comes in the form of torrential storms that can do more harm than good. Drought is a relative term. It can range from long dry spells, such as is often the case in California and the desert Southwest, to shorter spells without rain in temperate areas that tax the survivability of the plants grown there.

Fortunately, there are many techniques to make you a water-wise gardener. Your goal should be a landscape where little or no supplemental irrigation is needed once plants are established and where excess rainfall is held on site rather than allowed to wash away in storm drains. Fortunately, with a little attention to plant selection, soil improvement, garden design, and proper maintenance techniques, you can have a water-wise landscape that is beautiful as well.

OPPOSITE: Water-wise gardening is about accepting the reality of your climate and gardening accordingly. For some people, this may mean changing their idea of what a garden should look like. But practical doesn't have to mean unattractive. This hillside is planted with deep-rooted grasses and forbs to reduce runoff. The brick wall at the base helps hold the soil.

Start by assessing your site and determining what, if any, problems you have with regard to water use. Are you finding that you typically have to water more than once a week? Do you notice large amounts of water rushing down the driveway and into the street after a hard rain? Are there areas of your landscape that seem to receive little or no rainfall, possibly due to a canopy of large trees or the eaves from buildings? Do you live in an area where drying, heavy winds are common? Do you have large paved areas that exaggerate the drying effects in sunny areas?

You should also be aware of what the average rainfall amounts are for your area of the country to help you make better plant selections. Knowing your soil type is also important. Next to rainfall, it has the greatest impact on the amount of water available to your plants.

Water-Wise Actions to Take Right Away

- Mulch bare soil
- Start a compost pile
- Raise mower blades
- Install a rain barrel
- Build a berm or terrace to help hold water on site

REDUCING WATER USE

Xeriscaping refers to landscaping that promotes water conservation by using carefully chosen plants, maximizing the use of rainfall runoff, and minimizing maintenance. It is most common in western and southern states where rainfall is lower and water use is more regulated, but xeriscaping really is a good approach to any landscape design. Even if you live in a temperate climate with regular rainfall, daily watering is wasteful and costly.

Xeriscaping incorporates several basic principles: soil improvement, plant selection and design, reduced use of turfgrasses, smart hardscapes, efficient irrigation systems, properly timed maintenance, and use of windbreaks where appropriate.

Xeriscaped landscapes are not always comprised of only drought-tolerant plants and rock. They can be green, cool landscapes full of beautiful plants maintained with water-efficient practices.

Succulents have fleshy, thick stems and leaves, which allow them to store water and get by with less supplemental irrigation.

SOIL IMPROVEMENT

Your soil's texture determines how much water is available to plants and, in turn, how well they will survive dry periods. Good soil leads to good root growth, which leads to better water uptake by plants. Your best bet is to select plants that are adapted to growing in the type of soil you have, but this can greatly limit what you can grow in your garden. So, it may be necessary to improve your soil's texture to better hold or drain water. This will allow you to grow a larger variety of plants without increasing your water use.

Adding generous amounts of organic matter to any soil will improve its texture, but it is especially important with sandy, fast-draining soils. Organic matter improves a soil's moisture-holding capacity by acting like a sponge. It holds onto water, making it available to plants when rainfall is low. In heavier soil, organic matter can be mixed with coarse sand to loosen the soil and increase air space to help prevent it from baking into hard, dry soil that can cause damage to plant roots. Mix compost or organic matter, such as well-rotted compost or leaves, into soil before planting, if possible.

PLANT SELECTION AND DESIGN

Most people think that drought-tolerant plants are limited to cacti and succulents, but there are many more plant choices. To get a better idea of plants that do well without supplemental water, look to those that have evolved in hot, dry conditions. These include dry-soil prairie plants, desert plants, seashore plants, and Mediterranean plants. Plants that are native to your area usually are good choices because they have adapted to local climates.

There are certain characteristics typical of drought-tolerant plants:

- Plants have gray- and other light-colored foliage. It reflects the sun's glare so the plant stays cooler and doesn't require as much water.
- Plants are often covered in tiny hairs. These shade leaves and help reduce moisture loss.
- Blue-foliage plants are often covered in a waxy coating.
- Succulents store water in their leaves, allowing them to go a long time between waterings.
- Small leaves and needled foliage have reduced leaf surfaces and therefore lose less water through the foliage.
- Cool-season annuals—those that do best in spring or fall—require less water than summer-blooming flowers.
- Many drought-tolerant plants have deep tap roots.

Most people don't want their entire landscape to be made up of drought-tolerant plants, but you can still reduce watering by grouping plants with similar water needs: high water, medium water, and low water. You can be much more efficient with your water use if all the plants that need regular supplemental water are in one or two areas. That said, try to limit your high-water zones, giving careful thought to their placement. Usually you will want your lush, higher-water-use plantings in areas of your landscape where you spend the most time, such as near a deck or terrace.

Plants with higher water requirements should be grouped together and sited near the house for easier maintenance.

Install a Gravel Garden

Gravel gardens are a way to showcase small, delicate plants while reducing water use. They are created in sunny spots by laying several inches of gravel over the soil and using drought-tolerant plants, such as succulents and those found in arid, rocky places. These gardens can take light foot traffic and are good substitutes for turfgrasses. By allowing plants to self-seed and pop up throughout the garden, you can create a beautiful mosaic of color.

REDUCED TURFGRASS

Lawns are among the thirstiest surfaces you can have in your landscape. Each blade of grass—and there are often many—loses water through transpiration. Most lawns require about an inch of water a week during the growing season. Shrinking your lawn or replacing it with lower-maintenance groundcovers or hardscape is a great way to reduce water use. Less lawn also means less pollution from power equipment and less chemical use. And, because traditional lawn grasses offer little or no habitat value to birds, butterflies, and pollinating insects, replacing all or part of it with a garden will increase the number of visits from these beneficial partners.

Traditional lawn grasses make a great groundcover in areas where children play and pets require it, but lawns are used in many other places where they're just not necessary. Use high-maintenance turfgrasses as a planned element in the landscape, and avoid using them where they aren't needed. Avoid impractical use of turf, such as long, narrow areas, and use it only in areas where it provides functional benefits. Where you do have lawn, raise the mower blade a bit and mow less frequently. Taller grass encourages grass roots to grow deeper, making stronger, more drought-resistant plants.

Alternatives to Turfgrass

There are many good alternatives to traditional lawn grasses. If you want the look of a lawn, consider an eco-lawn, low-mow mixture, or native grass. These grasses require much less watering and mowing than traditional turfgrasses. They can take light foot traffic and will blend in nicely with other lawns in your neighborhood. Just be sure to choose a lawn substitute based on the area where you live. Buffalograss is a good choice for the drier parts of the country. Pennsylvania sedge makes a nice groundcover in shadier spots in the East and Midwest.

There are many spreading plants that make good groundcovers and lawn substitutes. These can be used anywhere you don't require foot traffic (although some do tolerate light foot traffic). If you choose plants appropriate to your soil and sunlight conditions, groundcovers are almost maintenance free. They are especially good for shady areas under large trees where lawn grasses do not do well. Remember, groundcovers do not have to be planted as a monoculture. You can mix several together to create a tapestry of different textures, colors, and leaf shapes.

Planting a Bee Lawn

Bee lawns are becoming a popular alternative to traditional lawns in places where you don't need the perfectly groomed lawn. They are made up of low-growing, foot-tolerant, noninvasive plants, such as fescues, white clover, thyme, and self-heal, that are attractive to pollinators. In addition to greatly reducing water use, they also eliminate the need for pesticides and fertilizers.

OPPOSITE: Look for places in your landscape where you can use water-efficient plants and mulch in place of thirsty turfgrass.

SMART HARDSCAPES

Hardscape is anything in your landscape that isn't living: patios, decks, fences, pathways, retaining walls, and so on. It usually serves a practical purpose, but there are many things you can do to make hardscape work even harder in the landscape to be water-wise.

Replacing areas of your lawn with patios, decks, and walkways will reduce water use, water evaporation, and maintenance. There are a wide variety of materials available in many colors and textures that can be used in imaginative and attractive ways. If you want to soften the look of a hard surface, consider using plants. For example, on a path, place creeping plants between paving stones (just be sure to choose drought-tolerant, low-growing plants that can take a little foot traffic). Or for a more interesting look, leave out a paver here and there and fill the space with a taller, bushier plant.

Properly placed trees and structures, such as arbors, pergolas, and shade sails, can help reduce water use because they provide shade. Shaded areas can be up to 20 degrees cooler than sunny areas, and this means healthier plants. You can also increase shade and cooling from structures by planting vines that will grow up and over them.

EFFICIENT IRRIGATION

Before you haul out the hose, be sure your plants actually need water. Don't automatically water twice or three times a week. Get to know your plants and how they look when they are in need of water. Check soil moisture by sticking your finger several inches down into the soil or using a soil moisture gauge. Put a rain gauge in your garden so you know how much rain you've gotten. Established plants can often get by with less water than is recommended.

When it comes to efficient watering, timing and quantity are key. Early morning is the best time to water most plants, because evaporation rates are lower when the sun is lower in the sky. Watering in the cooler evening hours is efficient, but it can lead to disease problems if the plants have wet foliage overnight. Watering on a calm day is obviously more efficient than setting up a sprinkler on a windy day.

Make sure that when you water, you water deep enough. This encourages plants to root deeply and therefore be more tolerant of drought. Frequent shallow watering not only encourages shorter root systems, but it can also bring alkaline salts to the surface. These salts can tie up nutrients and burn plant roots.

To add interest to a paved area, leave out a paver or a group of pavers here and there and fill the space with drought-tolerant plants.

Soaker hoses can be placed over or beneath mulch, and are an efficient way to deliver water to gardens.

<... />

For areas of your landscape that require supplemental water, consider installing a drip or trickle irrigation system along with timers and water-control devices to increase their efficiency. Soaker hoses are a good choice for large borders and vegetable gardens. They emit water along their whole length from tiny holes. Because the water is delivered at a slow, steady rate, it has a good chance of soaking into the ground and not running off.

Hose-end sprinklers, while popular and affordable, are not efficient ways to deliver water to your landscape. A lot of water is lost to evaporation and wind, and they often produce puddles where water runs off before it can soak into the ground. If you are going to use hose-end sprinklers, consider installing a timer to limit how long they run. All too often, these types of sprinklers are forgotten and run much longer than they need to.

If you do use or plan to use an automatic sprinkler system, there are few things you should do to make it more efficient. Use the manual setting. Doing so avoids wasting water and gives you a chance to learn just how much water your plants need and how much drought they can tolerate before becoming stressed. Too many people set the automatic timer to run at regular intervals even though extra water is not required. Save the automatic timer for when you are on vacation. Check the irrigation system regularly for leaks as well as problems that reduce the efficiency and function of sprinklers, drip emitters, and other water-delivery devices.

Make sure that your watering zones are set up to reflect the needs of the different areas and plant types in your landscape. Your goal is to provide the least amount of water needed for each garden or area of lawn. Sunny areas will require more water than shady areas and turfgrasses require more water than most garden plants.

TIMELY MAINTENANCE

Healthy plants can get by with less water than unhealthy plants. Properly timed mulching, planting, pruning, weeding, fertilizing, and lawn care not only improve plant health and the garden's appearance, but they can also help reduce water use.

Soil mulch is very important because it greatly reduces the amount of water lost from the soil by evaporation, improves water penetration, and helps suppress water-stealing weeds. Organic mulches, such as compost, wood chips, and cocoa shells, are usually best for plant health, but they do decompose with time and must be replaced often. They are not natural to dry ecosystems and do not always look appropriate in water-wise gardens. Inorganic mulches, such as pea gravel or grit, often look more natural in dry-soil gardens.

Sheet mulches are another way to reduce soil moisture loss. These types of mulches are usually used in vegetable gardens or on steep slopes where it is hard to keep organic mulches from washing away. Examples of sheet moss material are bonded fiber fleece, woven geotextile, black plastic, newspaper, and old carpet. These mulches are durable and effective at reducing water loss, but they make it difficult to add organic matter to the soil. They're available as porous, letting in water and oxygen, or nonporous, which does not allow rainfall or air to penetrate. Sheet mulches must be laid before planting but after the soil has been prepared.

Proper planting and pruning can go a long way in helping plants use water more efficiently. All newly planted plants need adequate water during establishment, but planting in the cooler days of spring and summer will help reduce their water needs. Build up the soil to create a water-holding basin around newly planted trees and shrubs to reduce water runoff and allow moisture to soak slowly in. Consider removing unnecessary lower branches from large trees to reduce evaporation (and often improve the tree's appearance). Prune in spring, because heavily pruning trees and shrubs in summer stimulates the growth of new shoots and foliage, and new foliage loses water faster than mature leaves.

Keep your gardens free of weeds, especially deep-rooted ones, which rob landscape plants of a lot of soil moisture. Remove weeds as early as possible to conserve soil

Mulch is a very effective way to cut back on water needs. Without mulch, a garden bed can lose up to 70 percent of its soil moisture to evaporation.

moisture and prevent seed production. Also remove weak and unwanted ornamentals so you won't waste more water on them.

Fertilize only when necessary, and don't overdo it. Nitrogen stimulates new growth, thereby increasing water needs of plants—this includes weeds as well as lawns and landscape plants.

On cool-season lawns, increase the mowing height to 2 inches or more; the additional foliage will promote deeper rooting and allow the lawn to go longer between watering. Use an aerator to remove small plugs of grass and/or soil on lawns and the ground around trees and other plants; this prevents compaction and increases water absorption. On the lawn, remove the accumulation of old grass roots, stems, and leaves, called thatch, with a heavy rake; it acts as a barrier and keeps water out of the soil. Remove thatch in spring, before temperatures get too warm, if it is more than ½ inch thick.

USE OF WINDBREAKS

Wind has drying effects on plants, greatly increasing water loss. You can decrease the loss by installing windbreaks. They slow down the wind and lift it up and over the breaks. A windbreak can be a wall, fence, hedge, or line of trees. If you don't like the idea of a fence or hedge, consider installing a temporary windbreak where needed that can be removed when plants are large enough.

Windbreaks are most effective when they filter wind rather than completely block it. Find out the wind patterns on your landscape before installing a windbreak; place it on the windward side of your yard or garden.

Evergreens are the most effective windbreak, but even deciduous trees without leaves slow down winds. Trees should be planted just close enough so that their branches touch as they reach their mature size. If you plant them too closely, it actually can lead to more turbulence. You can also use an open fence or a trellis planted with a vine.

Properly positioned, a wall offers protection from the wind and helps prevent a garden from drying out as quickly.

Pavers set in gravel make an attractive and water-permeable walk or driveway surface. Geogrid textiles can be installed to accomplish the same with less work.

KEEPING WATER ON SITE

Make sure the trees and shrubs you plant for a windbreak have strong limbs and trunks that can stand up to the wind. Hedge plants should be spaced slightly closer than their full-sized width. Fences should be well-anchored.

KEEPING WATER ON SITE

Not only is it important for gardeners to try to use less water, but it is also a good idea to try to keep what water you do have on your site. It just makes good sense environmentally, financially, and from a maintenance standpoint. Plus, plants prefer rainwater to tap water, which is often treated with chlorine and fluoride. Naturally soft and mildly acidic, rainwater helps plants grow and absorb important minerals from the soil.

In a natural plant community, most rainwater is absorbed into the ground where it is taken up by plants or stored as groundwater. But where roofs, roads, and parking lots replace natural surfaces, little rain is absorbed into the ground. Instead, the rainwater washes pollutants and trash from streets and parking lots into storm drains and deposits it, without treatment, into a nearby lake or river. Along with the run-off rainwater go fertilizers and other lawn chemicals into waterways, which can have serious consequences for water plants, fish, and other aquatic life. Storm-water runoff can also lead to stream bank erosion.

DESIGN CONSIDERATIONS

A well-designed hardscape will go a long way in helping to keep water on your site. Start by considering the materials you are using for your hardscape.

Common paving material, such as concrete and mortared stone, deflect water. To help keep rainwater from washing away, install permeable surfaces, such as gravel or stone, in large walkways or driveways. They allow water to flow through their surface, recharging groundwater and filtering pollutants and solids from the water as it percolates through.

Gravel is often the least expensive permeable surface. It's easy to spread and it lasts a long time. It does require weeding, however, and it can be difficult to shovel or plow if you live in a snowy climate. Because it can be washed away in heavy rains, it is best used on a level or nearly level area.

Flagstone is a very attractive paving material for patios and paths. Choose a local stone to help instill a sense of place. Leave enough space in between the stones for water to percolate down. You can cover the spaces with gravel or coarse sand. Or consider planting a low-growing groundcover that can take some foot traffic.

A berm can also be an effective way to help retain water on your property. Berms are built by mounding up soil on nearly level or very shallow slopes. Bermed soil helps hold runoff in place and allows it to percolate slowly down into the soil. A series of small berms on a gentle slope keeps water from washing down the slope.

You could also build a swale, which is the opposite of a berm. Soil is excavated to create a shallow gully that collects runoff that would otherwise flow down a hill. By installing several swales down a hillside, you can really slow down the water movement, giving it time to soak into the soil.

If your property is on a steep slope, consider terracing to help prevent water from washing down the hillside. Retaining walls will also greatly reduce runoff from slopes or hillsides. They can be planted with deep-rooted plants, which will increase the water-holding capacity and reduce erosion.

RAIN GARDENS

A rain garden is an attractive, ecological way to help control runoff from impervious surfaces and filter out pollutants before they reach streams and lakes. When properly designed, a rain garden helps keep water on site so it can recharge the groundwater and provide water to trees and shrubs.

Built in a shallow depression, a rain garden is usually about 6 to 8 inches deep, allowing the garden to hold water for a short period of time (usually less than 24 hours) while it is absorbed into the soil. Rain gardens can be as small as the area under your downspout or as large as several city blocks. The water can be collected from many sources: roofs, driveways, patios, other impermeable surfaces, and even lawns.

It might seem logical to place a rain garden in a low area of your yard where water already collects. However, this usually indicates that the soil drainage is very poor there. You would have to replace the existing soil with improved soil to make it a properly functioning rain garden. In other words, it would mean a lot of extra work. An ideal location would be an area of your yard that collects water after a rainstorm, but the water is then quickly absorbed into the ground. That spot will require only nominal site preparation and soil amending to properly function.

To determine the size and depth of your water garden, you will need to determine how much rainwater runs off your property and how much of that you wish to capture

Terracing creates water-absorbing planting beds and helps reduce runoff into the street.

in your garden. Take into account runoff from downspouts, hard surfaces where water runs off, and even turfgrass, because the soil in lawns is often compacted and prone to runoff. The final size and depth of your garden will be determined by runoff amounts as well as your soil type and how well-drained the soil is (the percolation rate, which is determined by doing a test of the drainage rate of your soil—read more on that at www.bluewaterbaltimore.org/wp-content/uploads/2014/03/Conducting-a-Perc-Test-FINAL.pdf). If your soil is well-drained or you have replaced it with a well-drained mix, a general rule is to make your rain garden 20 to 30 percent the size of your total drainage area. A depth between 4 and 12 inches works well for most rain gardens.

Planted with appropriate plants, rain gardens become attractive additions to the landscape while reducing pollution, saving water, and attracting butterflies and birds. Runoff from the lawn and driveway are filtered into this one.

Choosing Plants for Rain Gardens

The list of plants suitable for rain gardens is quite extensive and it varies by region and soil type. Your main goal is to choose plants appropriate for your site that will take care of the necessary business of managing storm water. A plant's suitability is based on where you live (hardiness and native species), where your rain garden is located on your property (sun or shade, front or backyard), and how you want your rain garden to look (plant height, year-round interest, flower color). Within these requirements, you can also make choices based on wildlife attraction, season-long interest, bloom times, and even your favorite colors. Native prairie species, especially those that evolved in seasonally moist prairies, such as *Monarda fistulosa* and *Silene regia*, are especially well suited to rain gardens. Most of them have deep root systems that will help them survive summer dry spells. These extensive root systems also create natural channels that help keep the soil loose and improve infiltration.

Although most rain gardens are heavy on herbaceous perennial flowers, there are also many grasses and ferns that will thrive in these gardens. And in larger gardens, there are several shrubs and trees for consideration. The end result should be a functional garden that manages your rainwater, fits your desired level of maintenance, and still looks good in your yard and neighborhood.

One important thing to keep in mind when selecting plants is that you are not looking for wetland or water garden plants or those that require very dry soil conditions. Rather, you are looking for plants that can tolerate saturated soil for a period of time, but are also able to withstand drought conditions, especially in the central, lowest part of the garden (Zone A on page 281). As you move toward the outsides of the garden, in Zones B and C, you can incorporate more traditional garden and landscape plants that grow well in average soil moisture. They will need to be able to tolerate some standing water, but not for very long.

Building a Rain Garden

1. Remove any existing vegetation from the rain garden site. To remove sod by hand, push a square shovel just beneath the roots and lift up the sod.

2. Remove the layer of topsoil found just below the sod and hang onto it; you'll reuse it in the garden.

3. Remove heavy clay or poorly draining undersoil to a depth of 12 to 24 inches, depending on the amount of soil you need to replace.

4. After digging, measure your garden's depth to make sure it is deep enough. Make sure the bottom is level.

5. Soil amendments, including the saved topsoil, sand, and compost, can be mixed together outside the garden and added as one mixture or they can be added individually and mixed together as you build the garden. A good ratio is about 50 to 60 percent coarse, sharp sand; 20 to 30 percent topsoil; and 20 to 30 percent organic matter.

6. Make sure the bottom area of the garden is loose so your plants will get established more quickly. Then add plants!

A well-designed rain garden will have several different soil moisture zones.

Zone A plants in the deepest part of the garden must be able to tolerate periodic or frequent standing or flowing water as well as seasonal dry spells. This is also where you will want to place taller plants, keeping in mind that they will appear a foot or so shorter because this area of the garden is usually lower than the outsides.

Zone B plants are generally found in the area right around Zone A. They should grow well in average soil moisture. They will need to be able to tolerate some standing water but not for very long. If your percolation test results show you have a high infiltration rate, you can consider using plants that like average soil conditions (Zone B plants) in the bottom as well (Zone A), because your garden will drain readily and not hold water for too long.

Zone C plants should be able to tolerate average to dry conditions. Zone C plants tend to be shorter plants because this zone is usually found around the outside of the garden. But don't be afraid to include some taller, fine-textured plants in this zone. Keep in mind that this zone is usually the most visible and it is the area where the rain garden will blend into the existing landscape.

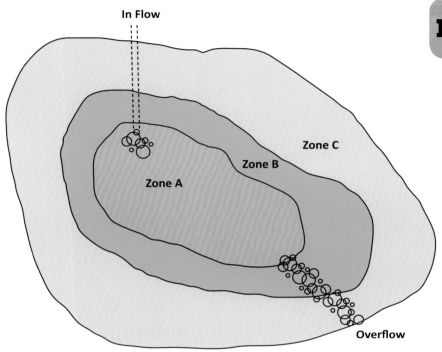

RAIN BARRELS AND CISTERNS

Harvesting rainwater is a great way to store it for drier times. It is easily done by connecting a water tank or barrel to a downspout or by simply leaving an open-topped container where it will collect rainwater. To collect water from a downspout, shorten the downspout with a hacksaw and add a curved section to the end to direct water into your barrel.

Rain barrels can be made of a variety of materials. Molded plastic barrels that hold from 30 to 80 gallons are popular. They should be opaque to keep out sunlight, which can encourage algae growth. Make sure your barrel is on a firm base that can support the weight of the barrel when it is full. A full barrel can be very heavy and dangerous if it were to tip over. The barrel should have a spigot and an overflow mechanism that will discharge excess water when the barrel is full. If you plan to connect a soaker hose to a rain barrel, the spigot should have a garden hose connector. Try to locate the barrel at a higher spot to improve the water pressure going through your hose.

A standard rain barrel can be placed under every gutter downspout in your home.

If the barrel is open at the top, install a fine-mesh screen to prevent mosquitoes from breeding and to keep out birds and rodents. Use rain barrel water within a week or two to discourage algae growth. Hose out the barrel twice each season when it's in use to remove debris. A rain barrel can be left in place year-round in colder climates as long as you leave the spigot open and empty the barrel before freezing temperatures arrive. If water freezes in the barrel, it could expand and cause damage. It is a good idea to cover the rain barrel in winter to keep it dry.

A rainwater cistern is really just a larger version of a rain barrel that has a pumping system to deliver the water. It is usually placed where it will catch the most runoff from buildings, and gutters and downspouts are often used to direct water into it. Cisterns can be made of metal, fiberglass, polyethylene (plastic), poured concrete, concrete blocks, stones, or wood. They typically have a secure cover and can be aboveground, partially buried, or underground. Because more runoff is generated from a typical roof than can be contained in cisterns or rain barrels at any one time, they are typically integrated into a design that also includes an adjacent rain garden.

A large cistern collects water from the roof for use in this garden.

CHAPTER 16

GARDENING FOR THE BIRDS AND BEES

By Rhonda Fleming Hayes

AS A GARDEN WRITER AND PHOTOGRAPHER, I AM lucky to visit a great number of beautiful landscapes. Among the sights I've been privileged to see are striking displays of colorful blooms, impressive stonework, unusual plant collections, and more. Scouting for garden stories to share with my readers, I seek out certain things, but not necessarily what nervous homeowners think as they scurry about pulling weeds and tidying up before I arrive. I look for liveliness, not only in thriving plants but also in flutter, buzz, and birdsong.

The presence of birds and bees is the tip off to what is truly a successful garden, one that speaks to me and makes my heart sing just like the robin or mockingbird watching from the trees as I wander about with my camera and notepad.

Back home, I pull together the elements for my story while sitting with my laptop on the front porch I call my outdoor office. Bumblebees and hummingbirds whizz by as I tap on the keys. A chipping sparrow ferries cabbageworms from my kitchen garden around the corner to her nest of bawling young in a nearby pine branch. My home sits on a modest urban lot, yet with a thoughtful selection of trees, shrubs, and assorted flowers, my garden shelters and feeds them and their friends all season long. In return they provide pollination, pest control, and the most delightful company.

OPPOSITE: Bumblebees feast on colorful blanket flower (*Gaillardia grandiflora* 'Arizona Sun').

Everyone benefits when they act to create a bird- and bee-friendly environment, because this powerful duo performs such vital services for the garden. Birds add beauty, music, and interest to our yards with their bustling activity while eating loads of harmful pests. Bees pollinate the flowers of both ornamental and edible plants. Together they contribute to a healthier, more productive garden. Even better, with the assistance of birds and bees, there's more time and energy to enjoy these outdoor spaces.

On a deeper level, gardening practices that support and sustain wildlife can be a boon for threatened and endangered species. Birds and bees face pressures to their survival with habitat loss first and foremost. Pesticides kill outright as well as cause indirect harm. Climate change will become a greater problem as erratic weather makes birds and bees vulnerable to more potent storms and sudden freezes. Crucial plant-animal relationships that have evolved over thousands of years may go out of sync.

Gardeners can't solve all the problems, but gardeners *can* help stem habitat loss.

BLOOMS, BUGS, AND BERRIES: WELCOMING BIRDS AND BEES TO YOUR GARDEN

When guests come to visit, you probably offer them something to eat and drink. Perhaps you've even done a little research to find out what they like or don't like. It's the same with hosting birds and bees in your garden, although you don't have to worry about who's dairy free or gluten intolerant. Still, it does help to do some homework and learn about their life cycles, behaviors, and diet.

Eat Like a Bird

A lot of people are under the impression that birds mainly eat seeds. After all, Americans spend more than 2 billion dollars on wild bird feed each year. It's a good-hearted hobby, but seed is only part of the needs of many backyard birds. Depending upon the species, region, and time of the year, various birds may consume insects, spiders, worms,

ABOVE: A hummingbird feeds at petunias.

OPPOSITE: A robin sings from the treetops, a reminder of one of the many benefits of attracting bees and birds to your garden.

bird eggs, fruit, grain, or even small mammals, reptiles, and amphibians. Hummingbirds may fuel up on nectar to fly, but surprisingly their diet is made up of mainly spiders and insects.

When it comes to raising their young, a whopping 96 percent of bird species feed insects to their new hatchlings in late spring to early summer. Insects provide much-needed high-protein nourishment to these growing young-sters. It's been estimated that songbirds feed their babies 4 to 12 times per hour. That's a lot of bugs! Indeed, a single chickadee feeds 5,000 caterpillars to her young before they leave the nest. So, where do all those insects come from?

One answer is native plants. Native plants have co-evolved along with other native species for thousands of years. These plants host the vast array of insects and other minute creatures that in turn feed birds and other wildlife, creating the intricate food web that supports our ecosystem. Native plants are a key part of the smaller ecosystem within your garden, even though it may seem counterintuitive to invite bugs to dine on your plants. You need a certain number of them hanging around to maintain the proper balance of birds and bugs.

But weren't some of those caterpillars going to trans-form into beautiful butterflies? Unfortunately, yes, but caterpillars are a necessary part of the circle of life. All the more reason to maintain and plant more natives. Thank-fully native plants include more than just members of the perennial border; native trees, shrubs, grasses, and vines are crucial to the cause. In fact, trees outrank herbaceous flowers in numbers of species they help to sustain. A native perennial may support perhaps 8 to 10 *Lepidoptera* species (butterfly and moth larvae) on average while an oak tree supplies food for hundreds of species. (Read more about gardening with natives in Chapter 14.)

Folks are surprised to find out that many trees are just as important as flowers to successful butterfly gardening.

This caterpillar is not a pest, but the forerunner of a tussock moth.

River birch (*Betula nigra*) is a larval host to the mourning cloak butterfly.

Seedheads are appealing in their own right.

Trees That Feed Caterpillars
- Birches
- Cottonwoods
- Elms
- Hackberries
- Oaks
- Poplars
- Tulip trees
- Wild cherries
- Willows

All are hosts to a number of showy butterflies (as well as moths). More trees mean more caterpillars and more baby food for birds!

Going to Seed

Once birds are done with child rearing, their diet often changes over to seeds and fruit that become available. At this stage, you can buy bird food or you can simply grow it!

There are a number of plants that are popular with birds such as cardinals, finches, sparrows, juncos, redpolls, buntings, and nuthatches, which all favor seeds as part of their sustenance. You can tell by their wedge-shaped bills, perfect for cracking the hulls. Of course, you'll have to leave these plants standing after the blooms have matured in order to produce seeds.

Fortunately, as the season comes to a close, the shapes and silhouettes of dried seedheads are often as appealing as the flowers. It's charming to see a goldfinch or other little fellow perched upon a swaying stem as they nibble on the treats. As winter nears, other birds will scratch around to find more seeds that have fallen. Among these plants are tough natives that are adapted to many conditions, along with a few annuals that are inexpensive and easy to grow.

Amaranthus 'Hot Biscuits' are good for both birds and autumn bouquets.

Flowers That Make Bird Seed

Perennials

- Asters
- Brown-eyed Susans
- Coneflowers
- Coreopsis
- Cup plants
- Goldenrods
- Liatris

Ornamental Grasses

- Big bluestem
- Blue grama grass
- Indian grass
- Little bluestem
- Prairie dropseed
- Switchgrass

Annual Flowers

- Amaranthus
- Bachelor buttons
- Cosmos
- Marigolds
- Sunflowers
- Tithonia
- Zinnias

Berry Good Plants

As autumn approaches, birds look to berries and fruits for extra nutrition they need to face overwintering in place or migrating to warmer climates. Studies have found that berries not only provide vital energy but also contain important antioxidants and other micronutrients that help them withstand the stresses of winter or long-distance flight.

Birds love the dramatic black fruit of chokeberry (*Aronia melanocarpa*).

For gardeners, these shrubs and trees offer beauty and interest in the garden throughout the season with flowers, fall color, and colorful fruit. Some species come in both multistemmed tree or bush form according to the variety. As berries ripen, birds have the opportunity to eat large quantities of fruit in one location so as not to use up their energy flying here and there in search of food. Planted as a single specimen, in groups, or as a hedge or a living fence, they are an attractive low-maintenance landscape solution that helps wildlife at the same time.

Trees and Shrubs with Berries for Birds
• Bayberries
• Blackberries
• Blueberries
• Crabapples
• Currants
• Dogwoods
• Elderberries
• Hollies
• Junipers
• Pokeweeds
• Raspberries
• Serviceberries
• Viburnums

You may see some precious berries on that list you hesitate to share. You may want to apply netting or gauze covers to valuable people-food crops. As an alternative, you could plant enough for everyone. Otherwise it's the early bird who gets the berry. Set your alarm clock!

Creating a Buzz

Bees are all over the news nowadays, and beyond the headlines, you see images of bees in art and on T-shirts, food labels, and billboards. While it's the honeybee getting most of the press, it's important to know there are also 4,000 native bee species in North America that need our attention as well.

Native bees range from tiny Perdita bees the size of a grain of rice to hulking carpenter bees. Many are striped with typical yellow and black, but others flaunt striking hues of metallic blue or green. Some have markings in shades of rust or orange. Once you start to notice them, their beauty will amaze you.

European settlers introduced honeybees to the New World, and since then they have been a dominant force in pollinating our food crops. However, many native bees are significant pollinators too. No matter the species, bees are hurting from habitat loss and gardeners are in a position to help make up for the deficit. The solution is simple: plant more bee-friendly flowers. Flowers = food.

Flower Power

Many native bees as well as honeybees are able to forage among a wide variety of flowers both native and non-native. They are called generalists, while other bee species are specialists, meaning they may only gather nectar and/or pollen from specific blooms. Native bees have co-evolved along with native plants, often adapting body parts, flower structures, and bloom time to accommodate each other. Tongue length often determines which flowers are utilized. Bumblebees with long tongues can probe tubular shapes to access food, but bees with shorter tongues, such as the green sweat bee, feed from daisy shapes where nectar- and pollen-producing parts are more exposed.

Flower traits that have evolved through natural selection by bees, other insects, and vectors are called pollination syndromes; they can include flower shape, color, and odor. Bees are most attracted to white, yellow, blue, and ultraviolet colors (colors that humans can't see). In addition, they seek flowers with markings or dots that act as nectar guides, sort of like a road map directing them to the nectar and/or pollen. They prefer flowers with fresh, mild scents.

A green sweat bee on an aster ('Purple Dome').

A mason bee is nectaring on an allium ('Purple Sensation').

Some bees have special pollination styles that allow them to better pollinate particular blooms. Bumblebees are especially nimble when it comes to pollinating tomato blossoms. They practice what's called "buzz pollination." To do this, they grasp the flower from the bottom and beat their wings at a high frequency to shake the pollen loose. Mason bees, or blue orchard bees, are valuable pollinators in apple and cherry production where they do a comical but highly effective "flop and wallow" form of pollination. That results in lots of pollen falling as they move from flower to flower. In fact, they are more efficient than honeybees at their job.

The moment bees emerge from their hive or nest in spring, they are looking for flowers. Blooms are scarce this time of year before the growing season is under way. Dandelions are an important source of nectar in spring, so think about leaving them to flower before mowing or pulling. Native ephemerals may be short-lived but provide much-needed food source this time of year too.

Spring-Blooming Ephemerals
- Bloodroot
- Celandine poppies
- Dogtooth violets
- Dutchman's breeches
- Pasque flowers
- Rue anemones
- Spring beauty
- Trillium
- Trout lilies
- Twinleaf
- Virginia bluebells

Purple coneflower (*Echinacea purpurea*) and blazing star (*Liatris spicata*) are beautiful native plants with high habitat value.

In supporting bees, the biggest challenge to home gardeners is keeping a constant supply of flowers, a seasonal buffet of blooms from start to finish. Honeybees can forage up to 2 miles, but some native bees may have a range as short as 500 feet. When flowers are few, it's like having the grocery store suddenly shut down. A good goal is to keep at least three plants blooming at a time when bees are active.

Instead of planting one of this and one of that, it's better to plant more of one kind of bee-friendly species. Bees are better able to find larger plantings and then conserve energy when they can forage from many flowers on a single plant at a time. You may notice that lots of bee favorites, such as salvias or anise hyssops, have multiple florets that bees systematically work over in their search for nectar.

Bee-Friendly Perennials
- Anise hyssops
- Asters
- Bee balm
- Coneflowers
- Eryngium
- Goldenrods
- Helenium
- Milkweeds
- Poppies
- Salvias
- Sedums
- Sunflowers
- Turtleheads
- Veronicas

Think outside the perennial border for flower opportunities. A layered, plant-rich landscape is much preferred to the sterile "lawn + tree + three shrubs" scenarios so often seen in cities and suburbs today. Flowering varieties of trees, shrubs, vines, and groundcovers should all be an integral part of your bee-feeding efforts. Bees count on fruit trees and bushes for a major part of "nectar flow" in spring as much as we count on bees for pollination.

Bees are the key to a productive vegetable garden when it comes to beans, cucumbers, squash, pumpkins, and more. Planting bee-attracting flowers near or among your vegetables will assure more thorough pollination that results in better-quality crops as well as higher yields. If you

Goldenrod (*Solidago*) is very popular with bees and other pollinators.

do nothing else for bees, plant an herb garden. Enjoy their culinary delights and fragrance for a while, and let at least half set flower. Before you know it, bees will be visiting.

Bee-Friendly Herbs

- Angelica
- Basil
- Borage
- Chamomile
- Cilantro
- Lavender
- Mint
- Oregano
- Rosemary
- Savory
- Sweet woodruff
- Thyme

Use colorful annuals to fill in gaps in the bloom sequence; a few cheap packets of seeds will provide a rainbow of blooms that beckon bees and other pollinators. Bees prefer the taller, old-fashioned version of garden flowers, such as zinnias and cosmos rather than the new shorter bedding

Plant annuals, such as orange cosmos, to help fill the gap between perennial blooms and attract bees and other pollinators.

varieties. Heirloom flowers with single-petal blooms are better than double or ruffled varieties. This is because often when plant breeders select for "improved" traits, the nectar structure is sacrificed, leaving them useless for bees.

Bee-Friendly Annuals

- Ageratum
- Alyssum
- Bachelor buttons
- Calendula
- Cosmos
- Forget-me-nots
- Heliotrope
- Honeywort
- Marigolds
- Nasturtiums
- Sunflowers
- Zinnias

ABOVE: A honeybee visits a rosemary blossom.

OPPOSITE: Mix flowers and herbs in the veggie garden to attract bees.

Endless miles of vast lawns and pruned up shrubbery do little to nothing for wildlife. It's time to bring back the blooms to our gardens!

WATER FOR BIRDS AND BEES

Water brings a joyful, life-affirming element to the garden. Even the smallest water source is guaranteed to lure more winged wildlife to your door.

Birds find some moisture in their food but also need to drink fresh water every day. They use it for bathing and grooming as well. Honeybees drink water and then carry it in their crops back to the hive for several purposes. In hot weather, they cool the hive with water by fanning their wings over it, much like a swamp cooler. Bees charged with nursing duty deliver it to growing larvae. In winter, when their honey supply crystallizes, they use the water to dilute it and make it edible for them again.

The simplest way to provide water for birds is to imitate the puddles found in nature. Pedestal birdbaths are pretty, but birds prefer a shallow basin, such as a large planter saucer, ceramic dish, or even a garbage lid, closer to or at ground level. A gentle slope to the sides helps them feel more secure with their footing; adding a few small stones increases that feeling of safety and also keeps them from getting their feet wet in winter. In summer, place the basin in the shade to slow evaporation and keep the water fresher for longer periods. There should be some type of plant cover nearby for quick escape from predators as well.

Moving water is especially appealing to birds, be it dripping, running, or misting. You can purchase water wigglers, solar or battery-operated devices that maintain a slight movement to the water making it more tempting for birds. Agitating

ABOVE: Place birdbaths like this decorative leaf one at ground level.

LEFT: Cedar waxwings pause from foraging to take a drink at this backyard water feature.

A female cardinal shelters among tree branches.

the water also discourages mosquitos from laying their eggs in it. In cold weather, an immersion heater will keep water from freezing so that wintering birds stay hydrated. Whatever the type of birdbath you decide upon, it's important to keep it clean and consistently full to draw in feathered friends. Of course, larger water features, such as garden ponds, and waterfalls, also work well to encourage birds.

Bees also need good footing and staging when they seek out water. Textured surfaces help them grip while drinking. They want to avoid getting wet because it hinders flying. Unlike birds, bees like their water "aged." It's thought that they find the odor of algae enticing. You can make simple "bee waterers" by filling planter saucers or other shallow containers with small pebbles or glass marbles before adding water. Some folks float tennis balls or corks in water features so that bees can drink while hanging onto them.

RESTING AND NESTING: SUSTAINING BIRDS AND BEES IN YOUR GARDEN

From top to bottom, it's easy to turn your garden into a five-star accommodation for birds and bees.

Safe Haven

Subject to the whims of weather and peril of predators while going about their busy lives, birds need safe spaces to rest and take cover. The same layered landscape that produces lots of food is just as important for these reasons. A garden with a great number of trees, shrubs, and other plant forms creates what is called "structural complexity," or simply put, a variety of places to hide from harm or sit out storms.

Evergreens are essential; they offer dense foliage year-round to protect birds from cold, wind, and rain. The prickly needles may also discourage some predators.

Shrubs planted in hedges afford a cage-like arrangement of stems and branches where birds can breathe easy between food runs. Areas between tall grasses are good hiding spots too.

Time your garden chores to give birds a better chance of survival. Prune in springtime so that foliage or branches remain denser for fall when it's needed more. Save your yard trimmings to make brush piles. You may have to arrange them with a bit of artistry to avoid neighbors' objections, but birds will be grateful for these convenient refuges. Place brush piles or any other handcrafted shelter so that it faces south and sits away from rain gutters or heavy snow accumulation.

There are times when birds prefer to perch and observe their surroundings in order to scope out possible mates or spot predators or potential food. Tall plants, support stakes, decorative poles, or rocks can serve as promontories for this purpose.

Feathering the Nest

Come spring, birds are preoccupied with scouting for nesting spots. In some cases, the female carries out this search alone, and at other times the male gives a second opinion on this important matter of real estate. The nest must be protected from the elements and hidden from predators.

Depending upon the species, it may be right on the ground, high in the treetops, or somewhere in the middle. Most birds build nests in trees and shrubs with found materials, while around 85 North American species are cavity nesters and take advantage of pre-existing nooks and crannies, holes in trees, building crevices, birdhouses, flowerpots, and even shoes left on the doorstep. Once again, a layered landscape with structural complexity offers the most opportunities to provide nesting sites for birds in your garden.

Birds use an astounding array of natural materials and human discards when constructing nests from scratch or lining cavities. Built nests vary from open cup-like arrangements to hanging sock–like structures. Birds are resourceful; they utilize all these materials with an eye toward strength, waterproofing, comfort, and elasticity

A chipping sparrow in a well-concealed nest.

that can last for the duration of their brood. Before you tidy up too much, think of your yard as a home improvement store for birds.

16

Nesting Materials from Nature
- Bark
- Feathers
- Fluff (cattail, cottonwood, dandelion, milkweed)
- Grass
- Hair (horse, cow, deer)
- Lichens
- Moss
- Mud
- Pine needles
- Roots
- Snakeskin
- Spider egg sacs
- Spider silk
- Twigs

It's not unusual for birds to use trash and debris such as twine, ribbon, tinsel, and even zip ties in their nest construction. Folks often think they are helping by leaving out string or yarn, but it can get tangled around birds' feet, cutting off blood supply. Don't put out dryer lint either; it crumbles once it gets wet. Instead, set out pet hair, coconut husks from hanging basket liners, sphagnum moss, and cloth strips.

BEYOND THE BEE HIVE

Honeybees raise their young in hives, where a strict division of labor makes sure they are properly cared for. Yet native bees must do all this on their own—more specifically, the female bee. Males are there for mating, but otherwise, all the work of childrearing falls to the female. Females have to find a suitable nesting site, create the nest, lay the eggs, forage for food, and then tend to the baby larvae until they mature and are ready to leave the nest. Gardeners can help out a girl bee by adjusting a few of their landscape practices to accommodate her nesting needs.

Give Bees a Chance

When it comes to nesting, native bees fall into one of two categories; ground nesters (70 percent) and cavity nesters (30 percent). Many people fear ground-nesting bees that choose to locate in areas where they play and work. Often it is actually wasps that create these problems; bees are often blamed for wasps' behavior (wasps are pollinators too, but require a wider berth than most bees).

Most native bees are solitary bees instead of social bees, unlike honeybees that live in colonies. Ground-nesting bees excavate and build a single nest, although according to the species, they may build these individual nests in large groupings or aggregates. Other species may share a single entrance to separate underground burrows.

Notice the intricate construction of this nest.

Leafcutter bees cut circular pieces from plant leaves to line the egg cells of their nests.

Bumblebees will nest in abandoned mouse holes found under tufts of grasses and sedges.

Bare soil on an eastern-facing slope is the ideal site for their nests. However, gardeners tend to mulch every exposed square inch of their yards so that bees find it increasingly difficult to find places for nesting. To help out, consider leaving some areas of the yard unmulched, especially in low-to-no traffic areas, such as slopes.

Cavity nesters take up residence in old beetle tunnels and other holes bored in dead wood. Others find pithy or hollow stems to call home. Cavity-nesting bees lay their eggs in a series of linear cells within the length of these tubular shaped spaces, and then, depending on the species, seal up each cell with waxy body secretions, mud, or even leaves in some cases, and then seal up the entrance as well. Mason bees got their name from using mud, just like the bricks-and-mortar profession. Leafcutter bees line their nests with a patchwork of leaf segments.

An overly manicured yard is of no use to these bees. When you can, leave some woody debris or deadfall, an interesting stump, or a gnarled log for rustic looks and valuable habitat. Arrange bundles of shrub trimmings or reeds in foot-long lengths. Some of the same plants that provide food and habitat for birds also offer nesting materials for bees.

Hollow- or Pithy-Stemmed Plants for Bee Nesting
• Bamboo
• Blackberries
• Cup plants
• Dogwoods
• Elderberries
• Hydrangeas
• Raspberries
• Sumacs
• Sunflowers

Bumblebees are social bees that live in a colony. The colony dies off at the end of the growing season when flowers are done blooming, leaving only the mated queen to overwinter and start a new colony come spring. She nests in old rodent holes and cavities under tufts of grasses. In small-space gardens, even a few ornamental grasses can create bumblebee habitat. On larger properties, thickets of tall meadow grasses are prime spots for homegrown bumblebee conservation.

SMART PEST CONTROL: PROTECTING BIRDS AND BEES IN YOUR GARDEN

Now that you've invited birds and bees to move in and raise their families in your garden, take measure to protect them from harmful substances.

People often think that pesticides only kill troublesome bugs and weeds. In fact, the damage and destruction from many pesticides is far reaching, affecting living creatures all the way up the food chain, including humans. *Pesticide* is a broad term for insecticides, herbicides, miticides, and more. Pesticides don't discriminate in what they kill besides the target species; spider spray doesn't just kill spiders. For birds and bees, pesticides can cause outright death but also a huge amount of indirect harm.

Recently neonicotinoids, a type of pesticide linked to colony collapse disorder in honeybees, have been in the news. Now studies show that this widely used insecticide also negatively affects birds. Neonics are systemic insecticides used for both agricultural and home garden use, meaning the plant takes up the active chemicals, effectively making the entire plant an insect-killing machine.

Flowers, pollen, and nectar become poisonous too. The pesticide is often delivered through coated seeds. During agricultural application, the pesticide escapes as dust created by planting activity. It can persist in the soil for years as well. Birds and bees ingest these chemicals through nectar, pollen, insects, seeds, and water.

Although the chemicals in neonicotinoids and other pesticides may not be considered lethal to birds and bees, they are sublethal, causing a number of problems that affect their behavior and reproductive systems.

Pesticide Issues for Birds
- Eggshell thinning
- Deformed embryos
- Inattentive parenting
- Lethargic behavior
- Lack of appetite
- Hormone disruption
- Inability to orient for migration

Pesticide Issues for Bees
- Impaired foraging
- Inability to navigate
- Impaired olfactory learning
- Inability to communicate information
- Reproductive disorders
- Inattentive brood care

Step Away from the Spray

Pesticide use in home gardens can be reduced or completely eliminated through a common-sense and scientific approach to pest management. Read more about this in Chapter 10. Be an advocate for birds and bees by asking your garden center to carry neonicotinoid-free plants. Be sure their greenhouse suppliers are complying too.

LEFT: Avoid spraying when bees like this one pollinating a cucumber blossom are active.

OPPOSITE: Pesticides in water harm birds in a number of ways.

What about Weeds?

Many think that herbicides only kill vegetation, so they don't affect birds and bees. However, birds eat grasshoppers and caterpillars along with other insects that depend upon so-called weeds for food. Birds eat weed seeds. A decrease in insects and seeds mean less food. Removing vegetation can reduce the amount of grasses and other plants that provide cover for ground-nesting birds. In addition, ground-foraging birds, such as the robin, are exposed directly to lawn chemicals as they go about looking for worms. Whenever possible, pull weeds by hand or spot treat rather than spray. Leave weeds around the wilder edges of your property where they will enhance habitat value yet won't detract from your landscape.

Unlike landscapes in nature, gardens are designed with human pleasure in mind; they provide places for people to play, relax, and connect with nature. That connection is made stronger when beneficial wildlife, such as birds and bees, are welcome; the chirping of birds and the gentle hum of bees creates a healthier, happier garden. A few simple steps can make meaningful changes that reach far beyond the garden gate.

ABOVE: Bees flock to poppies in bloom.

LEFT: This garden delights both people and wildlife.

CHAPTER 17
CONTAINER GARDENING

By Charlie Nardozzi

THERE ARE SOME DEMOGRAPHIC CHANGES IN OUR society that are converging to make container gardening more popular than ever. For the first time in human history, there are more people living in cities and towns than in rural areas. At the same time, these urbanites are more interested in gardening. According to the National Gardening Survey, there has been an increased interest among urbanites in growing gardens and food. This is particularly true among young millennials in the city.

While this is great news, it sets up an inherent problem. People in cities don't have as much room to garden as those in suburban or rural areas. The solution is container gardening. With new types of pots, potting soils, and plant varieties, we can grow food, flowers, and perennials in containers, even in small spaces.

While city dwellers need to garden in containers because of lack of space, even gardeners with space are understanding the benefits of growing in containers. Due to a lack of time, resources, or energy, many gardeners are downsizing their plantings. Containers are the solution for them as well. Even for gardeners who are keeping their big garden, containers can provide a solution to poor soil. Containers also provide accents in the landscape. They're movable, so you can place them in a yard to create a desired effect and change them out during the season.

OPPOSITE: You can grow flowering containers in sun or shade, and both in small space locations or as large focal points in the landscape.

The keys to successful container growing are choosing the right pot, getting good soil, selecting varieties that grow well in small spaces, and caring for them properly. I'll tackle all those issues in this chapter.

CONTAINER GARDENING BASICS

There are many advantages to growing food, flowers, and perennials in containers. Besides saving space, containers provide versatility in your garden. You can grow your favorite plants in containers but still have room for other outdoor accents, such as deck furniture, a grill, a fire pit, and water features. Containers allow you to move plants when you need more space. If you're having an outdoor dinner or party planned, simply move the containers to the side or off the deck or patio to create the necessary space for chairs, tables, and guests.

Containers extend the growing season so you can plant sooner in the spring and grow later into the fall. Containers also allow you to change the look of your garden throughout the season. For example, plant spring pansies and primulas for early season color. Once they fade, remove them and add heat-loving plants, such as verbena and geraniums. In the fall, wrap up the season by planting ornamental cabbage and kale in your pot. A similar succession can be made using different vegetables and herbs.

Containers do have limitations. Even though you can grow large plants, such as sweet corn and trees, in containers, they require a large pot and more work. You also have a more limited variety of plants that can easily grow in containers than in the ground. And you'll have to be more aware of your container plant's needs. Container plants generally dry out faster than plants in the ground. Because of the limited amount of soil in the pot, you need to supplement the potting soil with fertilizer throughout the growing season. Containers that aren't well cared for can look ragged quickly. You may need to prune and replace plants throughout the growing season to keep the pot looking great.

Many vegetables can be grown in containers. Look for dwarf varieties that can grow well in small spaces.

Clay pots have a classic look to them. Because they breathe and drain water well, select plants for them that like well-drained soil. Because they drain well, they also require more watering than nonporous pots.

Finally, many edibles and flowers need full sun to grow their best. Fruiting veggies, such as tomatoes, cucumbers, and beans, as well as many flowers, such as cosmos and salvias, need at least six hours of sun a day. This may be a limiting factor in a city or town. A spot on your deck or patio that was full sun in June when the sun is at its zenith could be in shade by August and September. The sun in late summer is lower in the sky, and nearby trees and buildings can cast shadows on your garden.

Luckily, containers give you options. You can plant vegetables, such as arugula and spinach, and flowers, such as begonias and impatiens, that grow well in part shade. Another option is to move the containers with the sun. As the amount of direct light changes on your deck or patio, move the container to where it will get the most sun to mature those tomatoes or allow those late-flowering dahlias to keep blooming.

START WITH THE POT

Before you even consider which flowers, vegetables, and herbs to plant, think a bit about your container options. Almost anything can be used as a container as long as it can hold soil and has adequate water drainage holes. I've seen containers made out of old buckets, suitcases, toys, boats, bathtubs, hats, and even old shoes. While these are fun to imagine with flowers, herbs, and vegetables growing in them, you do have to be practical. Use plants that will still fit in the container once they grow and mature. Also, realize that you're creating a certain "look" in your garden with these containers, so make sure it fits with your taste and the rest of your patio furniture, decking, and accessories.

The shape of your container can make a difference in the plant's growth and care. Tall, thin containers dry out quickly on the top but may remain soggy on the bottom. Wide, shallow containers may not be deep enough for large rooted plants.

Here's a rundown of the most popular types of containers.

Terracotta clay. What starts as a clean terracotta color when new often fades to a patina with age. Fertilizer salts get absorbed in the clay, creating white edges, and in shady spots, moss can grow on the pot, giving it an ancient look. Clay pots come in a wide variety of shapes and sizes. Terracotta pots breathe, so they dry out faster than plastic pots. They're good to use with plants that like a well-drained, dry soil, such as portulaca and geranium. Terracotta pots can break easily if dropped, banged, or left out during freezing weather.

Concrete pots are very similar to terracotta in terms of water drainage and weight, although they are not as inherently beautiful. They can be round or trough shaped and are very long lasting and more weather resistant than clay.

Ceramic. These are terracotta pots with a glaze on the surface. Because they're glazed, they will hold water longer than terracotta pots. But like terracotta, they break easily, so they need protection and care when moving them. Terracotta and ceramic pots can be heavy and hard to move when filled with soil and plants.

Plastic. You can get plastic pots in all the colors of the rainbow, including some that look like terracotta. The advantage of plastic is that it's more durable and the soil doesn't dry out as fast. That's good for many plants, but if you have plants that like drier growing conditions, such as Mediterranean herbs and lantana, you might consider using a terracotta pot, lighter potting soil, or a plastic pot with more drainage holes.

Ceramic pots are beautiful additions to a deck, patio, or small garden. Make sure they have drainage holes in the bottom so the plants can thrive.

To lighten the weight of large containers, fill the bottoms with empty plastic bottles, then cover them with landscape fabric before adding potting soil.

UV-stabilized polypropylene. These pots offer distinct advantages. They're longer lasting, more durable, and much more decorative than plastic but are still light weight. Some of these new UV-stabilized polypropylene containers come in bright colors with smooth finishes. Some are also made from a polymer resin and won't chip or crack in temperatures down to -20°F. Others are made with recycled materials.

Self-watering containers. These polypropylene pots contain a false bottom with a reservoir below it that you fill with water. Using a capillary mat, water is wicked into the dry soil from the reservoir, keeping the pot moist for days. You'll find self-watering containers in all shapes and sizes, including railing planters and hanging baskets.

Wood. Wooden containers look rustic and are excellent choices for long-lived perennial flowers, shrubs, and trees, as well as annual plants. They can be made from old whiskey barrels, composite wood materials, or rot-resistant boards such as redwood. They are durable and don't break easily. But while they last for years, they will eventually rot. And they can be fairly large, making them heavy and hard to move. Like terracotta, wood breathes, so these wooden containers dry out faster than plastic pots.

Metal. For durability, you can't beat metal containers. Some are painted bright colors while others have a corrugated, galvanized look. Metal containers heat up fast and hold water well. Plants that like the heat and moisture, such as sweet potatoes and canna lilies, grow well in them.

Grow bags. Polypropylene fabric grow bags are lightweight and breathe like a terracotta pot but are thick enough to hold moisture like a plastic pot. You can grow a whole range of vegetables and flowers in them. They come

in many colors and have handles, so they are easy to lift and move around. The biggest selling point for grow bags is their storability. In fall, simply empty the potting soil into the compost bin, flatten the bag like a pancake, and store it.

Hanging containers. These are a great way to use vertical space for growing plants. You can turn a small 4×6-foot balcony into a Garden of Eden by using railing planters, hanging baskets and vertical wall gardens.

- **Railing planters** are perfect for creating a growing space on narrow metal balcony or deck railings. One side of the railing planter is fashioned into curved plastic and the other has a plastic planter. The curved side hooks over the railing and the weight of the soil, water, and plants holds it in place. Deck railing planters fit over 2×4-inch or 2×6-inch wooden railings. They're shaped like a saddle and straddle the railing on both sides. Both types are available as self-watering containers.
- **Hanging baskets** can hold cascading plants, such as petunias, fuchsia, ivy, and cucumbers. Some are made of plastic, while others use metal frames lined with coir, a coconut-husk-fiber product, or sphagnum peat moss. The coir or peat moss gives the planter a more organic look. Self-watering styles are also available.

Vertical garden kits. You can buy kits that attach to a wall. They're great for growing lettuce, arugula, herbs, and other small plants. Place them where they'll get proper sunlight for the plants you're growing, then keep them well watered and fertilized. (Read more about vertical gardening in Chapter 18.)

Elevated containers. These are partly decorative and often used like a piece of furniture, but they also save planting space. They can be made from wood, metal, or plastic. The beauty of them is that they make it easy to garden without bending over. The downside is that when filled with soil, they're heavy and hard to move.

Strawberry jars. These are made from plastic or terracotta and feature holes in the sides where you tuck in strawberry plants. Don't limit yourself to growing just strawberries, though. Any cascading plant, such as thyme, lobelia, and petunias, will grow well in a strawberry jar.

TOP: Wooden containers have a rustic look. Large ones are good for growing shrubs, trees, and big perennial flowers.

ABOVE: Almost anything can be used as a container as long as it can hold soil and has holes to drain water.

DRAINAGE AND WEIGHT

One of the keys to a successful container planting is proper drainage. If water doesn't drain well from the pot, it creates a soggy potting medium. Waterlogged soil will kill plant roots because of the lack of oxygen, causing plants to die.

The first step when buying or making any container is to be sure it has adequate drainage holes. Most commercial containers already have drainage holes in the bottom. As I mentioned earlier, ceramic containers sometimes do not. It's not easy to drill a hole in a ceramic container without damaging it. The solution is to create a false bottom by placing an upside-down plastic pot in the bottom of the container and dropping another plastic pot, one size smaller than the ceramic pot, into the ceramic container to sit on top of the turned-over plastic pot. The excess water will drain into the space in the bottom of the container.

For homemade wooden containers, drill holes in the bottom. For example, drill six to eight ½-inch-diameter holes in a 14-inch-diameter pot.

For any pot sitting on the ground, make sure it's elevated off the deck or surface for proper drainage. Use pot feet, bricks, or pavers to prop up a pot at least a few inches. To prevent staining your deck or patio, place water drainage trays under the pot.

Weight is another concern with pots. A container that's too heavy to move suddenly becomes a fixture on your deck or patio, and loses some of its appeal. A simple way to ensure mobility with your pots is to buy ones with casters on the bottom or place pots on trays with casters.

BELOW: Most plant roots don't grow below 1 foot in your container. To save space and money in large containers, fill the bottom of the pot with empty water or soda bottles, place screening on top of the bottles, and add potting soil on top.

LEFT: A small-space garden may need to be mobile. Look for containers and raised beds on casters or wheels so you can move them out of the way or protect them from inclement weather.

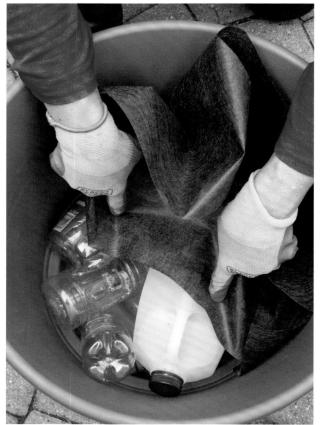

POTTING SOIL

Once you've found the right pot, you need to fill it with soil. You shouldn't use regular garden soil for a variety of reasons. Garden soil may harbor insects and diseases that will attack your plant. Also, garden soil might be too sandy and drain too much water and dry out or have too much clay and compact in the container. Compacted soil makes it hard for roots to grow.

It's best to purchase commercial potting soil. Potting soil is not living soil. It's usually a mixture of organic materials that roots grow well in. It provides bulk to hold the plants, drains water properly, and holds nutrients for plant growth. There are lots to choose from, and it can get confusing. Let's start with the ingredients that are common to most of them.

The main component of most potting soils is peat moss. Milled peat moss is lightweight but can absorb water and provide the bulk plants need to grow. A mix of straight peat moss will not drain water properly. That's why many mixes contain the materials perlite and vermiculite to help with proper water drainage and retention. Perlite is a white-colored, heated volcanic rock that is lightweight and helps with water drainage. Vermiculite is a golden-colored mineral that helps retain water and nutrients for plant use.

Some mixes contain coir, which is shredded coconut husk fiber. Horticulturists have found that coir absorbs water better and drains it faster than peat moss.

Compost is another material you'll find in some mixes. It adds bulk and fertility to a potting mix. It's best used in large containers when growing big plants, shrubs, or trees. It still should be mixed with peat moss, perlite, and vermiculite for proper water drainage.

Finally, some potting mixes have chemical fertilizer added to them. Unless you add compost, most potting mixes offer little fertility for your plants. You'll need to fertilize regularly to keep them healthy. By adding fertilizer to the potting mix, you'll help support early plant growth. Some gardeners would rather not use chemical fertilizer on their plants, and this starter fertilizer is often gone from the mix after a few waterings. (Read more about fertilizing containers later in this chapter.)

When selecting potting soil at the garden center, look for bags that contain peat moss or coir, perlite, and vermiculite. Lift up similar-size bags of different brands of potting soil. The bag and potting soil should be dry and lightweight. Remember that you can always add more bulk to your

ABOVE: Most potting soils are a mix of peat moss or coir, perlite, and vermiculite. These materials are blended to aid in proper water drainage and nutrient and water retention.

TOP: Use potting soil in containers. Garden soil may contain insects and diseases and can compact, making it hard for your plants' roots to grow well.

How to Plant a Container

Here's a step-by-step process for planting your container.

1. If you're reusing old pots, make sure you've washed them out well with a 10-percent bleach solution. This will kill any diseases that might be lurking in your pot from last year.

2. Check the bottom of your container for adequate drainage holes.

3. Fill the container about two-thirds full with moistened potting soil. (For larger containers, consider not filling it entirely with soil. Most annual garden plants need about a 1-foot-deep layer of soil to grow properly. If you have a 3-foot-tall container, you can fill the bottom 1 to 2 feet with empty plastic water, milk, or soda containers. Then lay landscape fabric or plastic screening over the empty containers so soil doesn't wash through. Add potting soil on top of the fabric. This also reduces the amount of soil you'll need to buy and makes the containers lighter and easier to move.)

4. Think about the size of the plants you want to grow in your pots. Small flowers and vegetables, such as pansy, lettuce, basil, and dwarf marigolds, will grow fine in 8- to 10-inch-diameter container. For larger flowers and vegetables that grow 2 to 3 feet tall, select larger containers that are 12 to 14 inches in diameter.

5. Plant your seedlings at the same depth as they were growing in the original pot. Tomatoes are the exception and can be planted deeper because they have the unique ability to root all along their stem.

6. Fill the container with potting soil, pressing it down. Leave a 1- to 2-inch space between the rim of the container and top of the potting soil.

7. Gently water at the top of the container, watering thoroughly and letting the soil soak up the water. You can also place small containers in a basin of water and let the water naturally soak into the dry soil through the drainage holes.

8. Place your containers in their new location, making sure they're elevated off the ground so water drains properly out the bottom. If you wish, place water drainage trays under the containers to prevent staining.

6. Fill the container with potting soil loosely packed around the rootball.

5. Plants should be planted in containers at the same height they were in their original pots.

7. Gently water the container.

potting mix by adding sterilized compost, but it's much harder to lighten a heavy mix.

Once you have a successful season of growing in your container, the question of what to do with old potting soil often comes up. The short answer is that unless your plants were diseased or insect infested, you can reuse it again next year. It is important to remove all the dead plants from the pot and not plant the same type of vegetable or flower in that container next year. This will reduce the risk of diseases attacking the plants. By spring, the old potting soil in the container will have settled, so amend your container with a new batch of potting soil, filling it to the top and mixing it in with the old soil. You should be able to use the same potting soil for two to three years before needing to replace the whole batch. For potted perennials, shrubs, and trees, simply apply a topdressing of fresh potting soil and compost to the container each spring.

SELECTING PLANTS

The type of vegetables, herbs, flowers, and fruits you plant in your containers depends on the size of your pots and the size of the plants. You also need to consider sun, shade, and how much room you have to grow these beauties in your yard or on your balcony, deck, or patio.

SINGLE VERSUS MIXED CONTAINERS

A single plant in a container can be beautiful. I still have fond memories of my mom planting different colored geraniums in individual pots around our home when I was growing up. But one of the fun parts of container gardening is getting creative, like mixing annual flowers, vegetables, and herbs in single pots.

Grouping different-size containers together on your deck or patio creates a beautiful visual effect. Single-plant containers can be arranged together to give the illusion of a mass planting. Place tall, medium, and short containers together so each can be seen from the most common vantage point. Use railing planters, hanging baskets, and vertical wall gardens to create a whole area of flowers and edibles.

When you start combining plants together in a container, it can get exciting. But you also need to be smart about the types and numbers of plants you put in any one container. Gardeners often overplant containers because they forget a

Tomatoes can grow well in containers. Select a dwarf or determinate variety, keep it well watered and fertilized, and support the plant with a cage or stakes.

The simplest flower container design is to grow one type of flower in the pot. Geraniums (above) and coleus are two examples of beautiful plants that look great by themselves.

basic fact: plants grow. A single tomato, eggplant, pineapple sage, or coleus can fill up even a large container by summer's end. Unless you know the ultimate size of your flowers, vegetables, and herbs, your container can quickly turn into a weedy mess. Garden centers and nurseries often will sell pre-planted containers. In order to make the container look attractive for sale, they often overplant. It will look good for a few weeks but then may need a makeover (more about pruning and sprucing up a container later in the chapter).

Start with a large container and mix and match plants with complementary growth habits. One method to use is the thriller, filler, and spiller technique.

THRILLER, FILLER, AND SPILLER

You can take advantage of the various growth habits of plants by mixing them together in a container. Not only can you add more plants than normal, but you can also create color and interest from a few feet above the container rim to the ground. It's called the thriller, filler, and spiller technique. Here's how it works.

Select a large pot that can fit five to seven plants. In the center, plant one tall, narrow-growing thriller plant, such as angelonia or purple fountain grass. Around the base of this thriller, plant two or three mounding filler plants that will grow about 1 foot tall. Some good examples are profusion zinnias, marigolds, dusty miller, and begonias. These will fill in the base of the tall thriller plant, giving the flower container some bulk.

Finally, add two or three spiller plants around the edge of the container. Select plants that naturally cascade over the edge of the container and can eventually grow to the ground. Some good examples of spiller plants include sweet potato vines, nasturtiums, dichondra, bacopa, petunias, and lobelia.

By planting thriller, filler, and spiller plants together in a container, you can have color reaching three to four feet off the ground from one container. The best way to keep the plants in proportion is to use filler plants that are roughly half the size of the thriller plant. You don't want the filler to overwhelm the pot.

You can also mix and match herbs and vegetables in the same pot using this technique. For example, grow a pepper as the thriller, lettuce around it as the filler, and cucumbers cascading over the edge of the pot as spillers. For herbs, basil can be your thriller, sage your filler, and oregano your spiller. You can get creative about the types of plants your use as thrillers and fillers. Sometimes a filler plant is large enough and can be pruned into a thriller plant. A kale plant with the bottom leaves trimmed away and the top leaves allowed to flourish can become a thriller.

COLOR COMBINATIONS

One of the challenges for many container gardeners is matching the right colors and leaf textures together in a container. It certainly is a trial-and-error process and is very personal. Sometimes the combinations work out beautifully and other times they just aren't right. Luckily, with containers you're never wedded to any one combination and you can always start over.

There are some rules that may help you create an attractive container with pleasing colors. Although a container with a riot of different colors of flowers is exciting, containers with simple color schemes are often the easiest to put together and more universally appealing. Use the color wheel as a starting point. Look for colors that complement each other and stick with just two or three colors in any one container. For example, plant blue salvias and orange marigolds together, or try pink celosia with yellow profusion zinnias. These complementary colors are soothing to the eye. You can even add a contrasting color, such as a white dusty miller or black-flowered petunias, to help the other colors pop.

Don't forget to use leaf colors as a way to bring color to your container. Plant breeders have been working hard

To maximize the amount of space in your container, use the thriller, filler, and spiller technique. Thriller plants grow tall and narrow, fillers grow low and bushy, and spillers cascade over the pot's edge.

to produce flowers with interesting colored foliage as well as blossoms. These are great plants to grow in a shady area where a flowering plant may not thrive. One of my favorites is coleus. There are so many different leaf colors and shapes that you can create a whole garden of colorful coleus. Look for colorful leaf versions of other annual flowers, such as dusty miller, begonia, sweet potato vine, Persian shield, and caladium.

THEMED CONTAINERS

A fun way to grow containers is to create themes for them. One of the simplest themed container gardens to grow is a salad garden. Think about what you like to add to your summer salads and grow those plants in a container. You can have individual pots of greens, cherry tomatoes,

cucumbers, and parsley or combine them, as mentioned earlier, into thriller, filler, and spiller containers.

Many gardeners are interested in helping pollinating insects and butterflies thrive. You can create a mini pollinator container garden by planting those flowers that provide nectar and pollen for these essential insects. Select flowers and herbs for pollinators, such as thyme, rosemary, oregano, anise hyssops, salvias, verbena, baby's breath, and dill. Not only will they help pollinators, but you can also pick some of the herbs for your cooking too.

For a low-maintenance container, grow a succulent-themed pot. These are perfect for a location with lots of heat and sun and very well-drained soil. You can mix and match agave, sedum, echeveria, and aloe in a container. These plants have interesting foliage and, if given enough sun, will flower too. Best of all, they require less water than

One of the simplest veggies to grow in containers is salad greens. Mix and match lettuces, arugula, kale, and other greens, and harvest them when they're young for the best texture and flavor.

Create themed container gardens, such as ones that attract beneficial insects, bees, and butterflies.

other plants, so you don't have to worry about them drying out over a long weekend if you're away. Some of these succulents are hardy, depending on where you live, and can be grown year-round in the yard.

Finally, create a kids' container garden. It's a great way to engage them in the garden. They can help come up with the themes and pick out the plants to fit in a manageable space. A container is not overwhelming and your child can help plant, water, and harvest their plants. Let them

suggest plant options. For young children, include some tried and true plants, such as beans, marigolds, and lettuce. You want to make sure they get a harvest from their container. Let your child decorate the container by painting garden images on the pot and adding signs, labels, and toys to the container. The more they feel like it's their container, the more engaged they will be in growing the plants. The key is for them to have a successful experience so they will want to continue gardening each year.

PERENNIALS, SHRUBS, AND TREES

You aren't limited to just growing annual flowers, vegetables, and herbs in containers. Perennial flowers, shrubs, and even trees can be grown successfully in pots.

Many small- to medium-size perennial flowers, such as salvias, coral bells, coreopsis, gaillardia, and veronica, can be successfully grown in a pot. There are many dwarf versions of popular larger perennials, such as purple coneflowers, bee balm, and asters, that can fit in a container as well. Look for cascading perennials, such as ivy, dead nettle, and ajuga, to create that spiller technique I mentioned earlier.

Of course, many of these perennials flowers only bloom for a short period of time, so combinations are important. You can mix and match early blooming perennials, such as violas, with summer-blooming salvias and fall-blooming asters. You can also select perennial flowers with colorful foliage, such as sedum and coral bells, to add color. Another approach is to mix annual flowers with perennial flowers. The annuals give a constant show all summer, while the

ABOVE: Small shrubs look beautiful in containers. To help them come back each spring, protect them in winter by bringing them into a cool room or basement or burying the container in soil or a mulch pile.

OPPOSITE: Even berry bushes and fruit trees grow well in containers. Look for dwarf varieties and protect them in winter in cold areas.

perennials add a pop at various times during the growing season. In warmer winter climates, you can leave the perennial flowers in the container year-round. However, in colder climates, you'll have to protect your perennial flowers in winter by burying the pot in the ground and mulching it or moving it into a shed, garage, basement, or other area where it doesn't get consistently below freezing.

Many plant breeders have created dwarf versions of popular shrubs and trees that fit much easier in a container and are easier to manage. You can grow fruit trees, such as the 'Northpole' columnar apple that only grows 8 feet tall. Dwarf blueberries, such as 'Northsky', 'Jelly Bean', and 'Tophat', only grow a few feet tall. I've grown figs in container for years. They're statuesque and produce delicious fruits every year. Even dwarf raspberry bushes, such as 'Raspberry Shortcake', are small enough to grow in a container.

Popular ornamental trees and shrubs come in dwarf versions too. 'Lo and Behold' is a dwarf butterfly bush great for attracting butterflies that only grows a few feet tall. 'Bobo' is a 3-foot-tall hydrangea that can fit in a pot. There are many miniature roses that are perfect for a container. Citrus, boxwoods, crape myrtles, and Japanese maples are all possibilities in large containers. Cruise through your local garden center looking for dwarf versions of your favorite shrubs and trees.

You can add color to your tree or shrub container by including cascading annual flowers, edibles such as strawberries, and perennial flowers. This will help give the container a season-long appeal. You can also grow just one plant per container and group them so tall trees are in the back, bushy shrubs are in the middle, and colorful low-growing flowers and edibles are in the front.

As with perennial flowers, in warm winter areas you can leave the shrubs and trees outdoors, but in cold areas they will need protection. As a rule of thumb, select shrubs and trees that are at least one hardiness zone colder than your location to ensure success.

Perennials, shrubs, and trees will need a potting mix that has compost added to it. You'll have to regularly fertilize through the growing season and keep the soil evenly moist. After a few years, your shrub or tree may need the tops and roots pruned. In spring, remove the root ball from the container and prune off any dead or rotting roots and any roots that are swirling around the base of the container. Add more compost and repot in the same pot or a container one size larger.

CONTAINER CARE

Now that you've got your containers all potted up and looking great, it's time to talk about container care. Proper watering, fertilizing, pruning, and pest control can help your plants shine throughout the whole summer. Containers will require more care than in-ground plantings, but if you're regular about checking your pots, you can stay on top of the care and not get overwhelmed.

Watering

Containers need frequent watering. The larger the container, the more soil mass it has, so less frequency of watering will be needed. The smaller the container, the more you'll need to water. What type of plants you're growing and the weather will also influence the amount of watering. In general, plants growing in full sun in medium-sized pots will need watering two to four times a week in spring and perhaps daily in summer. During hot, dry weather, especially with smaller pots, you might have to water twice a day. Drought-tolerant plants and those grown in shady locations will need less-frequent watering. Young seedlings and larger plants will require more-frequent watering. The way to know whether your plant needs watering is to check the soil. If you stick your finger down a few inches into the soil and it's still dry, water.

Growing plants in self-watering containers will help. You may be able to go two or three days without having to water, even in the summer, because the plant roots are soaking up water from the reservoir. The larger the container and reservoir, the less watering you'll need to do and the longer you can wait between waterings. Small containers, even with the self-watering mechanism, still may require daily watering in the heat of summer.

How you water is as important as the frequency of watering. When watering containers, be sure to soak the entire rootball. The common way to know if the root all is wet is to water from the top until water comes out the drainage holes. This works well in most cases. However, if you slipped in your watering schedule and the rootball dried out, you may have to try another technique. When very dry, the rootball of your container will shrink away from the side of the pot, creating a space. When you water from the top, the water will run down the space between the pot edge and rootball and out the drainage holes without moistening the

rootball. It may look like you watered well, but really the rootball is still dry and the plant didn't get relief.

For containers with very dry soil, a better technique is to bottom water. Place the container in a plastic tray one size larger than your container or in a bucket and add a 3- to 6-inch-deep layer of water to the tray or bucket. The water will naturally be taken up through the drainage holes by the soil, and eventually the whole rootball will be hydrated. Add more water as needed to the bucket or tray until the rootball is thoroughly moist. If you have the time, this bottom-watering technique is good even when you're watering pots that haven't severely dried out.

If your container dries out so much that the rootball shrinks, rehydrate the rootball by placing the container in a tray of water and letting the water soak into the rootball through the drainage holes.

A simple way to fertilize containers is to use time-release pellets. These pellets release fertilizer every time you water so you don't have to remember to fertilize.

Fertilizing

Most potting soils won't have adequate fertility for your plants to grow strong all summer. Even potting soils with time-release fertilizer mixed in will only last about three months.

There are two general options for fertilizers: liquid and granular. Liquid fertilizers are added to water and add fertility to your plants when you water. They're fast acting and good if your plants really are suffering and need a quick boost. You may need to add liquid fertilizers every other week, depending on how the plants are growing, during the growing season. You can purchase chemical and organic forms of liquid fertilizer, such as fish emulsion, from garden centers.

Granular fertilizers, such as cottonseed meal and 5-5-5, are dry and are sprinkled on the potting soil periodically during the growing season. They're slower acting and feed the plants gradually over time. You may only need to add these once a month.

The best way to know if you're adding enough fertilizer is to watch the health of your plants. If your plants are small, pale green, and not flowering or growing well, they probably need an additional boost of fertilizer to get them growing. On the other hand, if your plants are lush green, large leaved for that variety, and maybe not flowering a lot but are growing a lot, then you may be adding too much fertilizer.

Pruning and Deadheading

Many container-grown annual flowers will need a little sprucing up in midsummer. Petunias, lantana, verbena, and other cascading annuals may get rangy and will benefit from some pruning. Whenever branches get too long or are growing in the wrong direction, simply pinch them back with a scissors. Cut the branch back to right above a cluster of leaves. This will not only shorten the branch and make it fit better with the container, it will also stimulate new branching and flowering in a few weeks.

Deadheading removes the old flower and seedpod so the plant continues to send out more flowers to fulfill its purpose in life—setting seeds. Many newer varieties of flowers no longer require deadheading. They "self clean," either by having sterile seeds or being selected to drop the old flower once it fades. This includes varieties of impatiens, petunias, verbena, ageratum, and many annual flowers.

Succession Planting

Even the best planned container garden will need a makeover or touch-up during the growing season. Some plants will grow more vigorously than others, some will get diseased, and others will just give up over time. If you're growing a single flower, vegetable, or herb in a container, then you may just need to prune and deadhead to keep it looking great.

However, if you're growing flowers, veggies, and herbs in mixed containers, then you'll have to be more proactive. By midsummer, your nicely balanced container may have some brute flowers overrunning other plants and may have some dead plants that have been overcrowded. You have a couple of choices on what to do.

If most of the plants are still looking good but are just out of balance, simply prune back the large ones, add some fertilizer, and let them regrow. However, if the large plants have taken over, you can either pull all the other plants out and turn the pot into a one-plant container or start over. The nice thing about container gardening is that you can start over a number of times during the growing season. Because you're growing quick-maturing plants and flowers, starting over means you'll get back on track pretty quickly.

Some gardeners don't wait for the plants to look bad to do a makeover. With the cool weather of spring, they plant containers filled with pansies, violas, primulas, arugula, lettuce, and parsley. Once the weather starts heating up and they notice the plants are struggling, they pull out all those flowers and vegetables and plant a summer container filled

After pruning a container planting, water thoroughly to rejuvenate the growth.

Regular deadheading of dead flowerheads will jump-start new blooms.

with heat lovers such as verbena, lantana, dwarf zinnias, dwarf tomatoes, cucumbers, and basil. You can save those cool-weather lovers from spring, if still healthy, in another pot for use in fall. Come late summer when these heat lovers have run their course, you can go back to cool-season plants, such as kale, arugula, ornamental cabbage, snapdragons, and petunias. It's more work, but if you only have a few containers, it's worth having them look great and varied through the growing season.

For containers in the shade, you may not have to go to such extremes of replanting with the seasons. Begonias, impatiens, and fuchsia grow more slowly, so they may just need a little pruning and pinching to keep the plants in bounds all summer long.

Pest Control

Even if you have the right pot, right soil, and perfect plants and you're diligent about watering, fertilizing, and pruning, you still may have problems with pests in your containers. In general, containers have fewer pests because they don't have garden soil and often are on a deck or patio away from the natural world. But that still won't stop powdery mildew disease, aphids, chipmunks, or squirrels from attacking your plants.

See Chapter 10 for detailed pest control information.

OPPOSITE: Some animals, such as chipmunks and squirrels, are best controlled by placing netting over the container and plants to act as a barrier.

BELOW: Use the sprays least harmful to bees, beneficial insects, pets, and the environment when controlling pests on your container plants. Sometimes handpicking is the best option.

CHAPTER 18
VERTICAL GARDENING

By Dr. Jacqueline A. Soule

VERTICAL GARDENING IS NOT A NEW CONCEPT. Ancient writers tell us of the "hanging gardens of Babylon," where water was carried upwards by water screws, applied to the top tier of plants, and subsequently encouraged to flow downward to water the lower tiers. These gardens are said to have covered acres and required the labor of numerous slaves.

Modern-day vertical gardens are much smaller in scale and hopefully *save* us labor. They help us fit more plants in smaller spaces, such as balconies or smaller yards now common in urban settings. And they help us create beautiful spaces.

In this chapter, "vertical gardens" include those created using containers that may be placed on the ground or hung on walls, those created by putting plants in the ground and training them up structures, such as arbors and trellises, and espalier plantings, where plants are trained to grow flat against a wall.

OPPOSITE: An arbor for plants is one type of vertical gardening; as an added benefit, it provides a shady seating area.

18 VERTICAL GARDENS IN CONTAINERS

Before you purchase any plants or containers, it is important to objectively assess your ability to care for the plants you wish to put in the space. Plants are living beings and will need regular care. You need to be honest about how much time you have to devote to the care of your garden space. Unless you are already an avid gardener, it is better to start small and grow over time (pardon the pun).

Light

Plants need light so they can make their food and feed themselves. (Fertilizer is like vitamins that will help them grow strong.) Consider how much sunlight will reach your garden at various times of the year. A garden sunny in March can become shady in June when the giant maple tree in the neighbor's yard leafs out. Also consider the fact that the sun moves in the sky not just by day but also over the course of the year. Your space may be shaded in fall and winter.

You should also consider reflected light. This can be a real problem, especially in warmer zones. Plants that are rated for full sun can fry when additional light bouncing off a picture window or pool water is added to the equation.

Your Garden Style

Consider what overall style you like in your space. If you prefer clean-cut and modern, a wall-mounted manufactured vertical system may be for you. If you are more laid back, you might like the effect of using the metal insides of a bed's box springs for a unique trellis for your plants to climb up. Or you may prefer something purchased from a garden center or even something created by an artist. Options abound!

Your outdoor space is part of your home and should continue the same design style for a unified whole.

ABOVE: Bright light situations are not for every species.

OPPOSITE: Vertical gardening involves not only plants that grow upward, but also those that cascade down.

Temperature

The temperature of your vertical garden isn't just how hot or cold it is; it's also related to how much light reaches the area and how many heat-holding items there are by the garden. In summer, a brick patio can heat up and then not cool down at night, stressing cool-weather plants. Meanwhile, rooftops are notoriously warm in summer and chilly in winter. Select plants that will do well in the environment they will be exposed to.

Water

Most vertical gardens pack many plants into a small growing space. Because of this limited space for plant roots, water can be an issue. Plan ahead of time—how will you *easily* water your vertical garden? If you have many plants in containers, it can take a long time to water them all, and it could be hard to reach the ones that are up high. Drip irrigation is one option for vertical gardening. Drip irrigation companies now sell drip lines in neutral colors that blend in with outdoor décor.

Related to water is drainage. Unless you are growing water plants, the roots of most species of plants need to *not* stay wet. This means whatever they are growing in needs drainage. But you should also consider what surface, if any, your vertical gardens are dripping onto. You may not want to create stains on a patio or deck.

Airflow

The flow of air in a garden is important to plants. Plant health is helped by some air movement. A number of common garden pests will not become an issue in sites with good airflow. But while some air is good, too much is a problem. A windy site will cause plants to dry out quickly and require more watering.

A drip irrigation system can make it easy to water thirsty or hard-to-get-to vertical gardens.

Soil

Soil is discussed in Chapter 2, is revisited with relation to watering in Chapter 5, and is discussed again when rooting cuttings in the Chapter 6. We keep coming back to the fact that soil is more than just dirt: it must contain plant nutrients and it must be porous—allowing both air and water to flow freely through the media. It's no different for vertical gardens.

Ready-made potting soils contain three components: soil, compost, and perlite, vermiculite, or sand for porosity. It is *easiest* to purchase premixed soil but certainly not cheapest. Fortunately, you can make homemade potting soil quickly and easily with readily available ingredients. If you opt for ready-made, don't expect miracles. The promises made on the bags are when tested under ideal conditions with horticulturists doing the growing.

If you have a yard full of soil, you don't need to buy ready-made potting soil. You can mix your own.

Purchase compost at the garden center. Read the labels carefully and get compost and *not* composted steer manure, a type of fertilizer. Use sand for drainage; you can buy coarse builders sand or play box sand. Or, if you like, use perlite or vermiculite instead of sand. Mix these three components in equal parts: one-third soil, one-third compost, and one-third sand.

Ready-Made Vertical Gardens

There are numerous ready-made vertical gardens you can purchase and install in your yard. Options include slope-sided towers, systems with flat backs to mount on walls or fences, and more.

If you lack the time or inclination to DIY, there are many options for ready-made vertical gardens on the market.

ABOVE: Potting soil contains soil, compost, and drainage media. The white flecks here are perlite added for drainage.

TOP: When this fountain cracked, the owners turned it into a vertical garden to take advantage of the ample drainage and architectural interest of the feature.

VERTICAL GARDEN STRUCTURES

Thus far we have looked mostly at vertical gardens in containers, but vertical gardens can be based in the ground. In this case, plants are trained to grow vertically through a fence, a trellis, over an arbor or ramada, or to cloak a pergola.

Support structures, such as arbors, pergolas, ramadas, and trellises, have multiple benefits. They offer a vertical growing space, help create a garden "room," add overhead appeal to a garden too small for trees, frame an opening or entrance, hide an unsightly view, provide privacy, and offer shade in a sunny area. Support structures are especially ideal in small or narrow gardens. They break up the narrow space and give it more interest.

Here are some things you should consider when deciding on design and materials:

- **Select the style and materials based on the architectural style of the home.** A Victorian pergola behind a Frank Lloyd Wright–inspired home creates a disjointed landscape that will reduce home resale value.
- **Size matters.** The arbor may look large enough for table and chairs, but will it also accommodate people sitting around the table? Unless it's strictly for kids, don't build an arbor smaller than average door height and width standards.
- **Select plants for the arbor based on its construction or select the support structure based on what you want to plant.** Different plants need differing supports. For example, wisteria and Cape honeysuckle are aggressive growers, resulting in larger mass and heavier weight than less woody vines, such as passionflower and clematis.
- **Consider maintenance.** Plants have leaves, petals, and maybe even fruit that drop and will require cleanup. Plants will require attention to train the new growth. The structure itself will require care. Durable metal rusts, decorative wood rots, low-care plastic can crack and spall, and materials will wear out.

An overhead structure allows a patio to have places for a garden to expand upward.

Plants to Clamber and Climb

Generally, vines or loose shrubs (such as climbing roses) are planted to cover trellises and arbors. Many such plants have beautiful flowers and the bloom period can be months long, offering another opportunity to fill your yard with color.

Vines are classified for landscaping by the way they climb. They can twine, grasp with tendrils, or grasp with aerial rootlets or holdfast discs. Some plants called vines are actually are better considered as weak shrubs with branches that must be tied into place. A "climbing" rose is one such plant that doesn't climb or twine, but simply has leggy branches that must be secured to a support structure. In this chapter, they're all being called "vines" to simplify the discussion.

Which vine you select for a vertical garden structure depends on what you are covering and how you are going to get the vine to cover it. For example, vines that grasp with rootlets are fine on unfinished brick or block, but when they grow large, they can pull the stucco off walls.

For arbors where you want summer shade and winter sun, plant vines that are winter deciduous. On the other hand, if you want a year-round leafy bower, plant an ever-green vine. Vines can be used for their green foliage, sea-sonal color, screening, shade, overhead cover, and even to grow fruit. If your arbor is 10 feet high or more, however, it might be better planted with an ornamental plant rather than a fruit you wish to harvest.

LEFT: Select or construct a trellis of material that can support the weight of the mature plant. So-called climbing roses can get very heavy.

OPPOSITE: A large plant in a sunlit area is ideally supported with a durable trellis.

How to Espalier

Espalier is the term used to describe the process of training trees, shrubs, and woody vines to lie flat against a vertical surface, such as a wall. You can also train plants to a freestanding fence or trellis. In a sense, grapevines in a vineyard are espaliered.

To espalier, you prune to create a main vertical stem, then train the side branches to achieve the desired shape. Depending on the plant, this can take a year or two to establish and at first requires constant monitoring. Afterwards, an espalier requires only light pruning to hold its shape.

Step 1: Choose the location. Almost any solid wall will do as long as there is enough light for the plant and space for the roots. You could use a container for the plant, provided it is large enough to hold the plant when it is mature. In warmer regions, the wall should not bake in the summer sun.

Step 2: Choose the plant. Most plants can be espaliered, but those with naturally spreading branches work best, such as apples, quince, figs, loquat, pyracantha, and camellias. At the nursery, look for the individual that already has a start on the branching pattern you want. Make sure the species of plant is suitable for your location.

Step 3: Prepare the support. Run wires between screws or nails set in the wall (or posts set in the ground) to create three to five horizontal lines. Use heavy-gauge wire and strong anchors that can resist the pull of the branches as they try to grow toward the sun. The lowest wire should be at the height that the lowest side branches will be once the plant is in its forever home (ground or container). Wire isn't necessary for vertical branches; they will grow that way naturally.

Step 4: Plant! Depending on the mature size of the plant, set the plant a small distance (6 to 12 inches) in front of the structure that will support it. This will give it room to grow. In most cases, center the plant in the middle of the espalier space. Position the plant so that at least two of the strongest branches run in the direction of the wires.

Step 5: Train the branches. This is the easy part! Simply tie the two lowest branches loosely to the lowest horizontal wires. Use soft ties that won't damage the plant. Trim off any other branches between this and the next horizontal wire, but leave the plant leader intact. As the leader (central trunk) grows, keep removing any side shoots. When the leader reaches the next wire up, allow two side shoots to develop (remove the rest) and attach them to the wires. Repeat as needed.

The Vertical Vegetable Garden

Peas trained up a fence in the vegetable garden are a prime example of gardening vertically. Don't stop with peas; space-hogs, such as squash and even pumpkins, can be trained to climb. Training vegetables to grow vertically takes some early planning but provides four key benefits:

- **Saves space.** You can grow more vegetables in the space that would otherwise be covered with a single crop.
- **Improves air circulation.** Plants grow better with some air movement to promote the exchange of oxygen and carbon dioxide.
- **Decreases chances for disease and pest damage.** Up in the air helps prevent mold, soilborne disease, and crawling insects or pests from reaching leaves and fruit.
- **Results in early harvest.** Vegetables are easier to see and easier to reach for harvest.

Training Young Plants to Go Vertical

Until a vine gets a firm hold on its support, you may need to tie it in place with twine or plastic garden tape. For clinging vines, you might tack plastic mesh over the stems until you see the aerial rootlets adhering. Once the stems of twining and scrambling vines gain some length, you can weave them through any open spaces of your structure. To encourage bushy growth on young vines, pinch or snip off the leaders or terminal buds.

Once a vine is established, you'll need to prune it periodically to keep it in bounds and to clear out unwanted or dead growth. For fruiting plants, this is done when plants are dormant but for flowering vines, this is done after flowering. Some vines are so vigorous that they can be pruned at any time.

ABOVE: Vegetables are more easily harvested when trained to grow vertically.

RIGHT: Even plants that have tendrils to climb with may need training to grow in the place where you wish them to grow.

READY TO GET STARTED?

Creating and maintaining a vertical garden is a process. Your garden space's benefits and drawbacks will dictate what you will be able to easily grow. What you choose to grow will somewhat dictate the type of vertical garden you create and your personal style preferences will dictate what that vertical garden will look like.

You may have some failures along the way, but know this: all gardeners have killed plants! Death of plants is part of gardening life. Just like learning to walk involved falling down a few times, learning to garden will mean some missteps and falls along the way. This is why I urge you to start small with vertical gardening and expand as your skills grow.

Trellises for vertical gardens can be large and make bold vertical statements in the landscape.

CHAPTER 19
RAISED BEDS

By Tara Nolan

MY FIRST TWO RAISED BEDS WERE BUILT FOR PURE aesthetics—I wanted to tidy up the in-ground vegetable garden I inherited when I moved into my current home a few years ago. It was a small, misshapen patch and I envisioned a tidy plot with mulch pathways. I enjoyed planting my favorite veggies—tomatoes, lemon cucumbers, onions, sweet peppers, herbs, kale (yes, I know, I'm one of the few who admits to liking it), and garlic. However, I soon realized a couple of things. First, there are multiple benefits to growing in raised beds that go beyond their neat and tidy appearance. Second, two raised beds weren't enough to hold the ambitious number of edibles I wanted to grow.

The opportunity to write my first book, about raised beds, came at just the right time. I needed to build projects to fill each chapter, and that satisfied my need for more gardening space. Suddenly, I had a plethora of raised beds to choose from! And they all have different purposes. I love to perch with a cup of tea on my raised bed with benches early in the morning, in between watering. My standard raised bed converts into a mini hoophouse in the fall to extend the gardening season. And my lettuce table, built from an antique table, is always teeming with fresh greens and microshoots for salads. And my collection keeps growing.

OPPOSITE: Raised beds are a benefits-packed alternative to a traditional, in-ground veggie garden.

I love discovering what others are building to conform to their space, whether it be a big or small raised bed. I also love to see raised beds being used for educational and benevolent purposes. I especially love that raised beds make gardening accessible to a vast demographic of new and seasoned gardeners.

RENEWED INTEREST IN RAISED BEDS

Raised beds have recently become quite popular—perhaps you've scanned inspiring photos on Instagram and Pinterest or you've noticed raised beds of all sizes bursting with veggies in a front yard, backyard, or beside a restaurant. You've maybe even seen a raised bed model at your local garden center. Raised beds have definitely undergone somewhat of a renaissance in the last few years—despite the fact that they're quite an old-fashioned invention and have been used for decades.

One reason for this renewed interest can be attributed to the fact that a great deal of the population has become more conscious about where their food comes from—there's been a big resurgence in farmers' markets too. But more and more people are also becoming interested in growing their own food, even those with limited urban or suburban spaces. Raised beds are a convenient gardening solution that spans multiple demographics. And they offer many benefits to both new and seasoned green thumbs.

With this newfound popularity, there is lots of raised bed design inspiration to be discovered, as well as savvy

Provided your space gets six to eight hours of sunlight a day, a smaller-scale raised bed can be placed on a balcony. Some edibles, such as greens, don't mind a bit of shade.

Raised beds may incorporate built-in seating, such as in this patio garden.

manufacturers who are creating kits for those who don't have the tools, time, or woodworking skills to build their own raised bed.

Why are raised beds an ideal option for any gardener? For starters, they can be built to whatever size you need them to be. Furthermore, you can place them absolutely anywhere, provided that space gets six to eight hours of sunlight a day. (Of course, if your raised bed is destined for a shady area, you'll want to choose your plants accordingly.)

Raised beds can be put wherever a traditional vegetable garden would go: on a driveway; along the side of a house; on a rooftop garden, patio, or balcony; on the corner of a deck—anywhere, really. You see raised beds often in community gardens because they're a great way to define a garden's boundaries and keep an allotment neat and tidy (like what I wanted to do with my original garden).

Wherever you choose to put your raised bed, there are lots of design and material options to suit your space. So, let's get started and talk about some of the benefits, inspiration, add-ons, and growing advice that will help you create and grow a flourishing garden in a raised bed.

A HOST OF BENEFITS

Not only can raised beds visually elevate your garden, but they can also present a number of benefits that are appealing to gardeners, such as solving accessibility issues; being able to plant earlier in spring because the soil warms up sooner; preventing pest problems (they can be made high enough that bunnies and groundhogs can't help themselves, or you can find ways to cover them); improving drainage; and more. You also don't need a traditional patch of soil—raised beds can be plunked absolutely anywhere.

Accessibility: Raised beds make gardening more accessible to those who have trouble kneeling down or bending over because you can design them to be at a height that allows gardening in a more comfortable way. Some designs have benches, while others have wider edges that allow you to perch on the side and reach into garden. The recommended height of a raised bed is at least 10 inches, but you can keep stacking boards until you're happy with the height.

Soil: One big advantage to a raised bed is that the gardener controls the soil quality by choosing what's added into the garden. This is great news for those who need to place their raised bed on pavement or gravel, or those who are worried about the quality of the soil underneath the raised bed. If a raised bed is placed over hard-packed or clay soil, the roots of the plants, especially root vegetables, will hit a wall as they try to grow downward. Raising the garden up higher ensures that plants are only reaching into the healthy, friable soil that's been placed inside.

Furthermore, by reaching to tend the plants in a raised bed instead of walking on the soil, you avoid compacting the soil and disturbing that beneficial web of activity (worms and microorganisms) that occurs beneath the surface.

Soil temperature: Because the soil in a raised bed warms up sooner than a traditional garden in the springtime, you can plant those cool-weather-loving crops, such as peas and members of the Brassica family, earlier. You can also garden later and extend your season by building a cold frame or by turning your garden into a mini hoophouse.

Pest control: Of course, despite your best efforts, some pests may find their way into a raised bed, but some can be thwarted. You can increase the height of your bed so that bunnies and groundhogs are not able to nibble. And you can use row cover and nets to prevent certain bad insects and birds from accessing your crops.

Raised beds also allow you to:
- garden in limited spaces,
- keep spreaders, such mint, in check,
- increase your yield,
- rotate your crops,
- extend your growing season,
- and more!

RAISED BED PREP

So, you've decided you want a raised bed. Now there's just a bit of prep work to be done before you pull on your gardening gloves and start planting.

Choose a Proper Location

You can put a raised bed virtually anywhere you'd like to place it, provided it gets six to eight hours of sunlight per day. And lack of space is not a limitation—tailor your raised bed measurements to suit a sunny area on a balcony, roof garden, small walkout, etc.

Remove Grass First

It's best to remove any grass that is growing where you want to install a raised bed. Digging up sod is a grueling task. An easier way to get rid of the grass is to mark out a perimeter and place a layer of cardboard on top of the grass. Secure it in place with a few heavy rocks so that it doesn't blow away. You may even want to cover it with mulch. Leave extra space around the raised bed, if you wish, for a mulch or gravel pathway. Keep the cardboard in place for several weeks (over the winter is a great time of year to do this) and the grass will break down underneath. Once the grass has died, you can place the raised bed on top of it.

TOP: It is traditional to first remove sod underneath a raised bed, but it is also possible to build one directly over lawn grass.

ABOVE: Choose the best-quality soil you can afford. Call around to see what's available in your area and to compare prices.

Concrete blocks can be fashioned into a raised bed in under an hour.

Fill the Bed with Soil

Buy the best-quality vegetable soil you can afford (do not fill a raised bed with topsoil). It's likely you'll need soil delivered to fill even one standard-sized raised bed. (Alternatively, you could pick it up yourself if you have a pickup truck.) You'd need to buy a lot of bags if you were thinking of going that route! Use an online soil calculator to help you figure out how much you'll need. It's also likely that the place where you purchase it will be able to guide you.

Once you've filled your bed with your soil, top-dress it with 2 to 3 inches of organic compost (see Chapter 7 on compost). Add a few inches each autumn or in the spring before your crops go in. It's also a nice idea to periodically replenish the bed throughout the season. Heavy rains and crops such as peas can deplete the soil of nutrients.

SIZE AND MATERIALS ARE UP TO YOU

Raised beds offer several flexible solutions. The size you choose and the materials you use are a matter of personal preference. Here are a few things to consider.

How Big Should You Build Your Raised Bed?

The easy answer is that raised beds can be any size at all, depending on your available space. If you're looking to build that standard rectangular raised bed that you'll find in many a yard, the following dimensions are recommended: 3 to 4 feet wide by 6 to 8 feet long and 10 to 12 inches high. This allows you to easily reach into the raised bed from all sides without having to step inside. You can simply modify the length and width measurements to suit your space, or modify the height to make it more accessible. If you're building multiple raised beds, be sure to allow space between the beds so that you can move easily from garden to garden. You may also want to allow space for a wheelbarrow to go between beds if you're getting fresh soil deliveries each spring.

Choosing Wood

Use rot-resistant, untreated wood for your raised beds—availability varies according to the region in which you live. Cedar and hemlock will both work well.

Use a rot-resistant, untreated wood, such as cedar or hemlock, to build your raised bed.

Using Non-Wood Materials

If wood isn't a viable or desired material for your project, there are other options to create a raised bed.

Stock tanks have become popular raised bed options, likely because they don't require any skills or extra hardware to put them together. They are oblong, come in various sizes, and are made of corrugated steel. You can simply remove the plug on the bottom and place it wherever you want it to go without having to remove any grass. You could even place a stock tank on a sunny driveway.

You can also get the corrugated steel stock tank look, but without a bottom. Prepare your site and place it right on top for an instant garden.

Find a Loaner

Is your tool collection rather small or nonexistent? If you don't know anyone who can loan you a particular tool, many towns and cities now offer tool-lending libraries. Big box stores also may offer a variety of big and small tools that you can rent.

Recycling vintage items is a great budget-friendly option. There are all sorts of items and materials that you can convert into a raised bed: old washbasins, apple or wine crates, recycling bins, etc.

Note: As much as I love upcycling, I don't recommend building a raised bed from wood that used to be a part of a deck or fence and is pressure-treated, especially if you're growing food. You do not want any remaining chemicals to leach into the soil.

Concrete blocks or old bricks are a fabulous time-saving option. With concrete blocks, you get extra planting space. You can put plants, such as marigolds, herbs, greens, or nasturtiums, in the holes.

Note: Be sure to choose concrete blocks with concrete as the only ingredient. They used to contain a toxic material called fly ash, which is not recommended if you're growing food.

Raised bed corners are an ingenious invention that allow a gardener to easily set up a raised bed. You simply place each corner in the desired, measured-out space and buy wood that is the right thickness and height to slide into each junction (you can get the wood cut to the dimensions you need at the time of purchase if you don't have the tools to do so at home), and attach in place with the hardware provided.

A little research will also reveal a whole range of **raised bed kits** in all shapes and sizes, available at various retailers. Most come with all the hardware and pieces you need to put them together. The only thing you might require are tools, such as screwdrivers or socket wrenches, to tighten nuts and bolts.

RAISED BED ADD-ONS

Once you get down to the nitty gritty of planning a raised bed garden, whether you are installing one or a several, there are a few useful add-ons you might want to incorporate into your design. This can be as simple as popping in a trellis for edibles, such as sugar snap peas or cucumbers, or installing something a bit more complex, such as an irrigation system.

Keep out the Bad Guys

If you're concerned about certain pests coming up from the bottom of your raised bed, there are a couple of things you can install at the time of building.

First, many gardeners use landscape fabric to ensure that weeds that reach way underground, such as bindweed, do not reach up into a raised bed once it's been installed. Staple it to the bottom of your frame with stainless-steel staples at the time you install the bed.

Another option is to attach hardware cloth to the bottom of a raised bed. This is used to prevent pesky critters, such as moles and voles, from getting into your garden from below and eating your root vegetable crops that live in the soil. There's nothing worse than pulling out a beet with great anticipation, only to find there's been a huge chunk of it removed—except maybe going out to your garden and discovering that tomato you've been patiently waiting to ripen has been eaten already! Sometimes, as a gardener, you're trying to combat pests both above and below the surface. Attach the hardware cloth before installing your raised bed in its garden spot using stainless-steel staples.

Stake It

One accessory that some gardeners will add when installing a raised bed is some type of midpoint stake along the longest sides. This prevents multiple levels of boards from shifting over time with frost. Some gardeners will even add rebar through the middle of a bed, from the midpoint of one long side to the other, to hold the bed firmly in place.

Add Some Hardware

Want to convert your raised bed into a mini hoophouse? Attach PVC conduit clamps to the inside of the bed, at even intervals, along each long side. Then cut ½-inch PEX pipe and create semi-circle hoops that span the width to align down the length of the bed. Cover with floating row cover and secure in place with spring clamps (or use rocks or tuck the fabric into the soil). Those same hoops could also be used to hold up netting to keep birds from eating your berries.

TOP RIGHT: Floating row cover can be used to protect your plants from insect pests in the spring and from frost in the fall.

BOTTOM RIGHT: Locking casters make it easy to wheel some raised beds into a shed or garage to store them for winter.

Plant supports are an integral add-on to any raised bed. Different styles hold up everything from bean plants to tomatoes.

Layer Up

Adding mulch to your garden helps keep the weeds down and the soil cool throughout the hot summer months. Straw, for example, is a popular option (don't use hay as it contains seeds) to spread on top of a raised bed.

Be Water-Wise

Once you've put in a raised bed, it is a perfect time to install an irrigation system. There are DIY kits on the market; check your local big box store, or call in a professional who will be able to set up a network that works for your raised bed and gardening requirements. (There are simple dripline options that are easy to place in the garden too.) Add-ons, such as timers, will allow you to leave your garden when you go on vacation without enlisting someone to water; rainfall gauges ensure you're not watering in the middle of a rainstorm.

Support Your Plants!

If you want to add plant supports, such as trellises, stakes, tomato cages, or obelisks, do so when plants are young. You risk breaking off stems if you try to maneuver a cage around a tomato plant, for example, once it's nearing maturity. Other trellising, such as a pole bean tunnel, needs a

bit more forethought as you'll likely be attaching it to your raised bed before the seeds are planted. Save this type of project for spring before your crops are sown, or in the fall so you're ready for early spring plantings.

A Wheelie Good Idea

If your raised bed isn't going directly into the ground—or if you want to store it for the winter—consider adding locking caster wheels. These will allow you to push a smaller raised bed into a shed or garage, rather than lifting it. Wheels also give you options if you want to move a raised bed during the season.

Adjust the Height

One major bonus of having a raised bed is that it brings the garden to whatever level you need it to be to garden comfortably. If you have difficulties bending down or kneeling (and getting back up again!), figure out a height that works for you. There's another benefit to higher sides: if you have a real problem with pests, such as rabbits or groundhogs, raising the bed up high is kind of the equivalent to building a giant moat around your garden. They're also great for plants that like to wander over the side of the garden. Strawberries, for example, like to trail, as do members of the cucumber family.

Even if you don't have land, that doesn't mean you can't have a raised bed packed full of delicious edibles. *Photo courtesy Les Urbainculteurs*

So, depending on the garden's height, plants can simply hang over the sides without interfering with other plants.

SMALL-SPACE IDEAS

Despite the square footage limitations of having a smaller space, one advantage is that you might not have to take on a big woodworking project in building a raised bed—although there are some really fun projects out there that you could choose to tackle if you want to get crafty and you have the tools and skills necessary for such an undertaking.

Look for Raised Beds with Legs

There are multiple kits on the market that provide all the materials you need to construct a cedar raised bed that comes to about waist height—kind of like a sunken table. Others are plastic with a stand and provide built-in irrigation options. Most options are generally deep enough to plant everything from peppers and tomatoes to root vegetables.

Build a Living Salad Bar

Imagine stepping out your door to snip fresh salad greens for dinner. You don't need a lot of depth to grow lettuce, so you could build a shallow tray (four to six inches deep) that sits on plain wooden legs. Or, you could take an old table with an easily removable top, attach some hardware cloth to the bottom (and some cedar strips to hold it in place and cover sharp edges), line it with landscape fabric, and voilà: a salad bar.

Basic Raised Bed Project

The beauty of raised beds is that they can be configured to any shape or size. However, if you're looking to build a basic rectangular one, one of the most popular styles, you'll like this project. It's easy to build, making it a great entry-level project for someone who is new to woodworking. You'll be able to plant it as an ornamental garden with cutting flowers and it is large enough to plant several types of edibles and enjoy a bountiful harvest. Just be careful—once you've caught the raised bed bug, you'll want more if you have the space!

Tools

- Tape measure
- Hammer
- Miter saw or circular saw
- Drill with driver bits
- Level
- Post-hole digger

Materials

- 1½" deck screws
- 1 × 6 cedar, 8' long (4)
- 1 × 6 cedar, 4' long (4)
- 4 × 4 cedar, 18" long (4)
- Potting soil

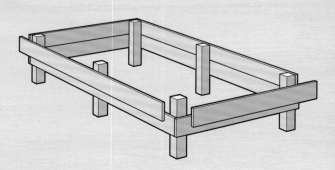

1. Outline the location of your raised bed on your yard using rope or a garden hose. Installation will be easiest on a relatively flat, level spot on your yard.

2. Cut all pieces to size with a miter saw or circular saw. We used 2 × 6 cedar, but the bed could also be built with 2× lumber for greater sturdiness.

3. If desired, seal all pieces with stain or wood sealer. Cedar has good durability, but treatment with a sealer will lengthen the life of your raised bed.

4. Using deck screws, attach the first row of boards to the four corner posts to form a 4' × 8' rectangle. Add one post to the middle of each long side of the raised bed too.

5. Attach the second row of boards to your posts, flush against the first row. If you live in a cold climate, you may also want to add a couple stakes to the long sides of your raised bed frame, as the boards can heave over time with freeze and thaw cycles.

6. Position the raised bed in its location and mark the location of the posts. Remove the bed and dig shallow holes for the posts.

7. Position the bed with the posts in the holes and check for level. You can prop up low sides of the planter to level it, if necessary. Fill your raised bed with a potting mix soil and you're ready to plant!

A Polygon Raised Bed Project

You can use this design to create various raised beds at different heights and with six, eight, or more sides. Hexagons or octagons are probably the easiest configuration to make, but, really, all you have to do is alter the angle of the corners. For the eight-sided figure shown here, each side piece was beveled at 22½ degrees.

For a six-sided hexagon planter, the bevel angle would be 30 degrees. Also, the dimensions of the box can be adjusted simply by changing the lengths of the sides. Our planter, with 20-inch sides, produces an octagon planter that is 4 feet across.

If you want a grouping of raised beds, odd numbers look better as a collection. Angle three together and either leave a path between them or bring them in close and snug together.

Tools

- Drill with twist bits and driver bits
- Tape measure
- Hammer
- Miter saw or circular saw
- Strap clamp
- Level
- Caulk gun

Materials

- 2½" deck screws
- 1¼" deck screws
- Bendable mending plates, 8" long (16)
- 2 × 6 cedar, 20" long (24), ends beveled at 22½°
- 2 × 2 cedar, 14" long (16)
- Cedar-toned outdoor caulk

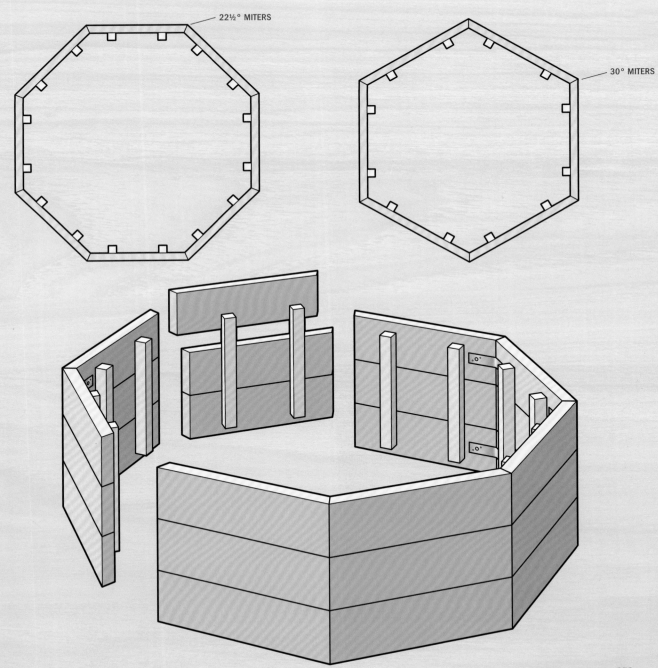

22½° MITERS

30° MITERS

Continued on page 358

Continued from page 357

19

1. Outline the location of your octagonal planter on the ground using rope or a garden hose. The best location will be a flat, level site. If you build your planter on an uneven or sloped site, you may need to dig out a portion of the building site.

2. Cut all pieces to size using a compound miter saw or circular saw, beveling at the appropriate angle. For our octagonal planter, the ends are beveled at 22½°. A compound miter saw makes this job much easier.

3. Assemble each side panel using three side pieces, each joined together with two interior 2 × 2 cleats attached with deck screws. Drill pilot holes first to avoid splitting, then drive 2 ½" deck screws through the cleats and into the side panels. This step will create eight side panels of three boards each.

4. If desired, apply sealer or stain to all panels. Cedar ages to a pleasing gray color and will be relatively durable, but stain or sealer will extend its life.

5. On your building site, use a strap clamp to assemble all eight panels upright in a circle. This may take a bit of adjustment to ensure the joints are consistent, and a helper will be useful. Try to position the pieces so all joints are tight. Level the planter; if necessary, you may need to dig down on the low side to level the planter.

6. Install bendable metal mending plates (two positioned across each joint) using 1" deck screws to secure the panels from the inside. The mending plates will prevent the weight of the soil from breaking the panels apart over time.

7. Reinforce the end joints with 2½" deck screws driven at an angle from the outside. This is to strengthen each outside joint. Drill pilot holes first to prevent splitting when driving the screws. If desired, you can caulk the outside seams with cedar-toned outdoor caulk to seal against water and provide a more finished look.

8. Fill your raised bed with quality soil for growing edibles, and install your plants.

Recycle old items into small-scale raised beds that will suit a small area. *Image provided by ProvenWinners.com.*

Discover the Simplicity of Fabric Raised Beds

For green thumbs concerned about the weight of a traditional wooden raised bed, perhaps on a balcony or rooftop, fabric raised beds are a clever solution. These are generally made from post-consumer recycled items, such as plastic bottles, and can actually benefit the plants through a process called air pruning. What does this mean? Because the fabric raised beds are permeable, air can flow through the soil, strengthening the root structure of plants. The best part about these gardens is that you can empty them at the end of the season, give them a shake, fold them up, and store them for the winter.

Grow Up!

Keep an eye out for vertical raised bed options, or get creative and build a garden out of an old pallet. You can also buy fabric pockets that can hang on the side of a brick wall, over a balcony—really, anywhere that you can attach a hook. (See chapter 18 for more on vertical gardening.)

Get Your Upcycling Groove On

Keep an eye out at antique markets and yard sales for miniature stock tanks, fruit and wine crates, colanders—anything that can be converted into a small raised bed.

Did You Know That Some Plants Don't Like Each Other?

When you're figuring out where you're going to put your plants and seeds, consult companion-planting charts (there are some great ones online!) to see which plants grow well next to each other and which ones are foes.

THE NITTY GRITTY OF PLANTING, WATERING, AND MAINTENANCE

Once your raised beds are placed in their forever home, put together, and filled with soil, all that's left to do is plant. There are various theories on how close together your plants should go. Some say that if plants are packed in too close together, the air can't circulate through the garden and plants could become vulnerable to mold and mildew. Some gardeners swear by planting everything closer together to suppress weeds. If you're new to gardening, read the plant tag or seed packet and follow the directions accordingly. The square foot gardening method, invented and perfected by Mel Bartholomew, is also a great technique for beginners.

Planting

If you start plants from seed, be sure to follow the directions on the packet carefully so that you start your plants in time (indoors or outdoors) and then dig them into the ground, giving them the space they require. The same goes for seedlings that you purchase from a garden center or nursery. Read the plant tag so you know what the plant is going to require to thrive.

Raised beds will thrive if you choose a good-quality soil, follow the seed packet or plant tag for planting directions, and hydrate and feed your crops all season long.

Feed Your Plants

As plants gobble up the nutrients in the soil, it's a good idea to establish a regular fertilizing routine. Look for an organic brand that's safe to use on edible crops and follow the directions for measuring and frequency. It's also a good idea to have a bag of compost on reserve (if you don't have a compost pile) to top-dress the soil throughout the season. If you're pulling out garlic or peas in July, you're bringing soil with the roots. Adding a bit of compost to your raised bed will add some nutrients back into the soil, which will benefit the plants that are still in there, along with any new ones you add.

Maintaining a Raised Bed

For a raised bed that you're going to leave out over the winter, the soil can stay inside—you don't have to empty it. Just be sure to replenish the soil with fresh compost in the autumn and/or spring. Furthermore, you can plant a crop, such as

garlic, in the fall, which will provide a couple of harvests (scapes and heads) starting in late spring/early summer.

Each spring, inspect all the hardware of your raised bed to make sure it's still in place and the bed is still sound. Eye each board carefully to see if any have rotted away. Rot-resistant wood should stand the test of time, but, over the years, you may have to replace a board here and there.

Succession Planting

Depending on which state or province you live in, there are different benchmark dates throughout the season for planting edibles that thrive in the heat, such as tomatoes, cucumbers, peppers, eggplants, and zucchini. However, you can generally plant cool-weather-loving crops, such as peas, brassicas (broccoli, cauliflower, kale), greens (lettuce, bok choy, spinach), and root vegetables (carrots, radishes, beets) in early spring. You can also plant these in mid- to late summer to ensure a fall crop. This will all depend on your growing zone (see the zone map in Chapter 1).

ABOUT THE AUTHORS

KATIE ELZER-PETERS

Photo credit: Kirsten Boehmer Photography

Katie Elzer-Peters has been gardening since she could first walk, a hobby (turned career) nurtured by her parents and grandparents. She earned a bachelor of science in public horticulture from Purdue University and a master of science in public garden management from the Longwood Graduate Program at Longwood Gardens and the University of Delaware.

After completing school, Katie served as a horticulturist, head of gardens, educational programs director, development officer, and manager of botanical gardens around the United States.

Katie has authored eight books for Cool Springs Press and she serves as the editor in chief of *The Designer*, the quarterly journal of the Association of Professional Landscape Designers.

Today, Katie lives and gardens with her husband and dogs in the coastal city of Wilmington, North Carolina (zone 8), where she owns The Garden of Words, LLC, a marketing and PR firm specializing in garden industry clients.

Books by Katie Elzer-Peters:

Beginner's Illustrated Guide to Gardening: Techniques to Help You Get Started (Cool Springs Press)

Carolinas Fruit & Vegetable Gardening: How to Plant, Grow, and Harvest the Best Edibles (Cool Springs Press)

Mid-Atlantic Fruit & Vegetable Gardening: Plant, Grow, and Harvest the Best Edibles (Cool Springs Press)

Mid-Atlantic Gardener's Handbook (Cool Springs Press)

Midwest Fruit & Vegetable Gardening: Plant, Grow, and Harvest the Best Edibles (Cool Springs Press)

Miniature Gardens: Design & Create Miniature Fairy Gardens, Dish Gardens, Terrariums and More—Indoors and Out (Cool Springs Press)

Northwest Fruit & Vegetable Gardening: Plant, Grow, and Harvest the Best Edibles (Cool Springs Press)

Southern Fruit & Vegetable Gardening: Plant, Grow, and Harvest the Best Edibles (Cool Springs Press)

RHONDA FLEMING HAYES

Rhonda gardens in an urban neighborhood surrounded by woods and water. Her abundant quarter-acre is home to many bees, butterflies, birds, and beneficial insects. She loves to share the fruits (and veggies) of her garden with friends, family, and wildlife.

While Rhonda became certified as an Extension Master Gardener in 2000, she has been gardening in some form or fashion since she was a child at her grandmother's knee. She is a member of the Garden Writers Association, The Herb Society of America, The Xerces Society, and the Minnesota State Horticultural Society. She is a trustee of the Minnesota Landscape Arboretum.

Books by Rhonda Fleming Hayes:

Pollinator Friendly Gardening: Gardening for Bees, Butterflies, and Other Pollinators (Voyageur Press)

Rhonda Fleming Hayes is an award-winning writer and photographer who applies her passion for all things plant-related with wit and solid, research-based advice. She is a monthly columnist for the *Star Tribune*, and she contributes unique feature stories as well as her popular "Pollinators" column to *Northern Gardener* magazine. Rhonda has also been published in *Southern Living, Mother Earth Living, The Herbarist, Wichita Eagle, Savannah Magazine,* and many online sites.

A native Californian with Southern roots, Rhonda now lives in Minneapolis, Minnesota. Following her husband's nomadic career, she has lived and gardened in Tennessee, Kansas (twice), Illinois (twice), Iowa, and even England. Regardless of location, she learned to bloom where she's planted. In between writing assignments in Minnesota, she shovels compost or snow, depending upon the season.

CHARLIE NARDOZZI

As a consultant, Charlie works with companies such as Velcro, Hilton Garden Inn, Stonyfield Yogurt, and Gardener's Supply Company. For the past four years, Charlie has worked with the Vermont Community Garden Network to promote school and community gardens, as well as veterans' and employee gardens through their Green Thumbs at Work and Grow It trainings.

Books by Charlie Nardozzi:

Foodscaping: Practical and Innovative Ways to Create an Edible Landscape (Cool Springs Press)

New England Getting Started Garden Guide: Grow the Best Flowers, Shrubs, Trees, Vines & Groundcovers— Connecticut, Maine, Massachusetts, New Hampshire, Rhode Island, Vermont (Cool Springs Press)

New England Month-by-Month Gardening: What to Do Each Month to Have a Beautiful Garden All Year— Connecticut, Maine, Massachusetts, New Hampshire, Rhode Island, Vermont (Cool Springs Press)

Northeast Fruit & Vegetable Gardening: Plant, Grow, and Eat the Best Edibles for Northeast Gardens (Cool Springs Press)

Vegetable Gardening for Dummies (Wiley Publishing)

Urban Gardening for Dummies (Wiley Publishing)

Charlie Nardozzi is a nationally recognized garden writer, speaker, and radio and television personality who has been delivering expert gardening information to home gardeners for more than 25 years. He delights in making gardening information simple, easy, fun, and accessible to everyone.

Charlie is the author of six gardening books, including *Foodscaping* and *New England Month-by-Month Gardening*. He is a nationally known presenter at venues such as flower shows, Master Gardener conferences, gardening trade shows, and garden clubs. He has three radio shows in the Northeast and a television show in his home state of Vermont. He is the edibles editor for www.GoodGardeningVideos.org, vetting accurate and informative gardening videos for the gardening public. Charlie also leads food and gardening tours to Europe, England, and throughout the United States.

TARA NOLAN

Photo credit: Marsha Z.

Workshop magazine, and currently does work for the Canadian Garden Council and volunteers at the Royal Botanical Garden.

Follow Tara and her adventures in gardening online (and share your raised bed projects):

Raised Bed Revolution

Facebook.com/RaisedBedRevolution

Savvy Gardening

www.SavvyGardening.com

Facebook.com/SavvyGardening

Twitter and Instagram: @SavvyGardening

Tara Nolan

Twitter: @thatTaraNolan

Instagram: @Tara_E

Books by Tara Nolan:

Raised Bed Revolution: Build It, Fill It, Plant It... Garden Anywhere! (Cool Springs Press)

Tara Nolan is a writer, author, editor, and speaker. Her first book, *Raised Bed Revolution*, was published by Cool Springs Press in 2016. In 2013, she co-founded the popular gardening website Savvy Gardening with three other writers. Together, these four green thumbs from two different countries and four different growing zones work to inspire both experienced and budding gardeners with innovative ideas, tips, and advice.

Tara's gardening and travel articles have appeared in *The Globe and Mail*, *The Guardian*, *The Toronto Star*, *Canadian Living*, *Zoomer Magazine*, and *Garden Making*, among other publications. She was also the award-winning web editor of *Canadian Gardening* magazine's website for six years, where she won Gold at the Canadian Online Publishing Awards for her "Seed to Supper" newsletter. Additionally, Tara has worked as an editor for *Canadian Home*

DR. JACQUELINE A. SOULE

Photo credit: Mark Turner

Jacqueline Soule published her first garden story when she was seven years old, and went on to become an award-winning garden writer. She is the author of a dozen gardening books and is a popular columnist with weekly and monthly columns in a number of local and national publications.

Jacqueline grew up in Vermont and Tucson, Arizona. Her degrees are from the University of Arizona, Michigan State University, and University of Texas, with a post-doc at Washington State University. Jacqueline has worked at the Morris Arboretum in Philadelphia, the Chicago Botanic Garden, and the Frederik Meijer Gardens in Grand Rapids, Michigan. She learned many of the techniques discussed in this book with her fingers in the dirt as she moved around the nation.

Jacqueline is active in plant organizations locally and beyond, including the international Desert Legume Program and the Garden Writers Association. She offers lectures and classes on gardening for all ages around the nation.

Her garden is the entire landscape around her home, filled with herbs, fruiting plants, raised beds, containers, and ample flowers for pollinators. With her busy life, she prefers plants that need as little care as possible. Her husband, Paul, appreciates this low-care approach, as he often gets called on to help.

Recent books by Jacqueline Soule:

Arizona, Nevada & New Mexico Month-by-Month Gardening: What to Do Each Month to Have a Beautiful Garden All Year (Cool Springs Press)

Southwest Fruit & Vegetable Gardening: Plant, Grow, and Harvest the Best Edibles—Arizona, Nevada & New Mexico (Cool Springs Press)

Father Kino's Herbs: Growing & Using Them Today (Tierra del Sol Institute)

Success with Succulents in Southern Arizona (Tierra del Sol Institute)

LYNN STEINER

Lynn Steiner is one of the Upper Midwest's best-known garden writers and a frequent speaker at gardening and environmental events. She is the author and photographer of several books that advocate for the effective use of native plants in a typical home landscape. The author and photographer of several other books, Lynn helped develop, write, and photograph Cool Springs Press' *The Complete Guide to Gardening* series of ten regional gardening books.

For 15 years, Lynn was the editor of *Northern Gardener* magazine, the official publication of the Minnesota State Horticultural Society. Under her direction, *Northern Gardener* received several Overall Excellence awards from the Minnesota Magazine & Publishing Association, and several individual contributors received Garden Writers Association Media Awards. She now writes a column titled "Northern Natives."

Growing up in northeastern Wisconsin, Lynn spent many enjoyable hours hiking and camping in the north woods. She has a bachelor of science degree in natural resources from the University of Wisconsin and a masters degree in horticulture with a minor in agricultural journalism from the University of Minnesota. She is a member of Wild Ones, the Nature Conservancy, the Prairie Enthusiasts, the Saint Paul Garden Club, the Parks and Trails Council of Minnesota, and the Natural Resources Foundation of Wisconsin.

Lynn lives with her husband and two cats on a 120-year-old farmstead in northern Washington County, Minnesota, where she enjoys tending her gardens and watching the progress of her restored prairie, savanna, and oak woodland.

Books by Lynn Steiner:

Grow Native: Bringing Natural Beauty to Your Garden
(Cool Springs Press)

Landscaping with Native Plants of Michigan
(Voyageur Press)

Landscaping with Native Plants of Minnesota
(Voyageur Press)

Landscaping with Native Plants of Wisconsin
(Voyageur Press)

Prairie-Style Gardens: Capturing the Essence of the American Prairie Wherever You Live (Timber Press)

Rain Gardens: Sustainable Landscaping for a Beautiful Yard and Healthy World (Voyageur Press)

JESSICA WALLISER

Books by Jessica Walliser:

A Gardener's Notebook: Life with My Garden (St. Lynn's Press)

Attracting Beneficial Bugs to Your Garden: A Natural Approach to Pest Control (Timber Press)

Container Gardening Complete: Creative Projects for Growing Vegetables and Flowers in Small Spaces (Cool Springs Press)

Good Bug Bad Bug: Who's Who, What They Do, and How to Manage Them Organically (St. Lynn's Press)

Horticulturist Jessica Walliser co-hosts *The Organic Gardeners,* an award-winning program on KDKA Radio in Pittsburgh, Pennsylvania. She is a former contributing editor for *Organic Gardening* magazine and a regular contributor to *Fine Gardening, Urban Farm,* and *Hobby Farms* magazines. Jessica also serves on the editorial advisory board of the American Horticultural Society.

Her two weekly gardening columns for the *Pittsburgh Tribune-Review* have been enjoyed by readers for more than ten years. In addition, Jessica blogs weekly for both www. SavvyGardening.com and www.HobbyFarms.com.

She is also the author of *Container Gardening Complete* and the Amazon bestseller *Good Bug Bad Bug.* Jessica's fourth book, *Attracting Beneficial Bugs to the Garden,* was awarded the American Horticultural Society's 2014 Book Award.

GEORGE WEIGEL

business, leads numerous garden trips, and gives dozens of talks each year at various garden shows, garden clubs, and Master Gardener programs.

George is a member of the Pennsylvania Horticultural Society's Gold Medal Plant Committee and the Garden Writers Association, and is a former board member of Hershey Gardens, where he helped plan the one-acre Children's Garden.

Books by George Weigel:

Mid-Atlantic Month-by-Month Gardening: What to Do Each Month to Have a Beautiful Garden All Year (Cool Springs Press)

Pennsylvania Getting Started Garden Guide: Grow the Best Flowers, Shrubs, Trees, Vines & Groundcovers (Cool Springs Press)

Pennsylvania Month-by-Month Gardening: What to Do Each Month to Have a Beautiful Garden All Year (Cool Springs Press)

Striking Back: The Trigeminal Neuralgia and Face Pain Handbook (Trigeminal Neuralgia Association)

George Weigel, from Harrisburg, Pennsylvania, is a garden writer, designer, and frequent speaker. He's best known for the garden columns he has written for 25 years for *The Patriot-News* and www.PennLive.com.

George earned a journalism degree from Penn State University and is a Pennsylvania Certified Horticulturist. Besides his newspaper column, George has written for numerous magazines, including *Horticulture*, *Green Scene*, *Pennsylvania Gardener*, *Central PA Magazine*, and *People, Places and Plants*.

He also posts a weekly column on his website, www.georgeweigel.net, which includes monthly garden tips, public garden profiles, plant profiles, and a library of articles on a wide variety of gardening topics.

Besides writing, George offers garden design and consultations to do-it-yourselfers through his Garden House-Calls

INDEX

A

allergens 249

all seasons interest: and bloom timing 148–149; and design techniques 135–138; and fall 144–145; and garden nursery as inspiration 132; and public garden as inspiration 132–133; and spring 140–141; and summer 141–143; and winter 146–147

Alternaria solani (early blight) 204

amendments 39, 42–43

animals and garden design 50

annuals: and birds and bees 290, 296; definition of 16–17; and seasonal interest with 141–142, 145; and selection and planting 66, 71, 322

appearance of plants 100

aquatic plants 16, 23

asexual propagation: by air layering 225; by crown division 219–221; by cuttings 223–224; definition of 211; by ground layering 224–225; by storage organs 216–219

asparagus beetle 180

Azadirachta indica (neem oil) 185–186, 202, 207

B

Bacillus subtilis based fungicides 201–208

Bacillus thuringiensis 183

bacterial pathogens 192

bacterial wilt (*Erwinia tracheiphila*) 201–202

basil downy mildew (*Peronospora belbahrii*) 200–201

bee lawns 270

bees: and helpful plants 293–296; and nests or hives 302–303; and pest control 183, 186, 304; and water sources 299, 300

beneficial insects 181–182

berries and fruits 145, 239–241, 290–291

biennials 17

bin composting 116

biopesticides 182–184; *see also* pesticides

birds: and berries and fruits 290–291; and herbicides 307; and insects 288–289; and pesticides 304; and seeds 289–290; and shelter and nesting 301–302; and water sources 299–300

black flies 183

black spot (*Diplocarpon rosae*) 202

blister beetle 173

bloom times 148–149

botanical oils 185

botanical order 11

Botrytis spp. (gray mold) 202–203

bubble diagram 51–56

bulbs 16, 21–22, 73, 140, 216–217

buying plants 66

C

Captain Jack's Deadbug Brew 183

care of new plants 67

caterpillars 183, 186

cell packs 66

Cercospora leaf spot (*Cercospora* spp.) 203–204

chemical fertilizers 35, 39, 94

cisterns *see* rain barrels

clay: as amendment 39; kaolin 186; in soils 29–31, 50; and water storage 43, 50, 87–88

coir 220

H

hanging containers 313

hardening plants 69

hardscapes 272

harvesting: fruits and berries 239–241; herbs 235–237; vegetables 228–233

heat zones 25

herbicides 160–161, 166–167, 307

herbs and bees 296

horticultural oils 185

houseplants 16, 20

I

inputs 38–39, 42–43, 97

insecticidal soap 185

insect pest control: and biological methods 181–185; by physical and mechanical methods 180; through pesticides 185–186

insect pest prevention: through biology 178–179; through design 175–177; through gardener behavior 177–178

insect pests: definition of 171–172; identification of 173–174; overwintering behavior of 178

intercropping 77–79

iron phosphate baits 186

irrigation systems 91, 272–273, 352; *see also* watering

J

Japanese beetle 183, 184, 186

jar test 32

K

kaolin clay 186

L

landscape: accessories 60; beds 40; fabric 122, 159, 351

late blight (*Phytopthtora infestans*) 206

leaders and plant direction 101

leaf color 133–134

leaves and compost 121

light and garden design 50

lime and soil pH 33–34

Linnaeus, Carolus 10–11

loam 29, 31, 87–88

low-till method 37

M

mail-order plants 66

manure and compost 121

meristem cells 101, 214

Milky spore (*Paenibacillus popilliae*) 184

milled bark 220

moles and voles 351

Monterey Bt 183

Monterey Garden Insect Spray 183

mosquitos 183

moss 43

mulch: and application methods 129, 198; and bees 303; benefits of 38, 40, 43, 122, 275; and disease prevention 198; inorganic 127–128; and new plants 66, 67, 73; organic 123–127; and raised beds 352; tools to use with 128; and weed prevention 158–159; *see also* inputs

Mycostop (*Streptomyces griseoviridis*) 205

N

naming systems: meanings of names 12–13; nicknames in plants 15; varieties or "cultivars" 14–15

native plants: and bees 293–294; benefits of 244–247, 288; and birds 288; care of 260, 262–263; designing with 252–254; in gardens and landscapes 250–251; misconceptions of 247–249; and municipal laws 254; and pruning 262–263; selection of 254, 256–260

natural pest control products: botanical oils 185; horticultural oils 185; insecticidal soap 185; iron phosphate baits 186; kaolin clay 186; neem oil (*Azadirachta indica*) 185–186, 202, 207; pyrethrins 186

neem oil (*Azadirachta indica*) 185–186, 202, 207

nematodes 184–185

neonicotinoids 304

PHOTO CREDITS

American Horticultural Society: 25 (bottom)

Ball Horticulture Company: 196

Bill Kersey: 80 (right), 87, 88, 96, 105 (top), 108 (top), 119 (bottom), 224

Christopher R. Mills: 354 (bottom left), 357

Corona: 104 (bottom left)

Crystal Liepa: 24 (bottom), 30, 32, 35 (bottom), 66, 71 (left), 74 (bottom left), 90 (middle left, bottom right), 91 (left), 114, 116 (bottom left), 118, 119 (top), 121 (both), 122, 123 (both), 124 (both), 125 (top), 154 (bottom left), 155 (top), 161 (both), 162, 163, 164 (both), 165 (both), 166 (both), 167 (left), 172 (right), 174, 180 (left, bottom right), 181 (left), 185 (both), 186, 197, 198 (both), 199, 263, 273, 311, 312 (left), 314 (both), 315 (both), 316 (all), 317, 324, 325, 326, 327, 328, 329, 335 (bottom left), 342 (right), 354 (top, bottom right), 355 (all), 356, 358 (all), 359 (all)

Donna Griffith: 351 (bottom)

Dramm: 86, 89 (bottom right), 90 (top left and right, middle right), 104 (top right, middle left)

Fiskars: 104 (middle right)

George Weigel: 10 (both), 11 (all), 12, 14, 15 (both), 16, 17 (both), 18 (both), 19 (both), 20, 21, 22 (all), 23, 25 (top), 46, 47 (both), 48, 49, 50, 51, 52 (both), 53, 54 (both), 55, 56, 57 (both), 58 (both), 59, 60, 61, 62, 132, 133 (both), 134 (all), 135, 136, 137, 138 (all), 139 (all), 140 (both), 141, 142, 143, 144, 145 (both), 146, 147 (both), 148 (both), 149 (all)

iStock: 8, 44, 127, 231 (right), 272, 277, 313 (top), 320, 321, 322

Jacqueline Soule: 89 (top, bottom left), 91 (right), 101 (top right, bottom), 103 (all), 105 (bottom right), 108 (bottom left and right), 109 (both), 111 (both), 212, 213 (both), 217 (both), 218, 220 (top left), 221 (bottom), 222 (all), 223 (both), 332 (bottom), 334, 335 (top), 343

Jerry Pavia: 278

Jessica Walliser: 153 (both), 154 (top left and right, bottom right), 155 (bottom), 159, 168, 170, 172 (left), 173 (both), 179 (top right), 195 (both), 200, 312 (right)

Katie Elzer-Peters: 39, 115 (all), 117 (top), 125 (bottom), 126, 129 (all)

Les Urbainculteurs: 353 (top)

Lynn Steiner: 67, 69, 72, 76, 80 (left), 156, 242, 245, 246, 247 (both), 248, 249, 250, 251 (both), 252, 253, 255, 256 (both), 257, 258, 259, 261, 262, 267, 268, 269 (top), 270, 271, 276, 282

Nigel Cattlin/Alamy Stock Photo: 209

Paul Markert: 226

Pixabay: 94 (left), 101 (top left), 102, 215, 219, 221 (top), 340, 341

Phillip Nicklay: 286, 287, 300

Proven Winners: 360

Rau+Barber: 231 (middle), 237 (both)

Rhonda Fleming Hayes: 284, 288, 289 (both), 290, 291, 292, 294 (both), 295, 296 (both), 297, 298, 299, 301, 302 (both), 303, 304, 305, 306, 307

Robert Domm: 279, 280 (all)

Shutterstock: 1, 2, 5, 6, 28 (all), 29, 36, 38 (both), 41, 64, 75, 78, 84, 95 (top), 98, 100, 105 (bottom left), 107, 110, 112, 116 (top right), 117 (bottom), 128 (all), 130, 150, 152, 157, 158, 160 (both), 167 (right), 171, 175, 176, 178, 179 (top left, bottom left), 180 (top right), 181 (right), 182, 183, 184, 187, 188, 189, 190, 192, 193, 194, 201, 202, 203 (both), 204, 205, 206, 207 (both), 208 (both), 210, 216, 220 (top right, bottom left and right), 225, 228, 229, 230 (both), 231 (left), 232 (both), 233 (both), 234, 235, 236, 238, 239, 240 (both), 241, 264, 269 (bottom), 274, 308, 310, 313 (bottom), 318, 319, 323, 330, 332 (top), 333, 335 (bottom right), 337, 338, 339, 342 (left), 346, 347, 348 (bottom), 352, 353 (bottom), 361, 376

Tara Nolan: 349, 351 (top)

United States Department of Agriculture: 24 (top)